ARCUS STUDIES IN HISTORICAL ARCHAEOLOGY 1

The Historical Archaeology of the Sheffield Cutlery and Tableware Industry 1750-1900

by Victoria Beauchamp and Joan Unwin

with a foreword by John C Bramah, Master Cutler

edited by James Symonds

ARCUS
Graduate School of Archaeology
Westcourt, 2 Mappin St, Sheffield S1 4DT
ENGLAND

ARCUS
Graduate School of Archaeology
Westcourt
2 Mappin St
Sheffield
S1 4DT
www.shef.ac.uk/arcus/

ARCUS Studies in Historical Archaeology 1 - *The Historical Archaeology of the Sheffield Cutlery and Tableware Industry 1750-1900*

Series editor: James Symonds

Technical editing, design and layout by Jenny Moore
Cover photograph and design: Anna Badcock

First published 2002
Printed in England by the Basingstoke Press

ISBN 0-9544240-0-X

British Library Cataloguing in Publication Data.
A catalogue record for this book is available from the British Library

This book is dedicated to Ken Hawley, M.B.E.

*A Sheffield man who long ago understood
the importance of things*

Contents

List of Figures

List of tables

Acknowledgements

James Symonds would like to thank Anna Badcock and Jo Mincher for their help with the illustrations for this volume. Jenny Moore should be thanked for the excellent service she provided as technical editor. David P Davison of Archeopress showed characteristic patience and good humour during extended wait for copy. Finally, Victoria Parsons helped to assemble the bibliography and offered her unfailing support through the production process.

Joan Unwin would like to thank Ken Hawley of the Hawley Collection Trust, Julie MacDonald, archivist of the Culters' Company in Hallamshire and David Hey.

Victoria Beauchamp would like to thank Ken Hawley, Joan Unwin, Dennis Smith, Jean Cass, Neville Flavell, Derek Bayliss, Victoria Seddon, the Grenoside Local History Group, South Yorkshire Industrial History Society and members of the Fairbank and Cutlers' Company projects at the University of Sheffield. Local craftsmen at A Wright and Son, Wilkinson Scissors, F Howard, Stan Shaw and Billy Thornton gave up their valuable time to explain the processes involved in cutlery production and the tools required. David Crossley is thanked for supervising the PhD research on which this section is based.

Acknowledgements for illustrations

Figure 2 is reproduced courtesy of ARCUS. Figure 3 is reproduced courtesy of Local Studies, Sheffield Libraries Archives and Information. In particular Douglas Hindmarsh is thanked for his help in locating this print.

Figures 7, 8, 10, 12, 14–24 and 17 are photographs taken by Joan Unwin from a selection in the Hawley Collection Trust. Figures 9, 13, 17, 25, 26 and 28 are copies of documents in the Hawley Collection and are reproduced courtesy of the Hawley Collection Trust. Figure 6 is reproduced courtesy of the Cutlers' Company. Figure 11 is reproduced courtesy of *The Star* newspaper, Sheffield. Figure 29 is reproduced courtesy of ARCUS.

Figures 31 and 32 are reproduced courtesy of Local Studies, Sheffield Libraries Archives and Information. Figure 46 is reproduced by courtesy of David Crossley. Figure 71 is reproduced by kind permission of Sheffield Museums and Galleries Trust. Figure 74 is based on CA202/2284 and reproduced courtesy of Local Studies, Sheffield Libraries Archives and Information. Figure 77 is from a sales brochure, First Move, published in 1995.

FOREWORD

In a building unchanged for over a hundred years, a cutler of some forty years' bench experience was demonstrating to me the technique for serrating the edge of a curved knife blade. Without the aid of jigs or fixtures, he deftly reproduced a series of uniform grooves along the entire length of the blade. He seemed disinterested when I selected a sample of blades from the completed batch and began to painstakingly count the tiny indentations on each blade. They were all identical.

Now, the technology required to build a machine to perform his task is available to us, at an ever- reducing price. There are computers that create images, computers that style cars and buildings, and computer controlled machines that intricately fashion wood and metal.

Alongside the decline in the cutler's craft, there has been a similar deterioration in the cutler's traditional working environment. Many of the simple workshops have been abandoned or destroyed. City planners are always faced with the task of demolishing some of the past to build the future. Today we have to recognise that it is often better to preserve our architectural heritage by infusing different life styles into old structures rather than obliterating them to start again.

There are an increasing number of examples in Sheffield where this has been achieved with both practicality and elegance. In extreme cases, like the Magna Centre, we have even achieved this objective with a huge steel works. Yet, in the end, there remains that intangible emotion that comes with any material that has been fashioned and finished by human hand.

'Made in Sheffield' still carries a huge amount of credibility, both nationally and abroad. These pages chronicle the history of the men and women who originally gave these three simple words their standing in the world today.

John C Bramah
Master Cutler
November 2002

INTRODUCTION

James Symonds

This volume is the first in a new series of studies in historical archaeology. Bringing together the work of archaeologists, historians and others, this publication examines the Sheffield cutlery industry. The industry has been integral to the development of Sheffield as a city, yet there is little published that shows the extent of this. More to the point, there are no volumes that integrate the history of the industry with its archaeology. This fact has become increasingly important, as development work on brownfield sites is rapidly removing evidence of the industry. It may appear to many that if there are recent written records then the archaeology becomes less important, but the reverse could also be argued. Written records are not complete, are subject to biases and do not deal with specific details of developments which impacted on human lives. Historical archaeology can provide evidence of such detail, as this volume demonstrates. Therefore, it is critically important to integrate the remaining archaeological evidence into the history of the Sheffield cutlery industry. This industry has been the backbone of the development of Sheffield, its character and its people, and is central to the identity of the city. An understanding and appreciation of the industrial origins of Sheffield enables present day residents of the city to feel that they have firm roots; it also offers inspiration and encouragement for routes to the post-industrial future.

The name Sheffield has been synonymous with cutlery for more than two hundred and fifty years. The craft traditions from which the city's world-famous cutlery industry developed extend back much further, however, to at least the twelfth century. Sheffield's lengthy cutlery-making pedigree is well rehearsed. In 1297, *Robertus le Coteler*—Robert the Cutler—is recorded as having paid a hearth tax in Sheffield[1]. In 1340, a Sheffield knife was listed among the possessions of King Edward III at the Tower of London. A generation later, in the 1370s, Geoffrey Chaucer described the Miller of Trumpington as wearing a Sheffield *'thwitel'* or

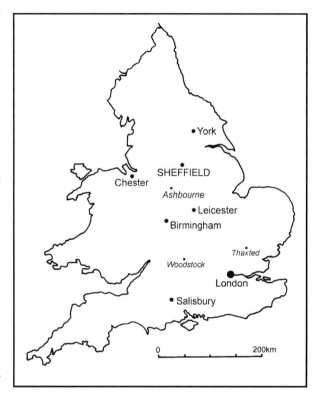

Figure 1 Map of England and Wales showing the position of Sheffield

whittle—a straight wooden-handled knife—upon his waist-belt in *The Reeves Tale*[2].

Throughout the Middle Ages cutlery made in Hallamshire—the region surrounding and including the parish of Sheffield—was generally aimed at the cheaper end of the market. The cutlery trade was not large, or for that matter particularly important, and competition came from several other provincial cutlery-making centres, such as Thaxted (Essex), Ashbourne (Derbyshire), Woodstock (Oxfordshire), Leicester, Salisbury, Chester, York and Birmingham. The national trade in high-quality knives was dominated by output from London. Cutlers were active in the City of London from at least the twelfth century and established a guild early on to control their trade[3].

1

Knives made in London continued to dominate the national trade until well into the eighteenth century. However, by the seventeenth century the quality of Hallamshire cutlery had improved sufficiently to overtake most of its regional rivals. Of the fore-mentioned regional competitors, only cutlers in Salisbury, known for their scissors and spring-knives, and Birmingham, renowned for their sword-making, continued production on any scale into the nineteenth century[4].

The Company of Cutlers in Hallamshire was formed to regulate the industry in 1624. Less than fifty years later, Sheffield had developed a highly specialised proto-industrial workforce, perhaps more so than that of any other English town[5]. Thomas Fuller, writing in 1662, observed that the majority of common English knives were made in Yorkshire, and that the parish of Sheffield was at the heart of the industry[6]. At that time as many as three out of every five Sheffield men worked in a branch of the cutlery trades[7].

This volume surveys the later history of the Sheffield cutlery and tableware industry, specifically the period between 1750–1900. It does not set out to provide a detailed or comprehensive economic history of the industry. Instead, the concentration here is upon two hitherto neglected aspects of the trade: the processes of manufacture, and the structures that housed the industry. Future volumes will explore other aspects of the industry, including the physical evidence that survives for archaeological interpretation above and below ground.

Sheffield cutlery and tableware products have been described in several popular books[8]. These publications provide an insight into the stylistic attributes of individual pieces, the chronological development of the industry, and the history of prominent manufacturing companies. Less satisfactorily, texts aimed primarily aimed at collectors tend, like the contents of many traditional museum collections, to emphasize attractive, valuable, or otherwise extraordinary items.

This volume, and future publications in the series, will seek to redress that balance. In the chapters that follow an attempt is made to reconstruct day-to-day working practices, and to offer an overview of the range of cutlery and tableware products that were made. Attention is given to the specific historical context of production, to the location, layout and use of workshops, and to human participation in the industry. Rather than seeking to examine the culture-historic nature of the artefacts, the lived experience of the industry is evaluated, through investigation of the processes of manufacture and examination of the buildings.

The rise and eventual 'take-off' of the Sheffield tableware and cutlery industry in the mid-eighteenth century has long been attributed to the local availability of natural resources: iron ore and coal for the fuelling and operation of forges; sandstones from which sharp grindstones could be made; and above all a plentiful supply of water-power from the rivers and streams surrounding the town[9]. While acknowledging the fundamentally important part played by these resources, and the contribution made by technical innovations, such as the development of cementation and crucible steel, the analyses in this volume stress the importance of highly localised social structures and the persistence of customary working practices in shaping the subsequent trajectory for industrial growth.

For these reasons, the descriptions of industrial processes and structures and how lives were lived are likely to be of interest to a wide readership. Firstly, this volume offers a contribution to local studies, and will be of value to all those with an interest in the local history and archaeology of the Sheffield region. Second, the volume provides a detailed case study of an historically significant regional industry, within the wider context of British industrialisation. Finally, throughout the nineteenth century Sheffield cutlery and tableware were exported to the British colonies of settlement in the Americas, Australasia and Africa. Information on Sheffield products and the context of their manufacture will therefore be of interest to historical archaeologists who work in these locations. The unique approach offered here considerably expands previous contributions, in understanding the operation of the cutlery industry and its influence on shaping the character of Sheffield.

Local histories and local distinctiveness

Sheffield has been relatively well served by urban biographies. In the last ten years various single and multi-authored volumes have explored the eighteenth and nineteenth century social and economic history of the city[10]. Although the subject of work has featured prominently in writing about Sheffield, comparatively little attention has been paid to documenting the overall material conditions of life and work in the industrial city.

A persistent theme running through histories has been the operation of the city's unusual 'dual' economy. The labour historian Sydney Pollard, writing in 1959, distinguished two forms of Sheffield industry: 'heavy', i.e. steel, and 'light', i.e. cutlery[11]. Pollard sub-divided the so called light trades into three groups

1. those involving the production of iron and steel goods, such as cutlery, joiners' tools, files, engineers' tools, saws, skates, pins and needles, agricultural implements and fenders
2. silver working, and silver plating
3. various ancillary trades, such as the making of cabinet handles and cases[12].

The manufacture of cutlery and tableware was by far the most common of these trades. In Sheffield terminology the word 'cutlery' refers to 'that which cuts', i.e. knives, scissors, but also other edge tools such as sickles, shears and scythes[13].

The decline of the cutlery trade, in the twentieth century, led to the abandonment and demolition of many former workshops. In an effort to arrest this decay, and to stimulate urban regeneration, English Heritage, in partnership with Sheffield City Council, has actively promoted the re-use of these buildings. An English Heritage press release in 2001, timed to coincide with the announcement of grant-aid to facilitate the re-use of former metals trades buildings, stated:

> 'Humble workshops as well as the great integrated works buildings played a crucial role in the metals trades. The surviving buildings are a powerful symbol of Sheffield's industrial past. Equally, they are components of the city's regeneration, providing and reinforcing its distinctiveness and unique sense of place'[14].

The legacy of Sheffield's industrial past has, at the same time, inspired the publication of an English Heritage popular booklet on the Sheffield metals trades[15]. The focus of this

volume, on the cutlery and tableware industry, will draw further attention to an important aspect of local history and archaeology and a key source of local distinctiveness, but in addition, the approach will be more than a functionalist exploration of industrial history and archaeology. The lives of the people of Sheffield during this period, their day-to-day experience, will be considered.

Figure 2 Archaeologists standing in line over a former crucible furnace (© ARCUS)

Post-medieval archaeology and British industrialisation

Moving beyond the local and regional scale to a national level, the development of industry has been one of the major themes of British post-medieval archaeology.

In a recent overview of the subject, David Cranstone has cautioned that archaeologists have dwelt too heavily upon the study of consumption and that the study of production has been neglected[16]. The current vogue for studies of consumption has been influenced by two important factors. First, a new wave of post-medieval archaeologists have embraced theoretical trends derived from cultural studies and anthropology. Second, the work of these younger scholars has reacted against the earlier tendency of post-medieval archaeologists to concentrate upon such things as the technological development of pottery kilns, to the detriment of wider social and economic questions[17]. In short, more emphasis has been placed upon the study of people, rather than things. It is gratifying to note that Sheffield's main industrial museum, Kelham Island, advocated this approach more than twenty years ago, and created displays which showed working conditions for men and women in the Sheffield cutlery industry[18].

Within post-medieval archaeology, the coverage of individual trades and industries has been distinctly uneven. Numerous thematic studies have focused upon heavy and large-scale industries, such as iron and steel making, or those, such as cotton spinning – that employed a factory scale of production. Far less attention has been paid to trades employing craft or domestic scales of production[19]. As Marilyn Palmer and Peter Neaverson have pointed out, at its simplest the difference between a craft and industrial scale of production is that in the former a skilled individual is responsible for completing a whole article, while in the latter several workers contribute to the manufacture of a finished item[20]. In Sheffield, the persistence of 'little mesters' – independent craftsmen – meant that an unusual form of out-working, defying normal definitions of industrial production, continued well into the twentieth century.

Forgotten small things: local products and global trade networks

Parts of a brass pocket knife that had been made in Sheffield were recovered from the wreck of the *Colebrook*, an East India Company ship that sank in the Indian Ocean in 1778. Bone scales from the handle of another Sheffield knife were recovered from the 1830s wreck of the *Manasquan*, off the coast of New Jersey[21]. To cite just one terrestrial example, a Sheffield boning knife was owned by George Cribb, a butcher who lived and worked in the Rocks district of Sydney, New South Wales, in the 1820s. Cribb's knife was unearthed from the back-yard rubbish pit into which it had been dropped by an archaeological excavation in 1994[22].

These far-flung examples are a testament to the global influence of the Sheffield cutlery trade. However, this was not always the case. Prior to the establishment of turnpike roads in the eighteenth century, the hills and moors that surround the city provided a natural barrier to trade. In the absence of a navigable waterway to the coast, cutlery was ferried to markets in London and elsewhere by packhorses. A colourful description of this weekly event has been provided by the Sheffield historian, A W Goodfellow:

> 'The products of the Sheffield smitheries and grinding sheds were bought largely by chapman, or travelling traders, who bought strings of packhorses into the town, loaded up their purchases, and set out across the winding moorland trails in much the same manner that a caravan of camels goes in procession across an African desert.'[23]

Within a few years of the introduction of turnpike roads this situation had changed. Sheffield cutlery, like Staffordshire crockery, accompanied British nineteenth century settlers as they colonised new regions of the world. Sheffield firms were keen to exploit overseas markets, whether they belonged to the imperial territories or not. Long-bladed Sheffield machete knives were used to cut down plantation growth in South and Central America. The same implements were favoured by Cuban insurgents, '[who] were wont to adjust their differences with the Spaniards with them' prior to 1898[24].

Many Sheffield firms established trading agencies around the world. In the 1880s, George Wostenholm & Son Limited had representation in New York, Philadelphia, Montreal and Sydney. The largest Sheffield cutlery firm, Joseph Rodgers, exported widely to America, but in addition, had also secured a reputation for quality in India and the Far East[25].

The study of Sheffield tableware and cutlery may thus serve to provide a type series of closely-dated and provenanced artefacts for archaeological contexts worldwide. Building upon this foundation it may one day be possible to comment upon issues of style and consumer choice. Did different tastes and preferences emerge as settlers of British origin developed new colonial societies in India or elsewhere, interacting with and absorbing aspects of the indigenous cultures?

In an effort to stimulate demand and to cater to as wide a range of potential markets as possible, Sheffield companies devised ever more elaborate pattern books. There is evidence that this sometimes failed to have the desired effect, and it is debatable just how many of the designs in any given pattern book actually entered into production. Competition from American manufacturers of edge tools, from the mid nineteenth century onwards, clearly caused some consternation and led to no small amount of soul-searching among Sheffield agents:

> 'But it was not the mere fact of [Americans] manufacturing those [tools] that so much caused uneasiness as that, from the first, there was a superior intelligence brought to bear upon the design, shape and finish of the articles manufactured. If, for instance, it was an axe brought under our notice, we observed that it had been constructed with a scientific regard to the purpose for which it would be used.'[26]

In contrast, the variety of goods prepared by Sheffield firms for export to America was recognised by one contemporary critic as being:

> 'A vast mass of patterns, meretricious and gaudy design, absurdly numerous in variety, and all but useless in quality and strength.'[27]

The influence of trade with America has left its mark on the geography of Sheffield. Although the memory of this global enterprise has faded, many of the places and names remain. George Wostenholm (Fig 3) amassed a vast fortune, largely through the export of pocket knives, ranch knives and other specialist hunting knives to America. Wostenholm gloried in his New World connections and named the tenement factory which he acquired in 1848 the Washington Works[28].

Wostenholm's Kenwood mansion and estate at Nether Edge in Sheffield were modelled upon the country estates that he had admired during his visits to up-state New York. The wide tree-lined roads that approached his self-styled suburban retreat carried forth his idyllic American vision, imposed upon the sombre smoke-wreathed fields of a northern English industrial town[29].

Figure 3 George Wolstenholm in New York in 1856, the year he became Master Cutler (Local Studies, Sheffield Library Archives)

This raises important questions as to the extent of cultural and commercial interaction between nineteenth century Britain and America. It is interesting to note that Sheffield cutlery firms were quick to respond to the fashions of the American market. In an age long before the spread of multi-national corporations and the existence of global communication networks, it must be presumed that information was spread either by newsprint, or else by word of mouth.

The Bowie knife offers one such example. When, on 19th September 1827, the trader and land speculator James Bowie successfully defended himself in a fight on a sandbar in the River Mississippi, with a purpose-made hunting knife given to him by his brother, he became an American icon. Bowie's reputation was further enhanced by his heroic death at the Alamo in 1836. His trademark knife soon became a sought after personal effect for all would-be woodsmen and frontiersmen.

In the absence of an established American steel making and cutlery trade Sheffield cutlers quickly stepped in to service this demand. Bowie knives were made in Sheffield for export as early as the 1830s; the catalogue of firms manufacturing these knives included William Butcher, William Greaves, Samuel C Wragg and Unwin & Rodgers[30]. But it was George Wostenholm who gained pre-eminence in this field in the 1850s, and continued to dominate the American market until the 1890s[31].

America – mass production

The historic preservation movement in the U.S.A. has mirrored the activities of conservationists and industrial archaeologists in the UK, and has saved many of the buildings associated with early American capitalism[32]. The field of 'labor history', which is perhaps rather more developed than its equivalent in the UK, has highlighted the links between technological innovation and the de-skilling and control of industrial workers[33].

Michael Nassaney and Marjorie Abel have used a political-economic theoretical framework to examine social control and spatial re-organization in the American nineteenth-century cutlery industry. Their study of the Russell Cutlery in Turners Fall, Massachusetts, has shown how social and economic sub-ordination of workers took place both in the factory and at home, in the boarding houses provided by the company[34]. Control of this absolute nature was never achieved over the industrial workforce of Sheffield. Individual craft skills were fiercely guarded to resist the onslaught of proletarianisation, and company boarding-houses were never built. This kind of institutionalised social control existed for only the poorest inhabitants of Victorian Sheffield, who were confined to the Sheffield Union Workhouse on Kelham Street, or some other such institution of public charity, or correction.

If the dogged individualism of Sheffield cutlers was advantageous in resisting the corporate Leviathan, it also had its downside. It has frequently been remarked that Sheffield cutlers were slow to accommodate modernisation. American cutlery entrepreneurs of the 1830s introduced two key innovations to their industry: mechanisation and interchangeability. Together, these technological advances characterised the 'American system of manufacture'[35]. Although this method of working originated in the arms-manufacturing trade, it quickly spread to other metal-working trades in the Connecticut River Valley of Massachusetts. The implications for the production of finished metal goods were profound.

John Russell established his first cutlery factory on the Green River in 1833. By 1870 the company had grown in size and relocated to what was claimed to be the largest cutlery factory in the world, at Turners Falls[36]. What was the secret of Russell's success? The spatial organization of his factory, and the discipline imposed upon his employees, both in work and at home, certainly played an important part. However, the American willingness to mechanise and to dispense with the intensive use of hand-labour was probably of paramount importance. As early as 1844, Russell adopted the use of a water-powered trip hammer to speed-up the forging of blades. Heavy dies were also employed to press-out knives from one piece of steel.

Although not hand-crafted in the manner of Sheffield blades, 'Green River' hunting knives were regarded by many Americans as being superior in both quality and strength. A more telling comparison is perhaps the fact that using conventional methods it took two workers (a smith and a striker) to forge a blade and that they could produce approximately 150 blades per day. Russell's mechanised production methods produced 3000 blades in the same time[37].

Comparisons with other European cutlery industries

To what extent was the character of the Sheffield cutlery and tableware industry shaped by the topography and natural resources of the locality? As already noted, several authors have drawn attention to the importance of water-power, as well as the availability of other raw materials, such as coal, and sandstone, to the development of the metal-working industry in Sheffield. Did a similar clustering of natural resources encourage metal-working industries to grow and flourish elsewhere?

The historian David Hey certainly believes this to be the case. In his view 'The crucial importance of water-power in the triumph of the local cutlery trade' is evident when comparisons are made with the continental cutlery-making centres of Solingen and Thiers[38]. At Thiers, in Laguiole, central France, the river La Durolle provided water-power for some 28 grinding wheels, in a two kilometre stretch below the town. Additional metal-working sites were located in the countryside beyond. However, aside from the benefits of a plentiful supply of water, the cutlers of Thiers had few natural resources to call upon. They found it necessary, for example, to import grinding stones, as well as iron and steel[39].

These points aside, there are some striking similarities between the growth of industry in Thiers and Sheffield. At Thiers, as in Sheffield, the town was located at the centre of a wider rural metal-working region. Metal-working, for the manufacture of scythes, or other agricultural implements, was initially undertaken when time allowed, during seasonal lulls in the farming year. Prior to the rise of craft specialisation, in the sixteenth century, this allowed craftsmen the safety net of a dual occupation.

The cutlers of Thiers benefited from the patronage of a family of local noblemen. This mirrors the impetus that was given to the cutlers of Hallamshire by the Earls of Shrewsbury between 1406 and 1617. By 1582, the cutlers of Thiers were sufficiently numerous and well organised to form a company to regulate their trade and issue individual makers' marks[40]. The guild at Thiers preceded the establishment of a similar company in Hallamshire by 42 years.

The capacity for water power has been identified as a major factor influencing the early development of cutlery manufacturing at Solingen, near Düsseldorf, in the *Berghishes Land* district of Germany[41]. Here, in an area of high rainfall, the run-off from five ridges empties into the River Wupper. The resulting flow of water was sufficient to power the grinding wheels of Solingen, as well as several tilt-hammer forges in the neighbouring steel-making town of Reimscheid.

Between the fifteenth century and the mid nineteenth century the manufacture of cutlery in Solingen was divided-up between four different kinds of craftsmen. Individual pieces were first worked on an anvil by a *forger*. In smaller forges support was offered by a *second forger*. Once forged, the pieces were heated and quenched to give strength by a *hardener*. The final stage involved the assembly of parts to complete the product by the *finisher*. This contrasted with working practices in Sheffield, where forging by hand was the preferred technique, and individual cutlers did not specialise in particular phases of production until the early twentieth century[42].

The comparatively early division of labour at Solingen prefigured the adoption of drop forge technology and flexible, or serial production methods. In the 1850s steam engines were introduced to power grinding wheels on the ridges above the town. In the German period of 'high industrialisation', after 1871, several new cutlery workshops were established within the town. As with the example of the Connecticut River Valley of Massachusetts, cited above, the cutlers of Solingen worked alongside, and to some extent borrowed technology from the weapons manufacturing industry, in particular the Solingen company of Weyersberg, Kirschbaum & Co[43]. By the turn of the nineteenth century, the use of drop-forging machinery had been developed to allow the mass production of cutlery. The cutlery firm of Henckels dominated the town, exporting goods worldwide. In terms of bulk production, Solingen had effectively replaced Sheffield as the world's pre-eminent cutlery producing centre by 1910[44].

The rivalry that existed between the cutlers of Sheffield and their German and other counterparts is manifest in contemporary press and magazine articles. As early as 1884, one English commentator wrote: 'Wherever foreign competitors have chipped Sheffield trade the end has been accomplished by adapting machinery to common work, as in America, or by stooping to the wholesale production of cutlery that won't cut, as in Germany.'[45]

Not infrequently, this rivalry descended into acts of outright deception. In the 1880s, Sheffield cutlers made several complaints to the Foreign Office that German cutlers were marking goods destined for the U.S.A. with the name 'Sheffield' to give a false indication of origin[46]. It proved difficult to prohibit the use of this geographical name, however, as it was not a registered company name or trademark. The situation was complicated in the early twentieth century when German firms went to the extraordinary lengths of acquiring premises in Sheffield. Knife 'blanks' that had been forged in Germany were imported into England, finished in Sheffield, and marked 'Sheffield'[47]. It was not until 1924 that the Company of Cutlers of Hallamshire came up with a ruling that to qualify for the use of the mark 'Sheffield' at least 50% of the wages paid to labour in the production of a piece of cutlery should have been paid in respect of work undertaken within the City of Sheffield[48].

The same, but different: technology and variations in working methods

It has been shown that the early cutlery industries shared a number of characteristics. Foremost among these was the need for a plentiful supply of water to power grinding stones. In addition, industries generally grew up within an agricultural region with an existing rural metalworking tradition. Cutlers frequently received patronage, from a powerful, usually aristocratic, local dynastic family. This impetus undoubtedly propelled some individuals from being agricultural workers with an occasional seasonal sideline in metal-working to become full-time cutlers.

A study of the lists of indentures of apprenticeships held by the Company of Cutlers of Hallamshire has stressed that the distance over which the metals trades exerted an attraction as a source of employment was comparatively limited. Between 1624 and 1799 two thirds of the men who migrated to Sheffield to find work in the metals trades were from places less than 21 miles away, and less than one tenth were from more than 41 miles away. Significantly, nearly half of those who signed indentures were the sons of agricultural labourers[49].

Can differences be seen in the day-to-day working practices of Sheffield cutlers with their European or American counterparts? If so, how can these differences be explained? The first of these questions is easier to answer than the second, and may be illustrated with reference to the action of grinding.

In Sheffield a grinder sat astride a wooden saddle, or 'horsing', and leant forwards to bend over the grindstone, which rotated upwards, towards him[50]. In Solingen, a grinder stood up, and pressed his weight against the grindstone, which rotated downwards and away from him[51]. A different method of finishing blades was employed in Thiers. There, grindstones revolved towards the grinder, as in Solingen, but the grinder lay prostrate, on his stomach. Pictorial evidence suggests that the French grinder was sometimes assisted by a dog, which lay on the back of his legs, so as to provide a counterweight[52].

It is difficult to explain why continental grindstones revolved downwards, whereas Sheffield grindstones revolved upwards. It has been suggested that the Sheffield method was a more practical solution to the job in hand:

> '... the stone turns from the English grinder, who, by merely bending over it is enabled to throw all the weight of his shoulders into the friction.'[53]

Alternatively, it may be that the direction in which the grindstone rotated is of no real significance, and is a simple difference rather like the continental practice of driving on the other side of the road[54]. Nonetheless, the matter of the 'correct' way to grind a knife was treated with deadly seriousness by nineteenth-century Sheffielders. In some cases opprobrium was heaped upon unsuspecting foreigners for their failure to conform to Sheffield practices. In the following example, American cutlers are singled out for their perfunctory workmanship:

> 'The ex-major of Sheffield, Mr Michael Hunter, when in the States a few years ago, looked in at a grinding 'hull'. He found the workmen sitting bolt upright on their horses, grinding 'under the robin' as it is called, that is to say, holding their blades end-wise, and pointing downwards, much as youth 'rides' upon a walking stick. Why don't you 'finger' it? Exclaimed the English visitor but their disdain was their reply. By 'fingering' his blade the Sheffield grinder effects all those dainty touches and delicate gradations which no machine, nor no man using a machine can impart.'[55]

Sheffield cutlers took great pride in their work and even cited their skill as evidence of a form of patriotism:

> 'In dexterity of handling, rapidity of execution, perception of results, and honest zest, the Hallamshire forger and grinder are un-approached by any foreign workmen in their trade. With the latter the moral motive force is generally the bare necessity of earning bread and cheese; with the former there is the same incentive *plus* an inspiring local patriotism.'[56]

Sheffield cutlery and tableware certainly played an important part in the British imperial project, as already discussed. However, as the nineteenth century progressed, the unshakeable self-belief and inherent conservatism of many Sheffield cutlers sometimes came close to *hubris*.

As the first volume in this series, and by way of an introduction, the work of Joan Unwin and Victoria Beauchamp is brought together to provide an insight into the industrial processes and its buildings. Joan has recently completed her PhD at the University of Sheffield on *The Hallamshire Cutlery Trades in the late seventeenth century: a study of the Hearth Tax returns and the records of the Cutlers'* Company, and is a research assistant with the Hawley Collection. Victoria's research for her PhD was on *The Workshops of the Cutlery Industry in Hallamshire 1750–1900*.

The organisation of the volume

Chapter 1 outlines the historical development of the tableware and cutlery industry in Sheffield. The traditional nature of the industry is explored, along with the power and influence of the Cutlers' Company. The history of this prominent craft guild is examined in some detail, and attention is drawn to the long apprenticeships that had to be endured before a boy could register to become a freeman of the Company. The power of the Cutler's Company was substantially reduced in 1814. After this date far greater influence was accrued by trade unions and trade societies. The use of coercion and even violence, to control unruly workers, or to resist the power of masters, with the deliberate sabotage of equipment, or personal assaults, is discussed in a consideration of the 'Sheffield Outrages'. Reference is made to examples cited in the 1867 Sheffield Commission of Inquiry into the Outrages and the general intimidation of non-union labour. The chapter concludes with a short section that explores the rise of the 'Little Mester' and the importance of this stereotype in maintaining craft traditions, and bolstering the collective consciousness of Sheffield metalworkers.

In Chapter 2 the range of sources that are available for the study of the industry are set out. From the eighteenth century onwards two important sources are available: probate inventories and the apprenticeships and freedoms records of the Cutler's Company. By

the nineteenth century the number of first-hand descriptive accounts of work that were being published had increased to include books and magazine articles, as well as firms' histories and trade catalogues or 'Statements' of agreed rates and working arrangements. Published secondary sources, for the most part by economic and social historians, are then reviewed, followed by information on the various museum and private collections of cutlery and edge tools that are held within Sheffield at the City Museum, the Assay Office, the Cutlers' Company and the Hawley Collection at the University of Sheffield.

The making of cutlery and flatware is described in Chapter 3. This chapter begins with a brief consideration of the types of metals used in the trades. These included wrought iron, cast iron, and the 'blister' steel and crucible steel that were to become synonymous with steel and cutlery manufacturing in Sheffield. A detailed description is then given of the processes involved in the manufacture of table knives: from forging, to hardening and grinding the blade, to attaching the handle.

Chapter 4 extends the discussion of working practices to cover the making of forks and spoons. Fork-making does not seem to have been widely practised by Sheffield cutlers prior to the late eighteenth century. However, it eventually came to involve different methods, ranging from hand-forging from bars of steel, through to casting in iron. Closely related to fork-making was the manufacture of spoons. Spoons were mostly made from non-ferrous metals, such as pewter or silver, but were also made out of horn or wood, for the poor. Machine-assisted production is then discussed in relation to water-power, and the use of mechanically stamped, pressed, or decorated items. The chapter concludes with a discussion of the decorative techniques of engraving and saw-piercing, commonly used on non-ferrous cutlery and flatware.

Trade organisation is examined in Chapter 5. The influence of customary working practices, derived from the requirements of the agriculture year is highlighted. Bouts of intense physical activity were followed by relatively slack periods. In the early nineteenth century many cutlers did not work on a Sunday or a 'Saint Monday'; a mocking term that was used for a day missed from work to recover from the excesses of drinking on a Sunday evening. Prior to the introduction of steam-power, which ushered in the era of the tenement factory and more formal working conditions, a *laissez-faire* system of outwork and piecework dominated the industry. Evidence from the archives of the Cutlers' Company is used to explore the changing nature of apprenticeships from the seventeenth century onwards. As time passed specialisation inevitably increased, and divisions between different branches of the cutlery trade became more pronounced.

The importance of 'Statements' – i.e., agreed price lists for payment, negotiated between workmen, unions, and employers – to the reconstruction of working methods and levels of remuneration is emphasized. The chapter concludes with a non-exhaustive overview of basic products, and the proliferation of cutlery and flatware that occurred in the nineteenth century. This is illustrated with reference to the business records of Elizabeth Parkin's hardware business, and the contributions made by Sheffield manufacturers to the Great Exhibition in London, in 1851.

The second half of this volume examines the workshops of the tableware and cutlery industry. In Chapter 7, there is a survey of the spatial development of the industry in Sheffield. In the eighteenth century the majority of workshops were located in the river valleys upstream from the town centre. The introduction of steam power in the late eighteenth century enabled workshops to be relocated away from the traditional sources of water-power. By the mid nineteenth century a cluster of workshops sat cheek by jowl in the town centre. The conclusion is that the development of the industrial landscape of Sheffield owed more to the organisational needs of the industry than to the physical topography or underlying geology. In particular, the importance of a close interaction with the related trades of steel making, horn and bone working, the packing industry, and the quarrying of stone for grindstones, is stressed.

Chapter 8 examines the neglected subject of the small and medium-sized industrial workshop. The chapter begins by reviewing the contribution made by architects to the development of the form, and moves on to consider the range of construction materials that were commonly used, and the specific characteristics of workshops used by the trades. The evidence of trade directories is used to

chart the development of the building profession, and to illustrate the move that many builders made from craftsman to project manager. By the late nineteenth century speculative builders were responsible for the design and construction of the majority of workshops in the town.

The structural and external characteristics of workshops are explored in some detail in Chapter 9. Evidence for the size and scale of workshops is assembled, drawing upon fieldwork and documentary sources. An assessment of architectural features concludes that cutlery and tableware workshops had few distinctive external features, other than the provision of a large number of closely-spaced windows.

Chapter 10 extends the analysis of form and function to consider the internal characteristics of workshops. Here, features that are likely to survive archaeologically are scrutinised. Distinctions are drawn between forgers' hearths and cutlers' hearths, and the process of edge-grinding is described. Next, the possible residues left by a cutler assembling a knife and fitting a handle are considered. Finally, the buffing and polishing of knives is examined, and the contribution made by steam-powered machines is assessed.

These chapters give insight into what it was to be part of the cutlery industry between 1750–1900, and the everyday life of the people of Sheffield who were material in contributing to the development of this industry. Through work such as that presented here, it is possible to construct an historical archaeology of the cutlery industry, rather than simply extolling the virtues of pleasing or valuable artefacts. The contribution archaeology has to make to this understanding is represented in Figure 2, archaeologists standing in line over the remains of cutlers workshops – these remains are rapidly disappearing and along with them the information that they contain.

Notes

[1] William Brown (ed.), *Yorkshire Lay Subsidy 25 Edward il*, Yorkshire Archaeological Society Record Series, 16 1894, p 76.

[2] G I H Lloyd, *The Cutlery Trades*. London 1913 p 87-92 (reprinted 1968, London, Cass Library of Industrial Classics).

[3] David Hey notes that the Worshipful Company of Cutlers in London had its own guildhall in the City of London by 1285 and obtained its first royal charter in 1416, gaining a second

royal charter in 1607. Hey, D 'The Establishment of the Cutlers' Company' p 22. In Binfield, C. and Hey, D (eds) 1997 *Mesters to Masters: A History of the Company of Cutlers in Hallamshire*, Oxford University Press, p 18. Between the twelfth and nineteenth century no fewer than five cutlers' halls were built in the City of London. The most recent of these was opened in 1886 on a site close to St. Pauls Cathedral. This information is from Smithurst, P 1987 *The Cutlery Industry*. Princes Risborough, Aylesbury. Shire Album Series 195, Shire Publications Ltd, p 3.

4   Smithurst, P 1987 *The Cutlery Industry*. Princes Risborough, Aylesbury. Shire Album Series 195, Shire Publications Ltd, p.4.

5   Hey, D 'The Establishment of the Cutlers' Company' p 22. In Binfield, C. and Hey, D (eds) 1997 *Mesters to Masters: A History of the Company of Cutlers in Hallamshire*, Oxford University Press, p 12-25

6   Thomas Fuller, *The Worthies of England*. Folio Society, London 1987 p 423, cited in David Hey 'The Establishment of the Cutlers' Company', in Binfield, C. and Hey, D (eds.) 1997 *Mesters to Masters: A History of the Company of Cutlers in Hallamshire*, Oxford University Press, p 12-25

7   Hey, D 1998 *A History of Sheffield*. Lancaster, Carnegie Publishing. P. 60. Hey notes that the hearth tax returns for 1672 listed about 600 metalworkers smithies in Hallamshire and adjacent areas of South Yorkshire and Derbyshire. Some 224 of these smithies were contained within central Sheffield.

8   See for example, Tweedale, G 1996 *The Sheffield Knife Book: A History and Collectors' Guide*. Sheffield, The Hallamshire Press.; Grayson, R and K Hawley 1995 *Knifemaking in Sheffield: The Hawley Collection*. Sheffield; Ruskin Gallery, 1992 *The Cutting Edge: An Exhibition of Sheffield Tools*. Sheffield, Ruskin Gallery.

9   G I H Lloyd, *The Cutlery Trades*. London 1913 (reprinted 1968, London, Cass Library of Industrial Classics), p 89.

10 Cyde Binfield et al. (eds) 1993 *The History of Sheffield 1843-1993*. Sheffield: Sheffield Academic Press. Vol. 1 *Politics*; Vol. 2 *Society*; Vol. 3 *Images*.
    See also, Hey, D 1998 *A History of Sheffield*. Lancaster: Carnegie Publishing For a more popular approach to local history, see Jones, M (ed.) 1997) *Aspects of Sheffield: Discovering Local History*. Sheffield: Wharncliffe Publishing Limited. For a discussion of the historiography of Sheffield and a comparative critique of writing on other industrial cities see Reeder, D The Industrial city in Britain: urban biography in the modern style. In *Urban History*, 25, 3 1988 p 368-378.

11 The light trades were highly localised and were generally undertaken in small workshops, by skilled workmen with little capital, and an adherence to traditional methods. In contrast, the heavy trades were executed by large firms, with heavy machinery. They were more forward looking in outlook and were influenced by technological developments in other industries. Pollard, S 1959 *History of labour in Sheffield*. Liverpool: Liverpool University Press, p. vii

12 Pollard, S 1959 *History of labour in Sheffield* Liverpool: Liverpool University Press, p 50.

13 This definition is offered in Unwin, J 1999 'The marks of the Sheffield cutlers, 1614-1878.' *Journal of the Historical Metallurgy Society*. 33 No.2, p 93- 102

14 'Brighter Future for Sheffield's Historic Metal Trades Buildings'. English Heritage. News Release 943/11/01. 20th November 2001.

15 Wray, N. (2001) *One Great Workshop: The Buildings of the Sheffield Metal Trades*. English Heritage

16 Cranstone, D, 'Industrial Archaeology – Manufacturing a New Society', p 183. In Newman, R , D Cranstone and C Howard-Davis 2001. *The Historical Archaeology of Britain, c 1540-1900*. Stroud: Sutton Publishing, p 183-211. Cranstone cites the following edited volumes to support his assertion: Egan, G. and R.L. Michael (eds) 1999 *Old and New Worlds*. Oxford: Oxbow Books; Tarlow, S and S West . *The Familiar Past? Archaeologies of Later Historical Britain*. London and New York: Routledge; Funari, P P A M Hall and S Jones (eds) 1999. *Historical Archaeology: Back from the Edge*. London and New York: Routledge.

17 This viewpoint is neatly encapsulated in Mathew Johnson's comment 'most work in this area has concentrated on the archaeological elucidation of the development of the technologies involved, rather than the social and cultural parameters.' Johnson, M 1996 *An Archaeology of Capitalism*. Oxford: Blackwells, p 12. To be fair, it should be noted that the Society for Post-medieval Archaeology evolved out of the earlier Post-medieval Ceramics Group. For an explanation, see Barton, K 1968 'The origins of the Society for Post-medieval Archaeology'. *Post-medieval Archaeology* I, p 102-103.

16 See discussion in Palmer, M and P Neaverson 1998) *Industrial Archaeology: Principles and Practice*. London and New York: Routledge, p 14.

19 This problem has been addressed, to some extent, by recent initiatives from national agencies such as English Heritage. In addition to work on the Sheffield metals trades, building recording specialists from English Heritage have also documented the layout and operation of workshops in the Birmingham Jewellery Quarter, and Northampton's boot and shoe industry. See, Cattell, J and B Hawkins 2000 The Birmingham Jewellery Quarter: An introduction and guide. English Heritage and Birmingham City Council; Cooke, J, K Hilsden, A Menuge and A Williams 2000 *The Northamptonshire Boot and Shoe Industry: A Summary Report*. English Heritage

20 Palmer, M. and P. Neaverson (eds) 2001 *From Industrial Revolution to Consumer Revolution: international perspectives on the archaeology of industrialisation*. The International Committee for the Conservation of the Industrial Heritage, Millenium Congress. Cambridge: Maney Publishing, for the Association for Industrial Archaeology, p 10.

21 Public Art Research Archive: Sheffield Hallam University. *Sheffield's Cutlery Collection*. http://www.shu.ac.uk/services/lc/slidecol/pubart/canteen3.html

22 see Karskens, G 1999)*Inside the Rocks: The Archaeology of a Neighbourhood* Alexandria, NSW: Hale & Ironmonger. P 54.

23 Goodfellow, A W, 'Sheffield Turnpikes in the 18th century.' Transactions of the Hunter Archaeological Society, V, 1942, p 73. Cited in Lars Magnusson, *The Contest for Control: Metal Industries in Sheffield, Solingen, Remscheid and Eskilstuna during Indusrialisation*. Oxford, Provience, U.S.A. Berg Publishers, p 46.

24 quotation from Taylor, W 1927 *The Sheffield Horn Industry*. Sheffield: J W Northend Ltd, p 11.

25 Moore, S and G Tweedale 'The Cutlery Collection in the Cutlers' Hall', p 205. In Binfield, C and D Hey (eds) 1997 *Mesters to Masters: A History of the Company of Cutlers in Hallamshire*. Oxford: Oxford University Press, p 195-217.

26 Cited in Tweedale, G 1987 *Sheffield Steel and America: A Century of Commercial and Technological Interdependence, 1830-1830*. Cambridge: Cambridge University Press, p 144

[27] 'How Sheffield Lost the American Trade'. *Sheffield Independent*, 17 June 1875. Cited in ibid., p 133.

[28] Tweedale, G 1996 *The Sheffield Knife Book: A History and Collectors' Guide*. Sheffield, The Hallamshire Press, p 298-299.

[29] Ibid, p 300

[30] Moore, S and G Tweedale 1997 'The Cutlery Collection in the Cutlers' Hall' p 202

[31] Tweedale, G *The Sheffield Knife Book* p 299.

[32] Nassaney, M S and M R Abel 'Lessons from New England's Nineteenth-century Cutlery Industry'. In Delle, J S A Mrozowski and R. Paynter *Lines That Divide: Historical Archaeologies of Race, Class, and Gender*. Knoxville: University of Tennessee Press, p 239-276

[33] Some examples of labor historians exploring this field include, Braverman, H 1974) *Labor and Monopoly Capital*. New York: Monthly Review Press; Paynter, R. 1988 'Steps to an Archaeology of Capitalism: Material Change and Class Analysis'. In *The Recovery of Meaning: Historical Archaeology in the Eastern Unite States*, (eds) Leone, M and P Potter Jnr, p 407-33. Washington D.C.: Smithsonian Institution Press.; Shackel. P A 1996 *Culture Change and the New Technology: An Archaeology of the Early American Industrial Era*, New York: Plenum; Shaiken,H 1985 *Work Transformed: Automation and Labor in the Computer Age*. New York: Holt, Rinehart and Winston.

[34] Nassaney, M S and M R Abel 'Lessons from New England's Nineteenth-century Cutlery Industry'. In Delle, J S A Mrozowski and R Paynter *Lines That Divide: Historical Archaeologies of Race, Class, and Gender*. Knoxville: University of Tennessee Press, p 240

[35] Nassaney, M S and M R Abel 'Lessons from New England's Nineteenth-century Cutlery Industry'. In Delle, J S A Mrozowski and R Paynter *Lines That Divide: Historical Archaeologies of Race, Class, and Gender*. Knoxville: University of Tennessee Press, p 241.

[36] Nassaney, M S and M R Abel, p 242.

[37] Nassaney, M S and M R Abel, p 244.

[38] David Hey, 'The Establishment of the Cutlers' Company', p 14. In Binfield, C and Hey, D (eds) 1997 *Mesters to Masters: A History of the Company of Cutlers in Hallamshire*, Oxford University Press, p 12-25.

[39] Marc Prival, *Couteaux et Couteliers*. Thiers 1994), p 51-62. Cited in David Hey, 'The Establishment of the Cutlers' Company', p 14.

[40] Ibid, p 17-18. Cited in David Hey'The Establishment of the Cutlers' Company', p 15.

[41] Jochen Putsch and Manfred Krause, 'The Cutlery Industry from Production to Industrial Museum: Solingen and Sheffield Compared'. In *Engineering in Germany: Proceedings of a conference held in Cologne on 28th October 1994*. Transactions of the Newcomen Society. Volume 66 1994-95, Supplement no.1. Science Museum, London, p 43-52.

[42] Ibid, p 43-44.

[43] Ibid, p 44.

[44] Ibid, p 45-47. The authors estimate that by 1914 Solingen had achieved a 50% share of the global market in cutlery, whilst the share of Sheffield had fallen to 25%.

[45] Quotation from Henry J Palmer, 'Cutlery and Cutlers at Sheffield' *The English Illustrated Magazine*, August 1884. Transcribed, and and placed on the internet by Eric Youle: http://freepages.history.rootsweb.com/.../cutlery_and_cutlers. htm.

[46] David M Higgins, 'Trade Marks and the Defence of "Sheffield" '. In Binfield, C and Hey, D (eds) 1997)*Mesters to Masters: A History of the Company of Cutlers in Hallamshire*, Oxford University Press, p 85-114 (p 95).

[47] Ibid, p 103.

[48] Ibid, p 104.

[49] Information from E.J. Buckatzsch, 'Places of origin of a group of immigrants into Sheffield 1624-1799.' (p 296). In, Peter Clark (ed.) 1976 *The Early Modern Town: A Reader*. New York: Longman and the Open University Press, p .292-296

[50] Except in scythe-grinding, where the reverse was true.

[51] Jochen Putsch and Manfred Krause, 'The Cutlery Industry from Production to Industrial Museum: Solingen and Sheffield Compared', p 44.

[52] Evidence for this practice is quoted from the Maison des Couteliers et Musée de la Coutellerie, Theirs, cited in David Hey, 'The Establishment of the Cutlers' Company', p 15. Henry J Palmer, 'Cutlery and Cutlers at Sheffield' p 11.

[54] Although this is likely to be the case, there is a possibility that deep-seated customary practices may be at work here. Take, for example, the sunwise direction of movement i.e. from left to right (*deiseal*) which is practised in many routine agricultural and other tasks in the Western Isles of Scotland, and which may well derive from Norse or even earlier cosmologies. See James Symonds, 'Songs Remembered in Exile? Integrating unsung archives of Highland life' in Amy Gazin-Schwartz and Cornelius J. Holtorf (eds) 1999 *Archaeology and Folklore*. London and New York: Routledge, p 106-128 (p.121 for a discussion of *deiseal*).

[55] Henry J Palmer, 'Cutlery and Cutlers at Sheffield' p.10.

THE DEVELOPMENT OF THE CUTLERY AND TABLEWARE INDUSTRY IN SHEFFIELD

———————

JOAN UNWIN

Chapter 1

The development of the industry

Introduction

Sheffield has been a centre for tableware and cutlery manufacture since the Middle Ages. The area known as Hallamshire included the parishes of Sheffield, Ecclesfield and Handsworth, and together with adjacent Derbyshire parishes of Norton and Eckington, gradually became supreme in the production of knives, overtaking London by the middle of the eighteenth century, in both quantity and quality. Strictly speaking, cutlery means implements with a cutting edge, which includes items such as knives, scissors, razors, sickles, shears and scythes. In Sheffield's manufacturing terms, forks and spoons are called 'flatware' and other table items, such as dishes, trays and teapots are 'holloware', which grew out of the silver trades.

In the Cutlers' Company, the craft grouping of cutlers made a variety of knives, but evidence shows that this group also made forks, though the term 'forkmaker' is not generally used until the 1770s. No one was ever referred to as a 'spoonmaker', for which there is little specific evidence before the nineteenth century. Although many nineteenth century firms manufactured a variety of tableware, initially these trades were separate and developed many sub-branches and specialisations.

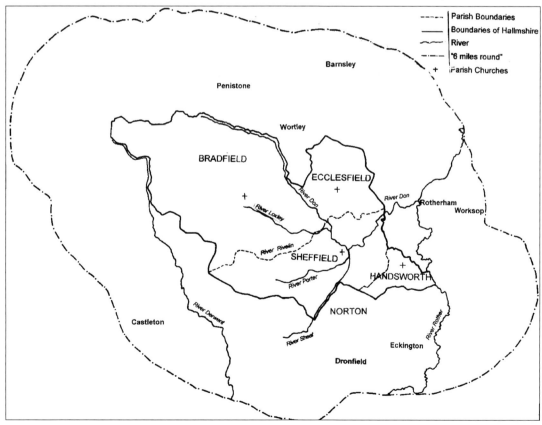

Figure 4 The area of Hallamshire[1]

Knife blades were usually made of ferrous metals, but the invention of Sheffield Plate and the expansion of the silver trades in Sheffield from the 1740s onwards, meant that many firms specialised in making a range of tableware with non-ferrous metal handles. Forks were made from both ferrous and non-ferrous metals, while in the eighteenth century spoons were often cast in pewter or sterling silver. By fusing silver onto copper, to produce Sheffield plate, many items for the table previously made from sterling silver could now be produced more cheaply. The silver trades benefited from the introduction of crucible steel in the 1740s. This steel could produce better quality dies for stamping spoons, candlesticks, etc which were made by the thousand from sheet material. Sheffield plate, Britannia metal and from c 1840s, electro-plated metals was used for most of the output. Although heavy stamps and presses were used in many manufacturing processes, handmade articles still made up a large proportion of Sheffield's output.

For centuries, the manufacture of knives, forks and spoons was by hand, with craftsmen operating with a minimum number of simple tools in small workshops. Power, other than the human hand or foot, was initially introduced at the waterpowered grinding wheels, heavy forging hammers and rolling mills. The introduction of steam power in the 1780s meant that power, via line shafts, could be transmitted to urban workshops in tenement buildings and used for a variety of processes, from boring holes in handles to stamping out forks and spoons. However, the gradual introduction of powered machinery for different processes did not totally replace the hand manufacture of tableware. The traditional manufacturing organisation of the 'Little Mester' in his workshop – an individual craftsman with perhaps two or three employees and apprentices – continued alongside an increasing number of factories with production-line processes. Fragmentation, specialisation and a complex trade organisation of sub-contracting ensured the survival of individual craftsmen, even into the twenty-first century.

The traditional nature of the industry

The earliest surviving reference to the Sheffield trade is that for Robertus le Cotelar who was listed in the 1297 lay subsidy; a few cutlers were mentioned in the Poll Tax returns of 1379[2]. Fuller documentary evidence for the organisation and the scale of operation for the cutlery trades begins in the middle of the sixteenth century when sufficient records survive to suggest that cutlers formed a large proportion of the working population. These records come from the courts of the Lords of Hallamshire, which established the Cutlers' Juries to oversee the organisation of the trade. In the mid sixteenth century, the manorial court drew up ordinances, which were later incorporated into the rules governing the Cutlers' Company. They were concerned with work practices, apprentice-ships and the registration of identifying marks of craftsmen. Some cutlers' marks were entered in the manorial court records around 1560[3] and the Cutlers' Jury later registered 182 cutlers' marks in 1614. Unfortunately, many of the records relating to the Manor of Hallamshire were lost in 1761 when fire destroyed Worksop Manor, another of the Shrewsbury's properties.

As lords of the manor, the powerful Earls of Shrewsbury had taken an active interest in the cutlery and metalworking trades, but on the death in 1616 of Gilbert, Earl of Shrewsbury, the manor passed to non-resident lords. The cutlers no longer had a controlling system for registering craftsmen's marks and regulating the number of apprentices, so they petitioned Parliament for an Act of Incorporation. In the face of opposition from the London cutlers, the Company of Cutlers in Hallamshire was established in 1624. It was given the responsibility for binding apprentices, admitting freemen, registering marks and administering regulations aimed at ensuring the quality of workmanship.

At the time, London was the pre-eminent centre for cutlery manufacture in England, having had a craft guild since the fourteenth century[4]. Surviving records show that the industry was fragmented into blademakers, cutlers and merchants. Because the freedom of the guild conferred civic rights and responsibilities, the merchants dictated much of the craft organisation[5]. They maintained a restrictive control over the selling of knives within London, struggling to exclude the knives from other centres, and requiring London-made knives to carry the mark of a dagger. The records of the London cutlers show that many facets of their trade organisation differed from those in Sheffield. Problems have arisen therefore, in publications about Sheffield cutlery over the varying trade terms for parts of knives and work processes (for instance, no one in Sheffield was ever called a 'blademaker').

One variation is in the registration of identifying marks by cutlers. Sheffield cutlers registered a mark when they applied for their freedom and, apart from a few exceptional cases, kept that mark for the rest of their working lives. The Sheffield mark books survive in an almost unbroken run from 1614 to 1878 and are an invaluable aid to the dating and identification of Sheffield-made knives. This is not so in London, where the mark registers have been destroyed and where marks could be bought and sold, often several times a year. This has meant that the identification and dating of London-made knives has depended largely on stylistic details; if such a method is applied to Sheffield-made

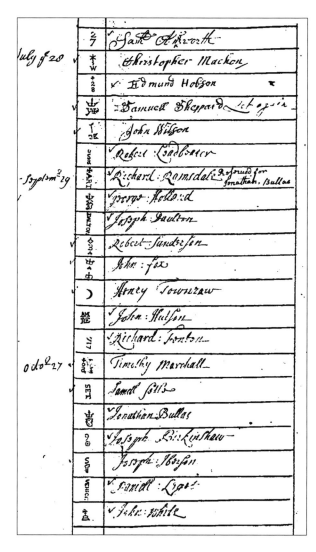

Figure 5 Page from the Great Mark Book, courtesy of the Cutlers' Company of Hallamshire

knives, discrepancies between style and mark date can arise.

Sheffield was fortunate in having natural resources which encouraged the formation of a metalworking economy. The exploitation of local ironstone, coal and sandstone established a local skills base but, although these resources provided craftsmen with some of their raw material, they were of insufficient quantity and quality to fuel the expansion of an industry requiring consistently good steel. Until the transport improvements in the mid-eighteenth century, Sheffield was geographically isolated, with arduous access to imported goods, such as iron and steel and with few good roads to carry away its manufactured products. To these physical restrictions was added the Cutlers' Company, which operated as a medieval craft guild, encouraging the traditional nature and outlook of Sheffield craftsmen. Their control over the industry remained until 1814.

The power and legacy of the Cutlers' Company

In 1624, the Cutlers' Company claimed jurisdiction over the working lives of cutlers, scissorsmiths and sickle and shearsmiths in Hallamshire 'and six miles round', which effectively only included the parishes of Norton and Eckington in Derbyshire. By the end of the seventeenth century, awlbladesmiths, filesmiths and scythesmiths had joined the Company, and by the late eighteenth century, forkmakers and razormakers (sub-groups of cutlers) were considered separate crafts when they registered their apprentices with the Company.

The Cutlers' Company was headed by the Master Cutler, who was elected for a year from among the 'Company', which consisted of 2 Wardens, 6 Searchers and 24 Assistants. The Searchers played an active part in the running of the trades. They were responsible for quality control, being entitled to enter premises and search out 'deceitful' wares, such as cutlery without a steel edge. They were also responsible for searching through the mark books to check that the proposed marks of freemen were not too similar to existing marks or carried covert messages about the quality of the goods ('BEST STEEL' for instance, was not allowed prior to 1814). The Company was a self-selecting group, but accepted nominations from the rest of the freemen craftsmen. These trained craftsmen were known as the 'Commonalty' and had little say in the running of the Company.

To practice the trade of cutler, boys had to serve an apprenticeship for at least seven years. References to apprenticeships were included in the ordinances issued by the manorial court of the Earls of Shrewsbury, so it is likely that this court played a role in recognising apprentices. From 1624, the Cutlers' Company performed a very important duty in controlling the numbers of apprentices by insisting that they were registered at the Cutlers' Hall, where the Company kept its records. Freemen were entitled to take one apprentice at a time, apart from their own sons. Another apprentice could not be indentured until the previous one was in his final year. It is assumed that the boy started at the age of fourteen and, at the end of the usual apprenticeship of seven years, he would reach the minimum age for a freeman. However, many boys were apprenticed for as long as ten years and some, especially parish apprentices, were specifically bound to serve until they were twenty-four years old. These long apprentice-ships occurred mainly in the seventeenth century and caused some concern in the Company, because boys younger than fourteen were being apprenticed. However, the main reason for these long 'apprenticeships', appears to have been to tie the boy as a journeyman to his master.

On completion of his apprenticeship at the age of 21 or 24, a man could choose to register his freedom. Sheffield never had a mayor and corporation and a freeman had no civic rights or duties, unlike the masters in medieval guilds in other towns. However, a man had to be a freeman if he wished to join the 'Company', with the opportunity to become Master Cutler. To become a freeman, a craftsman simply had to pay 3s.4d, register his mark and pay an annual mark rent of 2d. His freedom, with a summary of any background details, was recorded by the Cutlers' Company and an impression of the mark was stamped in the mark book. About fifty percent of the apprentices eventually took out their freedom, although some waited many years, perhaps until their father or master died[6]. As well as having the right to take apprentices and train his sons, a freeman's mark was perhaps his most important asset, since it allowed him to sell his own manufactured knives. Non-freemen, having no mark with

which to identify their work, could not do this and would always have to make knives for others. This led to a two-tier system of craftsmen. The non-freemen had to be employees or accept sub-contracting work from a freeman, possibly continuing work as a journeyman with their original master. They may have specialised in one aspect of production, perhaps becoming grinders or forgers.

Properly, the terms 'freemen' and 'non-freemen' were not used by the Cutlers' Company. A trained apprentice was deemed to be 'free of the Company', whether or not he registered his freedom and identifying mark. The Company considered *freemen* as men 'owning their own work' and the non-freemen were properly called journeymen-freemen. However, in this context, the terms freemen and non-freemen will be used.

The Company also sought to restrict the aspects of the craftsmen's production and periods of work. It insisted that cutting edges were of steel, but no limits were placed on the daily hours that could be worked. It did try to enforce rest periods which corresponded to work patterns in the agricultural year. This resulted in 'holidays' for two weeks after Christmas and during August. However, in 1680, the scissorsmiths tried to improve their working lives by limiting their hours of work. There were three petitions, each being signed by approximately 140 scissorsmiths[7]. The first one was dated 16 August 1680, which set out their complaints about being forced to accept commodities for their scissors, rather than money, and proposed the establishment of a storehouse for their goods. The second petition, a month later, repeated similar complaints, but the third petition, in November, dealt with the suffering of the scissorsmiths caused by having to work very long hours. They proposed therefore to work only between the hours of 6am and 8pm and continue the enforced holidays at Christmas and in August. It is not known whether these work periods were generally accepted, but one effect of the post-Christmas layoff was that the week prior to Christmas was, and is, termed 'Bull week'. This was the period when people worked exceptionally long hours, in order to earn enough for the time when there was no work. In the nineteenth century, 'Calf', 'Cow' and 'Bull' weeks was the period when every effort was made to fulfill orders before Christmas and cover the dearth of orders after Christmas.

One final restriction placed on Hallamshire craftsmen was that they were not to work with or for 'outsiders' or with anyone who had not been trained according to the regulations of the Company. This became an issue in the later nineteenth century, when 'outsiders' strove to enter the trade by becoming partners of poor freemen.

The control and administration maintained by the Cutlers' Company and its predecessor, the manorial court, created an organised manufacturing base in Hallamshire, which became an expanding centre for cutlery manufacture in the eighteenth century. The restrictive regulations on apprenticeships and work practices gave a structure to the trade and support to its craftsmen. Although the Company was a self-electing oligarchy bent on control and restriction, it did provide the focus for the many problems faced by the craftsmen, such as the numbers of parish apprentices and competition with the London cutlers. For decades after its foundation, the Company's control was generally accepted, but the restrictions became key features of internal dissension and conflict in the later eighteenth century.

The Unions and the Sheffield Outrages

At the beginning of the nineteenth century, the Cutlers' Company lost its power to control the numbers of apprentices. This coincided with the growing movement for workers' unions and groups such as friendly societies. From the middle of the eighteenth century, the Sheffield grinders had formed a friendly society for mutual support, followed by the development of 'box' clubs in the later eighteenth century. The national movement for recognition by various workers' groups is outside the scope of this work, except in the way such ideas impinged on the Sheffield trades and work practices.

In the later eighteenth century, many Sheffield cutlers had set themselves in opposition to the restrictive practices of the Company and the 'opulent masters' who, they thought, flouted many of the Company's rules[8]. A new Act of Parliament was granted in 1791, which relaxed many of the regulations, and in 1814, the power of the Cutlers' Company was reduced to registering cutlers' marks. There was a drawback to this loss of an organisation with control over the trades, especially in terms of working conditions, apprentices and pay. The

emerging unions and trade societies sought to fill the gap and societies developed in many sections of the cutlery trades, representing specific craft groupings, such as the grinders and forgers. By attempting to control the trades, these unions saw themselves as the natural heirs to the Cutlers' Company and wished to assume its powers. The Cutlers Company had enforced its ruling, by fines, that men could not work as cutlers unless they had completed an authorised apprenticeship and been recognised as a freeman or non-freemen. Craftsmen were obliged to be part of the Company and conform to its regulations, so the unions assumed that by practicing a trade, men were also deemed to be in its union. By equating the trade with a controlling organisation, as the Cutlers' Company had done, unions also strove to control the activities of the craftsmen, masters and apprentices. The unions also took over some of the socially responsible activities, giving support to poor workmen which the Cutlers' Company had done, but also developed a system of burial funds and paid men who were out of work. In Sheffield the national discussions about the role of unions or their existence had no meaning – unions were regarded as a right. The problem for the Sheffield unions was in the enforcement of their regulations.

Because these unions and societies represented specific sections of the trades, it was relatively easy to know who was doing what. Many unions were small enough for all the members to meet in rooms in public houses, whereby everyone knew what wages being paid, and whether masters were training too many apprentices. They also knew which men were not paying their union dues. To maintain high wages, the unions would remove men from the labour market, paying them to stay out of work and 'on the box'. The need to pay these men often put a severe financial strain on those in work, who had to contribute sufficient dues, and the unions resorted to extreme measure to force members to conform.

The most common pressure applied to wayward members was to remove a man's tools or the drive belt from his machine, thus preventing him from working. This was termed 'rattening'; tools were supposed to have been taken by the 'rats' and hidden away. These 'pranks' were age-old and were used to punish an unpopular workmate, discipline workers and masters who were 'obnoxious to the trade' or to intimidate a

17

craftsman into conforming to the rules. Often a threatening letter was sent, signed by 'Smite-em' or 'Mary Ann'. Masters could be accused of taking on too many apprentices, employing non-union men and under-cutting the prices for jobs. Tools were returned or their location revealed when the dues and grievances were remedied. 'Rattening' was hardly considered a crime in Sheffield, but these activities took on a sinister aspect during 1850s and 1860s, when the unions strove for control over the trades. Increasingly violent methods were used – placing gunpowder down chimneys, assaults and finally shooting at masters and employers who were deemed 'obnoxious to the trade'. Sometimes these crimes resulted in men being charged at York Assizes, but they were not always found guilty[9].

Three episodes were particularly violent. In 1857, the saw grinder, James Lindley, was accused by the union of taking on too many apprentices. He was followed around Sheffield for several weeks before being shot and killed. In 1861, a house in Acorn Street was attacked with gunpowder and an innocent lodger was killed; the house belonged to George Wastnidge, a non-union fender grinder. The Hereford Street Outrage in 1866 involved Thomas Fearnehough, a saw grinder at odds with 'the trade'. Gunpowder was placed in his cellar, resulting in damage, but no one was hurt.

This last outrage was reported in the national press, causing great anger and a reward of £1000 was offered for information; local unions offered £100. The demand for an inquiry into union activity and their involvement led to a discussion on trade unionism throughout Britain and unions, anxious to clear their name and to establish their rights, supported this demand. In 1867, the Government organised a Royal Commission into Trade Unions, with a sub-committee to enquire into the outrages in Sheffield[10].

Commissions of Inquiry met in various towns and cities and the Sheffield Commission met to hear evidence into the activities of the local unions and, in particular, the methods by which some union officials dealt with non-union labour, employers and recalcitrant members. Not once did anyone in Sheffield question the unions' right to exist, an issue which was being discussed in other towns and cities. Sheffield's Commission was more concerned with the violence and the methods used by some of the

unions. The Commissioners could inquire into outrages committed during the previous ten years, but rattening and similar activities were probably age old. They were generally considered reasonable activities, accepted alike by perpetrators, victims and townspeople.

The inquiry was held in the Town Hall and the Sheffield Commissioners, all of whom had legal training, were William Overend, a local man, Thomas Berstow and George Chance. The police had collected information on 209 cases of violence including 20 major outrages, with manufacturers, workmen and unions giving evidence. The Commission met almost every day for five weeks in mid 1867, calling 136 witnesses and asking 23,500 questions. Questioning rarely revealed the truth, which only came out after obtaining confessions by the granting of certificates of indemnity against prosecution. Initially, men confessed to minor cases of rattening, but the Commission succeeded in uncovering a complex system of trade union intimidation. At the centre of several shooting and gunpowder attacks was William Broadhead, secretary to the saw grinders. Broadhead was an important local figure, who also held a national position as the treasurer of the Alliance of Organised Trades, and had protested loudly at unions being unjustly incriminated in the outrages. He was questioned for nearly two days and had to answer almost 1400 questions.

A published transcript of the Commission's Enquiry makes fascinating reading[11]. It reveals the unshakeable belief of the Sheffield unions in their right to exist, their attempt to equate 'the trade' with 'the union' and to expect that all men in a trade would be members of its union. It followed that the unions must have some power to enforce their rules, possibly by distraining property, practices used by law-enforcement officers, or by fines – power that had been granted to the Cutlers' Company. The outcome of the inquiry concluded that, although several unions and their officials were guilty of intimidation to a greater or lesser degree, the union craftsmen were mostly honest, hardworking and upright members of society.

Although there were few grinding unions which had never turned to rattening, Sheffield unionists came out of the Enquiry in a good light and the Commission praised the great majority of unions who had not been involved in any outrages. The Commission concluded that the unions kept up wages, but it did not accept rattening as a legitimate means by which unions enforced their rules and it went out of its way to side with the 'poor workman' who was risk of being defrauded by union officials. Whereas unions in other places had to fight for recognition, Sheffield unions were taken for granted and aimed to extend statutory powers to benefit themselves. Rattening continued for some years after the Commission, and then gradually died down, at least as a method of union control.

This episode in the history of Sheffield has become a powerful image in the folk tradition of the city. It illustrates important features in the organisation of the trade. It demonstrates the traditional nature of the industry, based on control, firstly by the courts of the Lord of the Manor, then by the Cutlers' Company and finally by the unions. It also demonstrates that because Sheffielders had long equated the cutlery trades with the Cutlers' Company, the unions attempted to do the same. The Outrages reveal aspects of the trade organisation which were of paramount importance and which have been contentious issues for centuries – namely, the numbers of apprentices being trained, the hours of work and the payments due.

The 'Little Mester'

The institution of the 'Little Mester' is another image which has entered folk consciousness. The Little Mester is usually pictured working alone, in a small, constricted workshop, which is used to heighten the contrast between the poor working conditions and his fine craftsmanship. He is represented as the upholder of traditional work practices and values, maintaining the high quality of Sheffield goods. His pedigree is seen as descending through the masters and freemen of the Cutlers' Company.

Although the accounts and records of the Cutlers' Company use the term 'Freedom', the word 'Freeman' was not in common use by the Company until the late eighteenth century. The Company considered all trained craftsmen as 'free'. The 1624 Act does not mention freemen and the early byelaws talk only of 'masters'[12]. The men referred to here as freemen are the men whom Cutlers' Company described as 'owning their own work'. This referred to the practical advantage for a man who paid the fee to record a freedom and mark – his mark identified his knives etc, which he could sell for

himself. Those craftsmen, who chose not to do so, had to work for others and this later gave rise to confusing terms such as 'journeyman freemen'. However, here the term 'freeman' will be used for a man 'who owns his own work', who has registered his freedom and his mark, is a master of apprentices and who sold his own finished goods. The 'non-freeman' was a trained craftsman who had no identifying mark and no freedom. He was not allowed to train apprentices and always had to made goods for another man.

The Little Mesters may have worked alone and for themselves, but may also have taken on employees, taken on work as sub-contractors or given out work to specialists. As such, they were vulnerable to pressure to reduce prices and to accept conditions such as thirteen or fourteen items to the dozen. At times, far from being the upholders of all that was good, they were seen as employers who paid the lowest wages and worked in some of the worst conditions. They continued in existence even after the introduction of steam power, the building of tenement and integrated factories and the rise of the large cutlery firms, which employed thousands.

It is difficult to discover the origin of this term 'Little Mester', but it is listed in *A Glossary of Words used in the Neighbourhood of Sheffield*, compiled by S O Addy in 1888. R E Leader described the Little Mesters as being socially no different from any of the more affluent masters or officers in the Cutlers' Company. He went on to say 'the Little Mester continued as before to labour with bare arms and in leathern apron. But he was now the employer of others, not the employed by others …The employed might mean only a man and a boy; a striker and apprentice; but the cutler was his own master; a freeman in truth'.

Notes

[1] RE Leader 1905 *History of the Company of Cutlers in Hallamshire*, vol.I (Sheffield), p 3.
[2] D Hey 1991 *The Fiery Blades of Hallamshire.* (Leicester University Press) p 54-55.
[3] T Walter Hall 1928 *Descriptive Catalogue of Sheffield Manorial Records* Vol.II (Sheffield) p vi-viii.
[4] C Welch 1912 *History of the Cutlers' Company of London* (London).
[5] J R Kellett 1958 'The Breakdown of Gild and Corporation Control over the Handicraft and Retail Trade in London' in *The Economic History Review*,

Second Series, Vol. X., No.3, p 381-395.

[6] J. Unwin 1995 'Apprenticeships and Freedoms: the computer analysis of the Records of the Cutlers' Company in Sheffield' *The Local Historian*, Volume 25, No 4.

[7] Cutlers' Company archive, reference S1/1-3 Scissorsmiths' Covenant.
Sheffield Archives, MD571-574 – Freemen's protest, 1784.

[8] S Pollard 1959 *The History of Labour in Sheffield, Liverpool*, p 71-72.

[9] ibid, p 152-158.

[10] Trade Union Commission: *The Sheffield Outrages*, introduction by S Pollard facsimile 1971.

[11] R E Leader 1905 *History of the Company of Cutlers in Hallamshire*, vol.I (Sheffield) p 8

[12] R E Leader 1901 *Sheffield in the Eighteenth Century*, (Sheffield), p 14.

Chapter 2

Sources of information

Introduction

One of the problems in researching work practices is the general diffidence of craftsmen. They feel that what they do is 'nothing special' and often cannot explain in words the very complicated tasks they perform. Outsiders therefore describe these processes from observation and may not have the perception to understand the significance of seemingly trivial practices. Surviving eyewitness descriptions of processes which are no longer performed, must obviously be treated with care. Processes might have been recorded because they were unusual and therefore not representative of the general work pattern. Documentary evidence must also be taken in the context in which it was written and will undoubtedly contain omissions which are vital to a present-day understanding of two-hundred-year-old work practices. The descrip-tions given below are based on a variety of sources, which have been considered in conjunction with current practitioners of the crafts and skills.

Contemporary primary sources

Contemporary sources for the eighteenth century cutlery trade in Sheffield include probate inventories and the records of the Cutlers' Company. These two sources have been combined here to demonstrate their value. The probate records for the parish of Sheffield survive from the late seventeenth century to the 1740s and are held at the Borthwick Institute in York. The later ones are generally less informative since the inventories often list possessions of cutlers as 'goods in the smithy' or 'working tools', but where details are given, work practices can be reconstructed from the tools. However, there is rarely an indication of the specific products. Any finished goods would no doubt have been sold when the cutler perhaps became too old or ill to work.

The apprenticeships and freedoms records of the Cutlers' Company are particularly relevant. Boys wishing to become cutlers were required to register their apprenticeship to a master craftsman. On completion of their training, they became part of the Cutlers' Company, some men choosing to register their freedom and an identifying mark. The indenture documents and freedom certificates rarely survive but the Clerks to the Cutlers' Company kept books in which summaries of these occasions were entered. This data was collated and the published version has been used to assemble a computer database held at the University of Sheffield[1].

Several examples of probate inventories from the first half of the eighteenth century are given below. They provide lists of tools and equipment and two examples give details of the knives being produced. The inventory of Thomas Heaton, who died in March 1738/39, left one gross of 'rough blades' valued at 14 shillings. His inventory states that in his workshop, he had a pair of bellows, a vice, six hammers and a pair of tongs, amounting to total of £2.4s.4d. Although an anvil is not mentioned, these tools suggest that he was only forging blades, since there were no tools for grinding or assembling knives. Data in the Cutlers' Company records show that Thomas was the son of a cutler, apprenticed in 1694 for nine years, at the end of which, he never took out his freedom or registered a mark. His working life was approximately 35 years and it is assumed from the evidence, that he spent it making knife blades for other masters.

An earlier inventory however, does give a better idea of the value and variety of knives. Robert Rhodes died in February, 1729/30, and although he was described as a cutler, seems to have operated either as a merchant or shopkeeper. Robert was the son of a Barnsley collier and became a freeman in 1704. He therefore had the right to train apprentices and to strike his mark on his own knives, though his inventory makes no mention of workshops, smithies or any manufacturing tools. It does however list a 'shop' which seems to have been fitted out with over 60 drawers. He left a large amount of cutlery including one dozen case and one dozen table knives valued at 12 shillings, plus 51 dozen butcher knives and 2 dozen butcher steels. He also had almost 750 fork blades at £2.1s.0d. There were several oddments and parcels of knives as well as hafting material – 24 stone of boxwood (18s.0d) and 113 head of buckhorns (£1.8s.3d). This inventory suggests he was buying in finished and part-made items for resale, together with handle material and he was owed money by several 'tradesmen', some of whom were cutlers. This may be a false interpretation, since in his will he left his son Robert £5 and 'all my working tools and all utensils belonging unto them which belong unto the cutlers trade'. Robert junior recorded his freedom the year before his father died, and took the same mark as his father, who was possibly too ill to work.

Other probate inventories list the tools in a workshop, giving an indication of the type of processes being performed. Joseph Shimell (Shemeld) died in 1726, having a pair of bellow, stock, stithy and hammers (£1.1s.0d) – tools for forging, and his four vices suggests some assembly work. His debts included money due to specialist craftsmen and to traders for goods he himself bought. He owed Peter Wigfall £4 for grinding and Joseph Bennyson 10 shillings for pressing scales. Scale pressing to produce handle material will be discussed below. Joseph Shimell was a poor boy who was apprenticed in 1695, becoming a freeman in 1703. Peter Wigfall was a freeman of similar age, so the agreement between the two for Peter to do Joseph's grinding, would be an agreement between 'equals' and not a master/journeyman contract.

Another cutler who might have been contracting out his grinding was Joseph Smith who died in 1726. He had a smithy with two bellows, a plain stithy and two 'baitster' (bolster?) stithies and stocks, a cooltrough – equipment for forging but no hand tools are mentioned. He had workboards and six vices, suggesting assembly work. The numbers of stithies and vices suggest he was not working alone, but it is not possible to add biographical details because his was such a common name.

In contrast to these men who seem to have concentrated on forging and assembly, Isaac Staniforth's inventory of 1739 shows that he was a grinder. His inventory states that he had

'In the Wheel: 3 rough stones 1-1-0, 1 rough stone 2-6, 1 stone axel tree 2-6, glazier band 5-0, rough stone band 2-3, 2 wheele kitts 2-6, 1 horssing 3-6, witening stone and axel tree 8-0, horsen 11d, pulleys £1'.

All this equipment relates to different stages in grinding and putting finer finishes to the blades, which will be discussed below. From the mid-seventeenth century, several men called Isaac Staniforth were leasing the Nether Lescarr Wheel, a waterpowered grinding wheel on the River Porter and this particular Isaac may have been one of two men who became in freemen in 1676 and 1718.

Contemporary published sources

Descriptions of nineteenth century processes are found in a variety of published books and articles. These have generally been written by people outside the trades, or at least not actually involved in the manufacturing processes. In 1856, James Wilson presented a paper to the Society of Arts entitled 'On the manufacture of articles from steel, particularly cutlery'[2]. This gives a carefully observed description of forging, hardening, tempering and grinding. It also discusses the contentious issues of the correct marking of steel blades and the processes of casting cutlery.

Another source for descriptions of work processes are firms' histories. These are often produced to celebrate anniversaries in business or the removal to new premises. They are obviously self-laudatory but can provide detailed descriptions of the factory, machinery and processes. One such example is *Handicrafts that Survive*, purportedly celebrating the centenary of the firm of Thomas Turner, Suffolk Work, Sheffield. The title suggests quaintness and tradition but there are included photographs showing the manufacturing processes in making knives and forks. It was written in 1902 when Albert Hobson, the owner of Thomas Turner, was Master Cutler. This was obviously a good time for a public relations exercise, but there is no documentary evidence that his firm was founded in 1802. There were several Thomas Turners in Sheffield at that time, none becoming a freeman in 1802 or even starting their apprenticeships. Similarly, Thomas Turner's registered mark of 'ENCORE' was not registered by the firm until the mid nineteenth century. In 1802, it was owned by a cutler called Luke Brownell.

Of great importance in considering manufacturing processes are two types of publications arising from the trades themselves, the trade catalogues and 'Statements', which were price lists for the wages paid for the manufacturing processes in cutlery manufacture, agreed between masters and men. They cover every facet of production. These nineteenth century sources can be used to reconstruct work practices and can provide a more realistic assessment of the range of cutlery being made, than the surviving examples in museums and collections.

Published secondary sources

Turning from these contemporary sources, there is a large body of published material. The history of the Sheffield cutlery industry has long fascinated local historians and antiquarians, although the emphasis in early histories tended to be on the luminaries, and the cutlery trades were considered largely in terms of the Cutlers' Company and its civic role. One of the earliest histories is *Hallamshire*, written in 1829 by the Reverend Joseph Hunter, a general history which was revised by the Reverend Alfred Gatty in 1869. At the end of the nineteenth century, the antiquarian, Robert Eadon Leader must have been given unlimited access to the Cutlers' Company records in order to produce his comprehensive account of the Company from its inception in 1624[3]. Although there was an understandable tendency to deal with the issues and the personalities of the officers of the Company, rather than the craftsmen and processes of manufacture, it is nonetheless an invaluable and comprehensive history. The first volume covers the history of the Company, with emphasis on the Feasts and the powerful people associated with the Company. The second volume consists largely of printed lists of craftsmen; those present at the Company's incorporation in 1624; those who contributed to various undertakings and finally and most importantly, the apprentices and freemen of the Company from 1624 to the date of publication in 1906. Leader's sources for this part of the second volume were the books summarising the apprenticeships and freedoms[4]. Exactly how he, or others, extracted the material and arranged it in alphabetical order of apprentices' surnames is not known. One assumes it was achieved by several people compiling a card index. Despite errors in transcription and in printing, it remains a remarkable piece of work and makes a very important resource accessible to local

historians. More recently, in *Mesters to Masters*, edited by Clyde Binfield and David Hey, aspects of the Company's history and its work are described in a series of essays. This book was produced in 1997 by the Cutlers' Company as part of the celebrations for the 700 years' anniversary of the earliest surviving documentary reference to a Sheffield cutler.

The first substantial work to detail the actual processes of cutlery manufacture and work practices was written by G I H Lloyd in 1913. This book, *The Cutlery Trades*, provides an important insight into Sheffield's industry at the beginning of its long decline. Lloyd was able to observe processes common in the nineteenth century and the trade organisation of independent craftsmen and large firms, with a complex system of sub-contracting to out-workers. These outworkers and independent craftsmen continued to exist alongside massive firms such as George Wostenholm and Joseph Rodgers. A later publication, which also provides a careful description of work practices, is *The Story of Cutlery* by J Himsworth (1953). This has the advantage of good-quality photographs of processes and products. Focusing on the economics of the cutlery trades, Sydney Pollard's papers and especially *A History of Labour in Sheffield* (1959) have value in explaining the Sheffield trades in a wider context.

Since the 1970s, David Hey has produced a number of books on the Sheffield metalworking trades. His books are now the standard reference works on Sheffield's history especially for the later seventeenth and eighteenth centuries. *The Fiery Blades of Hallamshire* (1991) deals with Sheffield's population, industries, society and communications from 1660 to 1740. Another significant publication is *The Rural Metalworkers of the Sheffield Region* (1972), which considers the distribution of the metalworkers in and around Sheffield. Other publications by David Hey have been of a more general nature, giving an outline of the history of the cutlery trades. Written in honour of Joan Thirsk, the essay *The origins and early growth of the Hallamshire cutlery and allied trade* is noteworthy[5]. In this, Hey considered the geographic, topographic and social aspects, which contributed to the rise of the Sheffield trades.

Several books and pamphlets have been produced by museums and collectors, describing the cutlery produced in Sheffield and elsewhere. These books are descriptive of the types of knives and generally deal with the subject on a chronological basis, describing stylistic features, the materials used and the quality of manufacture. The most recent book of this type is *Cutlery for the Table* (1999) by Simon Moore. Although it is primarily intended for collectors and many of its illustrations relate to London-made knives, it provides a good record of the stylistic development of table cutlery. Along these lines another recent book is *The Sheffield Knife Book, a History and Collectors' Guide* (1996) by Geoffrey Tweedale. Aimed again at the collector, the book summarises the history of some Sheffield manufacturers. Of necessity, these firms are mainly those of the nineteenth and twentieth centuries, who have left records and examples of their workmanship; earlier manufacturers and craftsmen are dealt with more generally.

Collections of cutlery and flatware

The final source of information about the work practices of Sheffield cutlers are the knives themselves. Museums and private collections hold many examples of Sheffield-made knives, providing further evidence for materials, stylistic changes and the skills of the craftsmen. In Sheffield, there are extensive collections held at the City Museum, the Assay Office, the Cutlers' Company and the Hawley Collection (see below). However, it is necessary to identify and date them correctly, which is why the data held in the mark books of the Cutlers' Company is so invaluable[6]. Museums and collectors have understandably concentrated on knives that are attractive and valuable or demonstrate unusual features, but will not give a true picture of the general cutlery trades. Archaeological excavations of industrial sites in Sheffield by ARCUS (Archaeological Research and Consultancy at the University of Sheffield), as part of the regeneration of brownfield sites, have revealed knives in various stages of manufacture and although they are corroded, they can often provide information about processes and are usually examples of the more common types of knives.

If the collections of up-market knives are not overly helpful in any attempt to understand general manufacturing processes, then collections of industrial machines and tools are vital. The Industrial Museum at Kelham Island, Sheffield has reconstructed examples of cutlers'

premises, mostly from the mid twentieth century, but showing features which would have been recognised by cutlers from the previous century. The Museum also has several workshops that are rented out by cutlery craftsmen who demonstrate their skills to visitors, although unfortunately, there are no longer any hand forgers of knife blades.

A unique resource is the Hawley Collection at the University of Sheffield, which has had a deliberate acquisition policy concentrating on tableware, cutlery and edgetools of Sheffield manufacturer and on part-made items. The Collection also has acquired the 'tools that made the tools', which are essential for an overall appreciation of manufacturing processes. The collection of cutlery and associated tools is augmented by documentary ephemera, audio-visual material and the knowledge of Ken Hawley, the collector. The Collection, which is now owned by a Trust, also has hundreds of trade catalogues of cutlery and flatware manufacturers, dating from the late nineteenth century.

Notes

[1] R E Leader 1906 *History of the Company of Cutlers in Hallamshire*, vol.II (Sheffield). The apprentices and freemen were entered into a database as part of an ongoing project run by David Hey into the distribution of surnames at the Division of Adult Continuing Education, The University of Sheffield.

[2] J Wilson 1856 'On the manufacture of articles from steel, particularly cutlery', *Journal of the Society of Arts*, Vol.IV, no.177, p 357–366.

[3] R E Leader 1905,1906 *History of the Company of Cutlers in Hallamshire*, vol.I and II (Sheffield).

[4] Cutlers' Company archive, C6/1 and C6/2.

[5] D Hey 1990 'The origins and early growth of the Hallamshire cutlery and allied trades', *English Rural Society, 1500–1800, essays in honour of Joan Thirsk*, J Chartres and D Hey, eds, (Cambridge) p 343–367.

[6] J Unwin 1999 'The marks of Sheffield cutlers, 1614-1878, Journal of the Historical Metallurgy Society Vol 33, No 2, p 93-103.

Chapter 3

Making cutlery and flatware

Introduction

It will not be possible here to go into a detailed description of the metals used in cutlery and flatware manufacture. Those interested are referred to Barraclough's two-volume work on the steel industry before Bessemer, c 1860, there is an exhaustive description of the various types of iron and steel and methods of production. In simple terms, the crucial difference between iron and steel is the amount of carbon in the metal. Wrought iron has virtually no carbon and is malleable. Cast iron has approximately 4% carbon and is a brittle metal. Steel has less than 1% carbon, sufficient to give the metal properties which allow it to be hardened and once ground, retain a cutting edge. The type of steel generally used for knife blades in the eighteenth and nineteenth centuries was shear steel, which was being produced locally from the end of the seventeenth century, when the first cementation furnace was built in Hallamshire. Local and imported Swedish wrought iron was packed into these furnaces with charcoal to absorb sufficient carbon to turn it into steel. Shear steel was produced by hammering the resulting 'blister' steel to even out the carbon content and although crucible steel was invented in Sheffield in the 1740s, it was initially rejected by cutlers as being too hard to work with and was more expensive than shear steel. Crucible steel was initially used for razors, fine scissors and penknife blades. The first generally available bulk cast steel came in the 1860s after the development of the Bessemer and the Siemens open-hearth process.

Non-ferrous metals were also important in the tableware, cutlery and flatware trades. Pewter was used for casting spoons and sterling silver had been used for high-quality forks and spoons, handles for knives and the blades of such items as fruit knives. Since these were expensive items, substitutes for silver were sought. Sheffield Plate, invented in the 1740s, could be rolled into sheet and made into handles and from the 1830s, German silver, an alloy of copper, nickel and zinc, often replaced copper as the base for plating. German silver or nickel silver had the advantage that when the plating wore off, the silvery-coloured metal beneath was not as obvious as the reddish copper. Earlier methods of plating base metals were not too successful. 'Close plating' involved soldering silver leaf onto steel blades using a tin flux, but the leaf eventually peeled off in use. This process was used on dessert cutlery where fruit acid would discolour the steel blade, or on fish knives, which would become tainted by the fish.

In the 1840s, the process of electroplating metals with silver was perfected in Birmingham by Elkington. This method produced acceptable substitutes for sterling silver flatware and holloware. This process had the advantage that the spoons and forks could be completed prior to their coating with a thin layer of silver unlike the fused plate, which had to be treated carefully during the manufacturing processes.

The manufacturing processes that will be described here are those involving

- the making of table knives, forks and spoons
- the use of machines
- cast and non-ferrous metal cutlery and flatware
- decorative techniques

Making a table knife

It is impossible to know how many men were making table cutlery in Sheffield at any particular time between 1740 and 1900. The Cutlers' Company records record men simply as cutlers and grinders, without any indication of their specialisation, if they had one. However, from the 1780s onwards, the recorded occupations become more varied and a handful of men described themselves as 'table knife

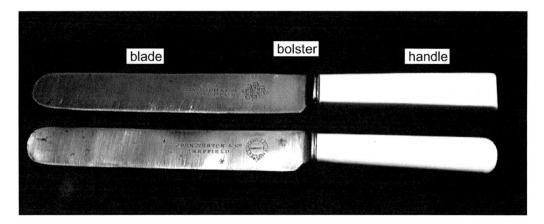

Figure 6 Table knives

makers' and 'table blade grinders'. Trade directories provide evidence for the names and locations of manufacturers of tableware. They indicate the minimum numbers involved; the time span of firms and the movement of craftsmen around the area. In the 1787 Gales and Martin directory for Sheffield some table knife makers are listed, together with their registered marks. They were three categories – 16 makers of silver and plated knives; 54 makers of table knives 'in general' and 11 makers of common table knives in the town centre and a further six in surrounding villages. These men had paid for their entries in the directory so were possibly the more affluent or more dynamic masters. They were freemen since they also had their marks printed and therefore represent only a part of the workforce – the non-freemen do not have any entries. A century later, in the 1898 Sheffield directory, there is a list of 224 table knife manufacturers.

Hand-forging a table knife blade, bolster and tang

The following descriptions have been compiled from the sources described above, together with reference to surviving craftsmen, audio-visual evidence, surviving knives and tools.

In Sheffield, the shaping of metal to form a blade was always referred to as forging and was carried out by the cutler or specialist forger; the term 'smith' was never used in the Sheffield cutlery trades. In the Cutlers' Company records, no one is described as a knife blade forger, though at the end of the eighteenth century, when more varied descriptions of occupations were given, six men described themselves as

table knife makers, which in Sheffield, refers to forging, not grinding or hafting. In the forging process, the metal is heated and hammered to form a blade. For most craftsmen in the eighteenth and nineteenth century, this was a hand process generally carried out in a 'smithy' or 'shop', while the forgers of heavier, larger items, such as scythe blades, were likely to work at water-powered tilts. Cutlers or forgers would need to acquire iron and steel in bar form and then forge them together in combination to produce a profitable object with a good cutting edge. Steel was more expensive than iron, so it was necessary to weld steel for the blade on to iron for the non-cutting parts – the bolster and tang.

Forging would necessarily be done as quickly as possible, while the metal was at the forging heat, since any reheating to complete the job would slow down production rates. This can take less than a minute, but larger blades could require reheating. The forgers worked at speed, but struggled to keep up such physically demanding work all day and every day. In order to join the two metals together, a bar of iron and one of shear steel would be cropped at an angle; heated to a welding temperature, the ends dipped in a flux of silicious sand and then overlaid. The two metals were forged together resulting in a slightly different appearance on the back or 'pile' side of the blade. This is caused because the iron, when glazed, will not take such a high finish. This is known as a 'cutler's thumb print' and is only seen on shear steel blades.

In the first heat in the metal, the iron near the joint would be shaped into a bolster. The forger placed the iron between two dies called 'prints'

Figure 7 The pile side of a knife blade, showing the cutler's thumb print

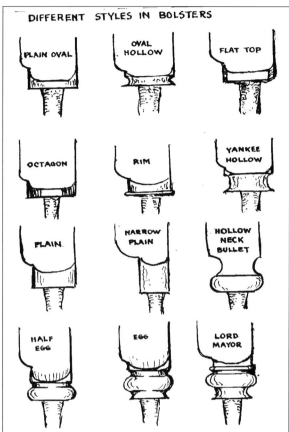

Figure 8 Bolster designs. Unpublished drawing by J Himsworth (The Hawley Collection)

which he held in tongs or in a bent hazel twig and the striker would hit the top die with a 14lb hammer. The forgers would have a range of prints for different sizes and designs of bolsters. The short section of iron bar was then drawn out as a tang.

The steel bar, having been cropped off on the aggon is called a 'mood', was heated and drawn out to form the blade. Small items such as pen- and pocket knife blades could be forged single-handedly, that is by one man, but table blades required two-handed forging. The forger was in control of the work, determining the shape of the blade, while the striker 'drew out' the metal. The forger held the mood in tongs and hit it at the point where the striker was to follow. The two men worked in a closely co-ordinated rhythm of striking the metal to produce the correct shape. It is unlikely that these processes of welding the iron and steel, forming the bolster, tang and blade, would take place on one knife sequentially. The forger would weld the metals, form the bolsters and draw out the tangs of a dozen or more knives, before reheating them and drawing out the blades.

The final process for the forger would be to strike the manufacturer's mark into the blade. This was done on the 'mark' side of the knife, near the bolster. If a knife is held in the right hand with the cutting edge to the left, the side of the blade facing is called the 'mark side'. The reverse is called the 'pile side', indicating the way that the wrought iron of the bolster and tang has been 'piled' on top of the steel of the blade. The mark punch is a short bar of hardened steel, with the device of the registered mark cut into the top. Making mark punches was a subsidiary trade for which there is no surviving documentary evidence prior to the later eighteenth century when men described as such were sending their sons to be apprenticed to cutlers. The marks struck on knife blades are as important in identifying and dating cutlery as assay marks on silver, yet because there is no published list, the valuable resource of cutlers' marks has been neglected.

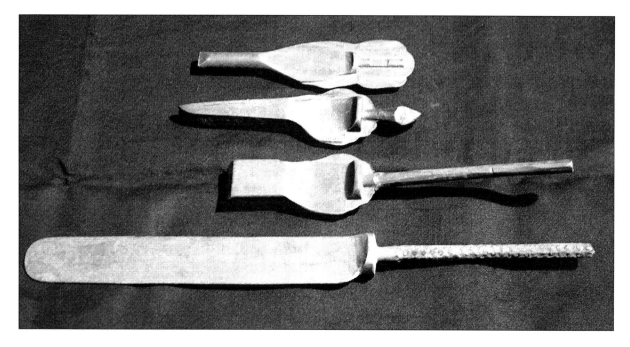

Figure 9 Forging a table blade

Hardening and grinding

One characteristic of steel was that it can be hardened and tempered, which allows a cutting edge to be retained. The forger could have done these two processes, but by the later nineteenth century, a specialist hardener would undertake this work. The steel blade was heated to approximately 1000°C; the temperature being judged by the colour of steel. It was then quenched in whale oil, brine or oil and water which hardens the steel in varying degrees, but made it brittle. Care was needed in quenching or the blade would 'skeller' or twist. Most of the oil was wiped off before the blade was returned to the heat, which ignited any oil residue helping the tempering process. The degree of hardness can be tempered by reheating to the desired temperature within the range of 150°C and 650°C. An increase in hardness is accompanied by a decrease in toughness; therefore, the tempering temperature could balance the degrees of hardness and toughness. If the knife blade had become twisted during these processes, it was 'smithed' or straightened by hammering while it retained some heat.

Grinding the blade and bolster

In the eighteenth century, cutlers ground the blades to brighten them and give them an edge. Alternatively, they might be passed on to grinders, a specialist group who seem to have appeared in the early eighteenth century. In the 1780s and 1790s apprenticeship lists, five men described themselves specifically as being grinders of table knife blades. Local fine-grained sand-stones provided grinders with their grinding wheels and different sizes were used by various branches of the trade and the table blade grinders having one about four feet in diameter and ten inches wide. A hole was made through the centre of the stone to fit it on an iron axle, originally using wooden wedges. However, these wedges could absorb water, expand and crack the stone. Later, the stones were attached with iron side plates and secured with a massive nut.

The grinder sat astride the heavy wooden 'horsin' or seat above and behind the wheel, holding the blade in a 'flatstick' and resting his elbows on his knees. In order to exert more pressure on the blade, the grinder might stand and put his whole body weight onto the blade. The knife blade is held against the grindstone

Figure 10 Newspaper cutting of 1936 showing a table blade grinder (reproduced by kind permission of Dennis Hound, *The Star* newspaper)

using a flatstick, a piece of wood protecting the grinder's fingers from the heat and helping him to control the grinding. It also kept the blade flat while he first did the rough grinding on both sides of the blade. The grindstone could be rotated by the hand or foot, but at a grinding hull, the power of a water-driven wheel was transmitted to the grindstone by means of leather drive belts running over pulleys and wooden drums. The grindstone (sometimes called a 'grindlestone') rotated away from the grinder. The faster the rotation, the faster the grinder could work, but the increased heat in the blade caused by friction could damage the temper of the steel plus an increased danger of the stone breaking. Recent discussion with a file grinder reveals that a 42in diameter sandstone grindstone would revolve at 250–300 rpm, giving a surface speed of 3000 feet per minute. This was considered the optimum, though they could be driven faster. Artificial grindstones introduced at the beginning of the twentieth century, could revolve twice as fast. The stone rotated in a 'trow' or trough in which was a few inches of water so that the surface of the stone was wet, cutting down some of the dust and helping to keep the blade cool. As the stone became too smooth to be effective, it was roughened with a 'racing iron' and if it wore out of true, it would be 'dressed' back into shape by hitting the grinding face with a hackhammer – a hammer with a chisel-like head. The stones

were used until they were reduced to half their original diameter, when they were sold on to other grinders requiring smaller stones.

The grinder also gave the knife blade its finished shape and cutting edge and while he ground the bolster, decorative features might be ground in. A skilful forger could produce blades requiring little work except for the cutting edge and the better the forger, the faster the grinder could work since he had less to do correcting bad workmanship. Further treatment of the blade would take place in the same location. Photographs show that at grinding wheels, either water or steam powered, the grinders sat in ranks, up to three men one behind the other. The men closest to and facing the windows were involved in the initial grinding of the blade. Behind him would be a man glazing blades. A 'glazier' or glazer was a wooden wheel of similar diameter, but typically with a two-inch wide edge, which was covered with leather. The leather 'head' was 'dressed' by being coated with fish glue and rolled in varying sizes of emery grit. Glazing would improve on the coarser finish left by the sandstone wheel and the blade may have further and finer glazing.

Hafting or attaching the handles

From the 1740s to the mid nineteenth century, natural materials, ceramics and metals were used for handles on knives and forks. Evidence for the materials and styles of handles comes from surviving knives and from the late nineteenth century trade catalogues. The different materials were used on different classes of knives, with the more costly goods having the more exotic handles, while the vast majority of knives in this period would have had bone or wooden handles.

For 'common' knives, the ends of long bones of cattle were cut to the general size and shape of table knife handles and hardwood was turned or cut into slabs forming scales and pinned on each side of the tang. For the middle quality range, animal horn would be used, stag and buffalo horn providing especially attractive handles, while the tips of antler, as well as the crowns (the part at the base of the antler), were used for carving knives and forks. Best-quality table knives might have handles of ivory or more exotic woods and pearl was commonly used for fruit and dessert knives. Ivory has been used in Sheffield for knife handles for centuries – the coat of arms of the Cutlers' Company, shows an elephant's head – and in the seventeenth century, Sheffielders had access to ivory 'teeth' supplied by London merchants.

Non-natural materials were also used for handles. In the eighteenth century, imported porcelain and English ceramic handles were made with a wide range of decoration and metal handles were common. Handles of Sheffield Plate, Britannia metal and later nickel silver, were stamped out of thin sheet using dies which could also impart surface decoration. The two halves of the handle were wired together, soldered and filled with resin. In the second half of the nineteenth century, plastics were introduced. Many types were developed such as 'celluloid', but they were flammable and the dust produced while working with it could easily catch fire.

To prevent such accidents in the factory, circular saws ran in a trough of water. The plastic 'xylonite' was also inflammable but was used for decades because it could be made in laminated layers which imitated ivory.

There was an enormous trade in the importation of exotic woods, ivory and pearl, buffalo horn which necessitated a whole series of subsidiary trades in Sheffield supplying handles and handle materials.

The photograph of a storeroom at Joseph Rodgers at the turn of the nineteenth/twentieth centuries shows the amount of ivory one large manufacturer might hold. All the raw materials were cut into handle sizes and any decorative carving was done before being sold to the cutler

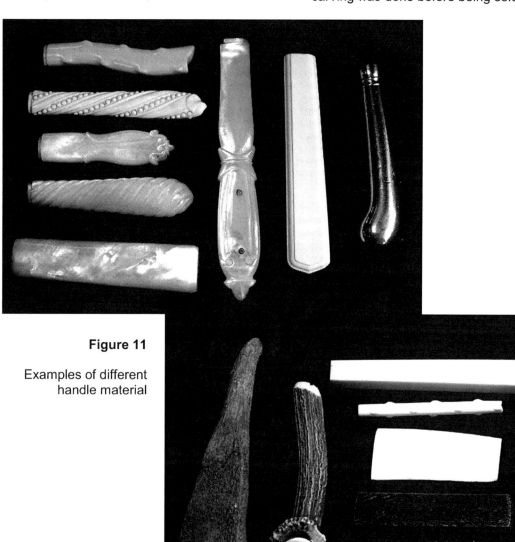

Figure 11

Examples of different handle material

Figure 12 Joseph Rodgers' ivory store from 'Under Five Sovereigns'

as a completed handle. Horn could also be 'pressed' into various shapes, a process whereby pieces of horn were softened by boiling before being pressed between two dies. The dies were cut with a variety of decorations, some imitating antler so providing a cheaper alternative. Evidence from probate inventories show that this was practiced in the seventeenth century.

Cutlers required few tools for the process of attaching the handles, and were often listed in seventeenth and eighteenth century probate inventories. There were vices for holding the work, saws for cutting up handle material, boring tools for making holes, hammers for riveting and files for minor shaping. Small wooden trays called 'workboards' held the parts of the knives, etc which were being assembled. A workbench would have been positioned under the window of the workplace.

The handle is attached to the tang, which can come in a variety of shapes and influence the type and method of handle attachment. Many methods have been tried, with patented ideas, since handle attachment was a weak point in the knife's construction. Natural handle materials could shrink and drop off, or swell in water and split. Pearl and ivory were delicate materials and could be easily damaged. Metal handles were produced in two parts, which were wired and soldered together, before being filled with resin which gave them weight and stiffness. Such blades were often soldered directly onto the bolster, especially on non-ferrous blades and forks.

There are two basic types of tang forged out of iron – a round section and those which are flat. 'Whittle' tangs are short round tangs and 'through' tangs are round tangs which go though the whole length of the handle. Round tangs are by far the most common, certainly for table cutlery. The 'scale' tang was a flat tang forged

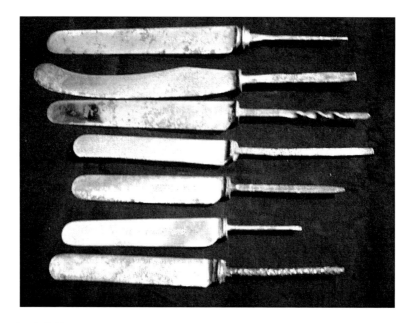

Figure 13 Examples of tangs

out of iron, but after the 1860s, with the availability of cheaper steel from the Siemens open-hearth process of steel making, a knife blade, together with its 'flat' tang, could be stamped out of metal bar.

Handles were delivered to the cutler without the central hole for the tang. It is not clear how the eighteenth century cutlers made this hole, though one assumes that they would use a treadle drill to bore the hole down the centre of the handle. Twist drills became available in the mid nineteenth century but prior to this, one might suggest that some tool similar to a spoon auger was used. The drilling would have to stop frequently to empty out the dust and the handle

would be rotated through 180° to ensure the hole continued exactly though the centre of the handle.

One method of ensuring the handle stayed on knives with round tangs was to rivet over the tang as it passed through the handle. Round tangs could be flattened slightly at the point where the rivet would go through. It will be appreciated that great skill was required in boring the handle and the hole through which the rivet was pinned. Not surprisingly, this pinning was only usually done on better quality knives. The problems of keeping the handle on the knife prompted manufacturers to experiment and at the Great Exhibition in 1851, Newbould

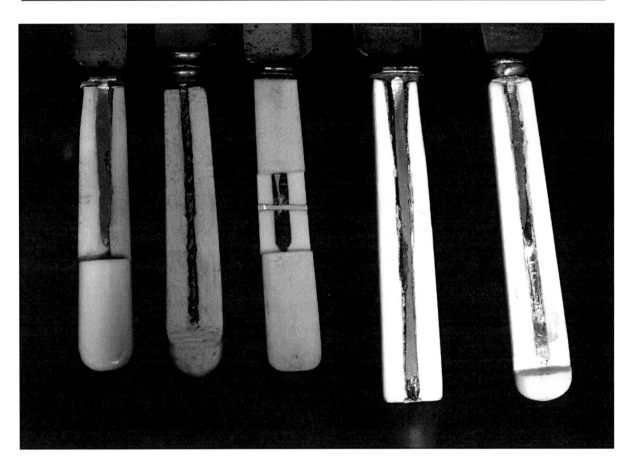

Figure 14 Cutaway handles showing the tangs

Figure 15 A variety of ferrules and endcaps

and Baildon of Surrey Works, Sheffield proudly announced that they were showing specimens of Roberts' patent table-cutlery, whatever that was. However, it seems that 'the blades are fastened by means of a dovetail, without cement, and cannot be injured by hot water'. They further showed ivory-handled table knives, where 'the tangs are made square, nicely fitted into the handles, without cement and riveted through at the extremity'. These descriptions reveal processes such as using rivets, cement to fasten handles to the knives, and suggesting that cementing handles was not an entirely successful method.

Another aspect of hafting was the 'balancing' of the knife. Better quality knives were 'balanced' by means of a small lead weight inserted in hole for the tang. This ensured that when the knife was placed on the table, the tip of the blade would not rest on the cloth.

Knives with scale tangs are stronger in construction and use and are typically found on food preparation knives. The handle material is cut into two matching halves and attached to each side of the scale with two or three rivets. Bone and wood are the most common materials for scales of table and food preparation knives.

The knife handle might be enhanced by the addition of a ferrule and endcap before the handle was pushed onto the tang. Thin strips of non-ferrous metal, often sterling silver, were embossed using dies. The strip would be rolled, cut and soldered providing rings of different sizes which were attached to the handle next to the bolster. Silver ferrules were assayed, locally from 1773, and they can provide dating evidence for the knives. Caps were punched out of flat sheet and a small spike fastened inside, which was hammered into the end of the handle.

Notes

[1] K Barraclough, 1984)*Blister Steel*, Vol 1, pp 2–4 and P T Craddock and M L Wayman, 2000 'The Development of Ferrous Metallurgical Technology', Chapter 2 in British Museum Occasional Paper No. 136, *The Ferrous Metallurgy of Early Clocks and Watches Studies in Post Medieval Steel*, ML Wayman, ed (London).

[2] Cutlers' Company archive, D19/1–5, The Storehouse records, 1680s.

[3] *The Great Exhibition, London, 1851. Official Descriptive and Illustrated Catalogue of the Great Exhibition, 1851*, Vol.II, p 608.

[4] Cutlers' Company archives, C6/2.

[5] Children's Employment Commission report, 1842 p 49.

[6] J & J Hatfield, 1974 *The Oldest Sheffield Plater*, (Sheffield), p 144.

[7] J Unwin 1999 'The Marks of Sheffield Cutlers, 1614-1878' in *Journal of the Historical Metallurgy Society*, Vol.33, No 2.

[8] Cutlers' Company archive, D19/1–5, The Storehouse records.

[9] *The Great Exhibition, London, 1851. Official Descriptive and Illustrated Catalogue of the Great Exhibition, 1851*, Vol.II, p 608.

Chapter 4

Making forks and spoons

Forks

From the later seventeenth century, Sheffield cutlers were the craftsmen making the forks, though the term 'forkmaker' does not appear in the Cutlers' Company records of apprenticeships until the 1780s. It is difficult to know whether cutlers specialised in forkmaking before the 1780s, or whether it was a sideline. The forkmakers who were identified in the later eighteenth century were concentrated in the suburbs north of Sheffield town centre and the 1787 Directory lists 16 forkmakers, six being in the outlying villages of Attercliffe and Shiregreen. None of these men has a mark printed by his name, though several were freemen with a mark, which they had registered as cutlers, while some of the forkmakers were non-freemen. However, the fact that non-freemen took the trouble to get themselves in the directory, perhaps indicates they were more the norm in this branch of the trade. In the 1898 Sheffield Directory, 56 fork manufacturers are listed, the majority located in the Shiregreen/Wincobank area to the north of the city centre. There were also ten men listed as fork casters making cast iron forks.

The forks produced in the eighteenth and nineteenth centuries had two, three and four tines, a long shank and bolster and various styles of tangs, to which handle materials were attached, often making a matching pair with a table knife. Forks were hand-forged from bars of steel, but by the later eighteenth century, were stamped using drop stamps. They were also cast from iron. The tines of the fork were ground but unlike the table blade grinders, the grindstone was run 'dry'. One reason was that fork tines cut into the stone and if it were wet, would wear it down too quickly, so the generated stone and metal dust created some of the worst conditions in the grinding trades. Hafting the forks would be done in exactly the same way as the knives.

Spoons

Generally, spoons were made of non-ferrous metals, pewter and silver being the most common, both of which can be cast. Silver spoons can be forged in the same way as ferrous metals – the metal is heated, hammered into shape and finally shaped and 'bowled' in a drop stamp. With the increasing use of stamps in the later eighteenth century and the availability of better quality steel dies, spoons could be 'blanked' out of sheets of metal, usually nickel silver after the 1840s.

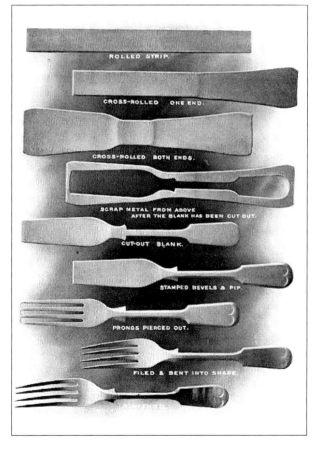

Figure 16 Thomas Turner – stages in the making of a fork, 1914 catalogue

Figure 17 Fork blanks, part-forged and stamped out

Spoon blanks were then passed between the ends of two steel rolls, which made the blank thinner and wider so that the spoon could be 'bowled'. The process was called 'cross-rolling' and women usually did the monotonous work of feeding thousands of blanks through the rollers. The next stage was 'bowling' spoon blanks on a drop stamp. The blank was carefully positioned on the bottom die and a falling weight, or 'tup' had the top half of the die. A range of dies would be needed for different sizes and design of spoons. The final processes were the buffing and polishing on a range of cloth wheels.

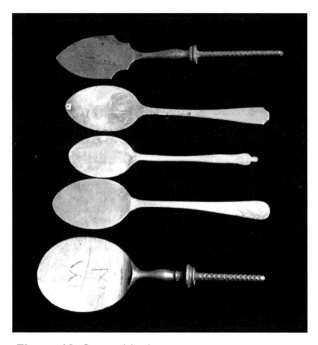

Figure 18 Spoon blanks

By the end of the nineteenth century, spoon manufacture was associated with fork manufacture, as indicated in the trade directories. Spoon manufacturers were also listed with the manufacturers of silver, Britannia metal and plated wares.

Machines

For generations of craftsmen, the only method of manufacture was by using hand tools and the power of the human or animal. The technology was simple and the tools were equally simple and easily acquired. Once waterpower could be harnessed to drive tilt hammers and grinding wheels, the trade organisation changed as specialist workers evolved and processes were fragmented. The grinders benefited from the power which drove a wheel faster than one turned by the hand or foot, thereby allowing them to do more work. Although waterpower assisted some craftsmen, it did restrict their work to specific places and their hours were then tied to the availability of power. This continued when steam power was became available in Sheffield from the 1780s, drawing grinders from the rural waterpowered grinding hulls into the town centre.

Table blade forgers did not use waterpowered hammers, used to forge large items such as scythe blades, but from the 1860s however, steam power was used to drive spring or goff hammers. Bars of steel were heated and placed between the top and bottom dies of these fast running hammers to draw out the blades. These hammers replicated the action of the hand forger, but were very much quicker. When cheaper steel became available after the 1860s, knife blades could be stamped or pressed out of sheet steel. However, although this produced a blade much faster than a hand forger could work, the blade was equal thickness throughout and therefore required more grinding to produce the correct profile.

The development of crucible steel benefited the men who made dies for the production of cutlery and flatware. The dies for machines could be engraved with the decorative pattern at the same time as they were cut to provide the 'blanks'. High quality dies and rollers can imitate the work of engravers, chasers and sawpiercers and allow cutlery to be produced for a fraction of the cost. The invention of Sheffield Plate followed by the use of nickel silver sheet to stamp out knife handles, spoons and forks, increased the demand for dies. The design for the article was prepared on a thin nickel plate and the outline is scribed on to the surface of a steel or steel-faced block. The diesinker then produces the design using chisels, engraving tools and riffler files to finish the die. The die would be tested for accuracy by using lead for trial stampings and if satisfactory, the die would be hardened. The quality of the finished item obviously depends on the skill of the diesinker and a considerable amount of a manufacturers capital could be tied up in his dies.

Cast metal blades and casting metal blades

It is necessary to appreciate the differences between blades forged from bars of cast steel and blades, made from cast iron. After the 1740s, molten steel was produced in crucibles and then cast into bars of steel, which could be forged into blades. Eighteenth century cutlers did not commonly use the metal because it was relatively expensive and harder to work with than shear steel. Once metal can be heated to the point where they become molten, it is possible to run it into moulds to produce objects directly, without the expense of forging. Part-finished cast objects can often be identified by a fine line of fash indicating where the two halves of the mould met. Cast iron is a useful metal and has properties which make it the most suitable metal for many things, but cutlery is not one of them. It cannot be hardened and will not retain good cutting edge. It is not surprising however, that men tried to make knives and especially forks, by casting them out of iron. Cast articles would be cheap to produce and, if polished, could fool many people into buying them as steel cutlery

From 1779, the Cutlers' Company tried hard to prevent the practice of casting goods out of iron, which was principally confined to forkmaking. The Company instructed its Searchers to enter 'all suspicious places' to seize these 'deceitful wares'. In 1780, new bye-laws were issued to try to eradicate the problems, initially seen as a manufacturing issue, in that the original Act of Incorporation in 1624 required goods to be made with a steel edge. The Company stated that the running of cast or pig iron into moulds meant that the fork blades did not have 'the strength, spring and elasticity of those that were forged or hammered out of steel'. Customers were being deceived because goods were 'polished so as to give the appearance of having been made out of forged or hammered steel.'

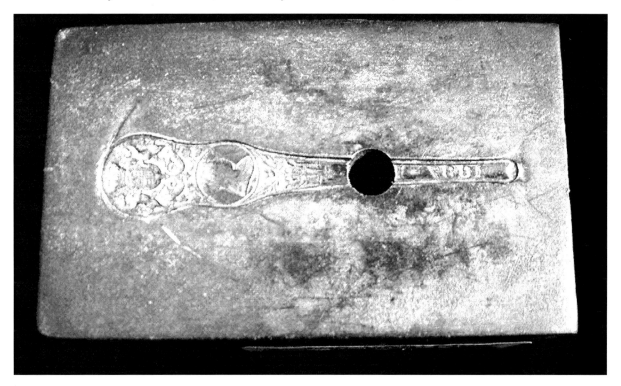

Figure 19 Die from C W Fletcher, silversmiths, showing the design for a teaspoon celebrating one of the jubilees of Queen Victoria. The die has been drilled to prevent its further use

Anyone making such blades would be fined ten shillings per blade. This seemed to have little effect and by the late 1790s, it was necessary to extend the bye-law prohibiting the sale of knives, razors, forks, scissors, etc made of cast or pig iron instead of steel. However, it seems to have had little effect and the Cutlers' Company declined to take much more action.

It was not until 1818 when a general Act of Parliament was introduced, designed to regulate the cutlery trades in England with the emphasis on the correct marking of such items. Cutlery, which had been hammered and forged from steel or iron and steel, was to be marked with a 'hammer' and it was illegal to stamp cast goods with the hammer. In 1827, the minutes of the Cutlers' Company record that 'common steel' was not to be marked 'cast or shear steel'. It is not clear exactly what 'common' steel was in this instance, though it probably refers to cementation steel, which has not been forged into shear steel. Problems continued and resulted in a spectacular occasion in 1839, when Samuel Naylor and William Sanderson were convicted under the 1818 Act of marking cast iron blades with 'Shear Steel' and 'Cast Steel'. Their penalties amounted to over £1800 and their goods were ordered to be destroyed. A cart carrying all their goods went to Paradise Square in the centre of the town, where a huge crowd cheered as the Master Cutler ordered the blades to be broken. Three men with hammers and anvils carried out the work.

Casting was held to be a cheaper process producing inferior goods. However, the lower costs in casting blades and flatware were enough to make it a common, though despised, practice in the nineteenth century[2]. A published paper given to the Society of Arts in 1856 refers to items made 'at a heat', that is, cast or run. It makes the point that 'the steel from which articles are 'cast' is very inferior, in fact, but one remove from iron.' It was called 'run steel' and blades cast in moulds were used to imitate first-class goods but when they were first run or cast, the articles were brittle and required annealing before being made up. Scissors, table blades and forks were being cast[3]. In the discussion which followed, the speaker, Mr Wilson, was corrected by Mr Sanderson who said that 'run steel' was actually pig iron and not steel.

Non-ferrous cutlery and flatware

Knife blades for the table have always been made of ferrous metals, except when silver was used to display the wealth of the owner, and later, when plated blades were introduced for eating fish or fruit. Spoons and forks have been fashioned from ferrous and non-ferrous metals, and for the poorest people, spoons were made out of horn or wood. Similarly, the production of forks and spoons came to rely less on the hand forger and more on machine processes, including casting the articles.

Sterling silver bar can be forged into knife blades, forks and spoons in the same way as the forgers worked with steel. The forks and spoons were hammered out into the shape of the particular design, but these items differ from knives in that they have to be 'bent' or formed into shape. The spoons have to be bowled in drop stamps, where care ensures that any decorative features are not damaged. This is achieved by lining the bottom die with tin.

An alternative was to stamp the spoon and fork out of nickel silver sheet – a process which probably resulted in these items being referred to as 'flatware'. Cast nickel silver ingots were rolled into sheet and blanking out tools used to cut out blanks for forks and spoons, which might be made in-house or bought in from specialist suppliers. Once the items had been shaped and formed, they could be plated by electrolysis with silver, known as E P N S. These processes were mechanised to some degree, involving machines such as stamps, presses and fly presses.

The final stage was buffing and polishing. Buffing flatware was traditionally done by women, and was a dirty job. Articles were buffed on revolving cloth wheels, using a mild abrasive. The buffer usually held several spoons in her hand at once, feeding a handful of a mixture of Trent sand and oil on to them. The cloth wheel spreads the abrasive onto all the contours of the spoons. Forks were similarly treated.

The manufacture of sterling silver and silver plated items involved more manufacturing processes than cutlery, largely because of the decorative nature of the objects. The improved quality of dies in the late eighteenth century, following the invention of the crucible steel process, meant that mass-production could be introduced. Steel dies could form an article and press the decoration into it at the same time.

Decorative techniques of metal

Sheffield cutlers were capable of producing many beautiful objects and increasingly in the nineteenth century, cutlery and flatware became more elaborate with decoration applied to the handles, ferrules and even blades of such items as fish knives and silver fruit knives. Pearl cutters and ivory carvers prepared an array of decorated handles for the better quality knives and forks, while metal handles could be stamped with decoration using dies. Expensive handcrafted decoration of the metal parts of the cutlery and flatware, such as engraving, was gradually being replaced by machine dies. However, surviving examples show the extremely high level of skill shown by the Sheffield cutlery community.

Engraving

The design is drawn on paper and the principal features of the drawing are marked out with pinholes. The pattern is fixed to the tray or bowl with adhesive tape. The pattern is then dusted with a bag of finely ground chalk so that when it is removed, a series of small chalk dots can be seen on the metal. To make the pattern more permanent, the outlines are marked with a steel point, which will be covered by the engraving.

The engraving is done using small chisel-like tools, which produce a variety of lines and dots in the surface of the metal. Engraving was used to enhance pierced designs on cutlery, such as fish eaters and fish forks. Decoration, which has the appearance of being engraved, can be achieved using dies.

Saw piercing

Saw piercing is a decorative technique commonly seen on dishes and trays, but was applied to fish knife blades, spoon and fork handles and the bowls of serving spoons. This process produces fretwork designs in the metal and involves great skill and concentration.

Initially, the design is drawn out on paper, which is then stuck on to a thin sheet of brass. A small punch pierces holes in the pattern through which the very fine saw blade is threaded. The pattern is sawn out, resulting in a 'scale' – a brass sheet with the pierced pattern on it. These scales then serve as reference templates for subsequent work.

The design can be transferred to items repeatedly by taking a paper rubbing of the scale, which is glued onto the object, holes are drilled for the saw blade and the pattern is sawn out.

Figure 20 Engraved serving spoon

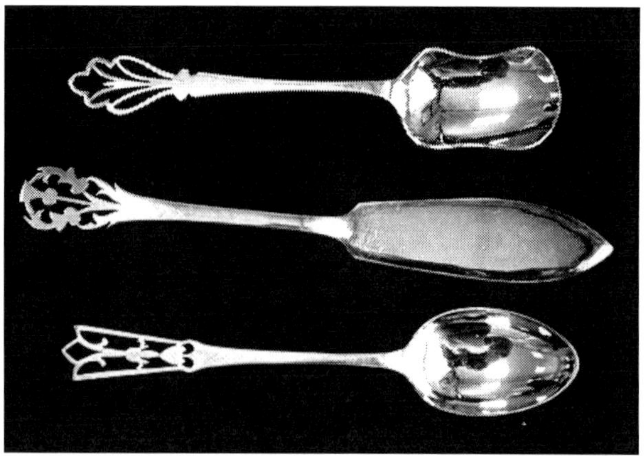

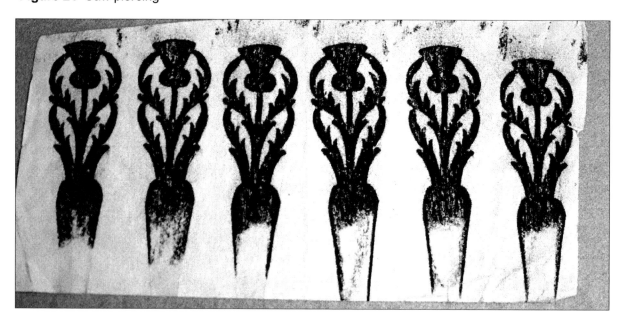

For mass produced items, 'punch pierced' designs using an array of punches and a fly press, can reproduce this fretwork effect. However, saw piercing by hand can produce more free-flowing patterns while the punched out designs tend to be simpler, heavier, more repetitive and rather 'mechanical' in form. Other processes, such as acid etching and gilding, could be applied to knife blades, though they were generally found on open razors.

Figure 21 Saw piercing

Figure 22 Rubbings of designs for spoon tops

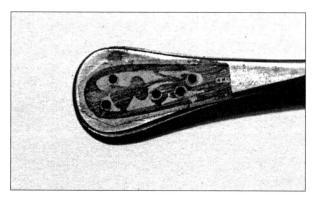

Notes

[1] From 1779, the Cutlers' Company tried hard to prevent the practice of casting goods out of iron, which was principally confined to forkmaking. RE Leader 1905 *History of the Company of Cutlers in Hallamshire*, vol I (Sheffield), p 118–121.

[2] J Wilson 1856 'On the manufacture of articles from steel, particularly cutlery', *Journal of the Society of Arts*, Vol IV, no177, p 357–366.

[3] ibid, p 359.

Figure 23 Rubbing on spoon top

Chapter 5

Trade organisation

Traditional patterns of work

The pattern of working in the cutlery trades was probably centuries old and originally linked to the requirements of agriculture – ploughing and harvesting needed men to work in the field. This resulted in the bye-laws of the Cutlers' Company enforcing the lay-off after Christmas and in August. Men did not work on Sunday and traditionally did not work on 'Saint Monday', a mocking name for the usual day off work. These traditions continued throughout the nineteenth century because large numbers of men in their own workshops worked without restrictions on their time, other than to earn enough money usually by piecework. Often they would only work to 'earn enough'. However, their time might be controlled by the need to work off 'sours'. Men would accept work at a fixed price per dozen, but might ask for an advance on payment. Therefore some of the work was already paid for and had to be finished first – the sours – before work could start on the 'sweets', which would be paid for on completion.

Further restrictions might be placed on a man's time by the availability of power. Waterpowered grinding wheels cannot be run continuously or the dam would empty and, depending on the water levels, work might only be done for a couple of hours at a time. Descriptions of grinders sitting around in the sunshine, drinking ale, were sometimes used to show the laziness and immorality of these men[1]. With the construction of steam-powered 'wheels' – tenement factories where power was rented out - the grinders were drawn into an unhealthier lifestyle in the town, where power was often available for twenty hours a day.

The large factories had more formal work practices. The details of the hours worked at James Dixon and Sons, silver and plate manufacturers, for instance, were given to the Children's Employment Commission, Fourth Report, 1862[2]. They were 7am–8pm on Mondays and Tuesdays; 6am–8pm on Wednesdays and Thursdays, with shorter hours at the end of the week, 7am–5pm on Friday and 7am to noon on Saturday. The employees were allowed an hour for lunch. The firm also had annual holidays – 10 days after Christmas and odd days throughout the year on feast days and gala days. The run-up to Christmas was reported as being very busy.

These restrictions imposed by the power supplies and the practice of getting the week off to a slow start, meant that many men were working late on Friday and Saturday to make up their wages. This aspect had tragic consequences in 1864. Late in the evening of Friday 11 March, Dale Dyke dam burst its banks. The floodwater roared down the Loxley valley causing devastation to riverside works and houses, before turning towards Sheffield after joining the river Don at Owlerton. The flood went on into the town centre then continued out towards Conisbrough. Approximately 240 people died. The stories of miraculous escapes and tragic deaths were reported in the local and national press and many confirm the work practices described above.

At Loxley Old Wheel, forgers were still working 'where it was usual for work to be kept up all night'. Joseph and John Denton, boys of 14 and 11 years old, were working with their father when the floodwater rushed in. John Denton climbed the shuttle pole (the pole operating the shuttle which opens the pentrough of the water wheel). He clung there while the water subsided, but his father and older brother were drowned. Further down the river at Rowell Bridge Wheel, William Bradbury, a grinder, was 'anxious to make a good wage on Saturday night, had stopped behind his companions, and was working all night. The last man except Bradbury, left the wheel at half-past eleven, only half an hour before the flood came ... No one saw what became of Bradbury ... his body was never recovered'[3].

Specialisation and the fragmentation of trades and products

There are no surviving descriptions of the work of a late eighteenth century cutler. One can only draw conclusions from the various bye-laws of the Cutlers' Company. It has been taken for granted that the cutlers were trained in all the processes of manufacture – forging, grinding and hafting – though nowhere does this seem to have been spelled out. In the early years of the eighteenth century, some indentures contain details of training other than the provision of maintenance and the odd reference to schooling[4]. Between 1713 and 1715, several masters were stipulating aspects of work which, one might have assumed, were standard practice. For instance:

> Josh. Brooks was apprenticed to Enoch Sanderson *'to make knife blades'*
> Peter Haward took John Platt and would *'learn him to make and grind'*
> Henry Downend would allow Edward White *' a day in a fortnight to make fork blades'*
> Ed. Newton took Richard Cooper *'to be instructed only in grinding and glazing knife blades'*
> Jer. Paramour would instruct Robt. Gibson *'to make fleams'*.

It was further assumed that at the end of apprenticeships, men would become either self-employed masters or journeymen/employees. Because the required tools and workspace were simple, there does not seem to have been much to hinder a man setting up on his own. In 1761, Joseph Collier published *The Parent's and Guardian's Directory and the Youth's Guide in the Choice of Profession*, in which he states that a cutler in London might set up shop with £50, with extra money to buy in stock. This seems to be a rather excessive amount for Sheffield.

The system operated by the Cutlers' Company encouraged small-scale work units with masters (freemen) and employees (non-freemen). The results of this two-tier system and the small size of the workshops was that employees did not necessarily work on the premises of their master. They would have their own workshop and tools and sometimes, these men would specialise in particular trades or practices. In 1742, a three-year agreement was signed between Robert Broomhead and John Goodlad[5]. Broomhead would supply steel weekly, provide *'utensils and necessaries'* and pay Goodlad 1s.4d to forge a gross of 'Jack penknife blades'. Goodlad was expected to produce eight gross of good blades per week, possibly earning 10s.6d for 1152 forged blades. It is not clear what size a 'Jack' penknife blade is, so it is not easy to work out how long each blade would take to forge. However, because cutlers usually worked only five days a week – not on Sundays or 'Saint Mondays', Goodlad would need to make over 200 blades a day. Goodlad's agreement with Broomhead forbade him to make blades for anyone else without Broomhead's agreement, but it seems unlikely that there would be much time to do so.

This document provides an interesting insight into several aspects of the Sheffield cutlery industry. It is evidence for the specialisation by some cutlers in one process; it gives an idea of rates of pay and it demonstrates the system of outworking. It also provides evidence for production rates. One forger was able to forge over a thousand blades a week, so assuming he took the required 'holidays' at Christmas and in August, he could produce around 48,000 blades a year! On a biographical note, both Goodlad and Broomhead served their apprenticeship to the same master, Peter Simon. Robert Broomhead was the son of a yeoman and became a freeman in 1727, and the following year, John Goodlad, the son of a button maker, began his apprenticeship. Broomhead, being a freeman, had a mark and the right to sell his knives, whether or not he made them himself, while Goodlad who was non-freeman had to make knives for masters. Robert Broomhead also trained John Goodlad's brother William from 1738, so the two men had obviously kept in contact from their training days. In the nineteenth century, men like Goodlad became known as 'outworkers', and might take work from one or more master.

The geography of Sheffield, with its cramped urban centre and the building of tenement factories and steam grinding wheels, all contributed to the continuity of one-man manufacturing units and outworkers. Some men did join together to form small firms, possibly one man providing the capital and the other the skill. By the beginning of the nineteenth century, some firms had expanded to employ hundreds and later thousands of people. Firms such as Joseph Rodgers and Sons and James

Dixon were able to build enormous factories, but individual craftsmen survived by being able to find niche markets and provide specialist services. They were also seen by merchants as cheaper alternatives to the large firms.

The evidence from the Cutlers' Company records shows that in the seventeenth century, there was a clear division of labour between the craft groups of cutlers, the scissorsmiths, scythe- shear- and sickle smiths, awlbladesmiths and filesmiths, who were all under the rules of Company. It is further assumed that in the early days of the Company at least, the scissors, knives, shears etc. were made by craftsmen, who could do all the processes of forging, hardening and tempering, grinding, glazing and attaching any handles. It is assumed that a skilled craftsman also did the additional processes for specific items, such as cutting teeth on files. The exception was the scythesmiths, who because they were making such large items, insisted on using non-apprenticed labourers to help them. Problems arise when attempting to discover the extent to which a man might concentrate on just one or two processes, sending work out to others who might do a better job on a particular process. It has been shown above that by the end of the seventeenth century at least, some men were clearly specialising in one or other process. Similarly, it is clear that among the cutlers, men were specialising in making different types of products; developing a range of spring knives, open razors, forks, carving and food preparation knives, as well as table knives.

The apprenticeship records of the Cutlers' Company give the occupation of fathers and masters of the apprentices and by the 1780s, there seems to be an increase in the variety of cutlery-related occupations, or clearer descriptions were being given. Men were listed as razorsmiths, forkmakers and grinders of these items, but any of these men had a registered mark, or if any of their apprentices registered one, they were recorded with the marks of cutlers. As well as the generic terms of 'cutler' and 'grinder' (there were no forgers listed), the following specific crafts were given:

> 3 table knife grinders
> 3 table knife cutlers
> 1 embellisher of knives
> 1 engraver of knives
> 1 silver cutler

All these descriptions appear after 1780 and imply the specialisation by men in activities that might have once been considered a part of the overall manufacturing process carried out by the same person.

It is evident then that a complex system of contracting work evolved and that in some relationships, one man might assume a superior role, being the instigator or the organiser, sending work perhaps to non-freemen, as in the contract between Robert Broomhead and John Goodlad. Men who developed particular skills, perhaps in hafting knives with ivory or pearl, or were able to forge quickly and competently, might find themselves sought after by many other cutlers and ultimately, by the large firms which developed at the end of the eighteenth century. It is remarkable that although firms might employ hundreds or thousands of people, they often sent out work to specialists or to 'outworkers'. For instance, large firms might find it uneconomic for the number of orders it received to retain a man skilled in attaching pearl handles. They might want to be able to offer a wide range of knives, but knowing few items would be ordered in large quantities, would chose to 'factor' the work to another firm or outworker and 'buy-in' items to maintain their product lines. This system of large and small firms, with inworkers and outworkers, existed alongside independent cutlers who would accept orders from large firms, considering themselves on an equal footing. One can imagine the town being criss-crossed by men and boys carrying part-finished and finished knives from one specialist to another and back to the manufacturer.

Not only was there a complex system of manufacture, which exists even in the twenty-first century, but there were also the specialist suppliers, who provided the cutlers with the raw or part-made materials for completing their knives. After steel, the most obvious items supplied to the cutlers were the handle materials. Natural material from plant or animal had to be dressed and cut most economically to approximate handle sizes. The costly materials of ivory and pearl, were not only cut to size, but might also be carved and fluted by skilled men. Bone, the horn of buffalo and buck, together with stag, would be cut to size for table knives and carving knives and forks and horn might be softened and pressed into different shapes, often to imitate more costly items such as stag. The production of metal handles involved not only metal production in molten or sheet form, which needed casters, rollers and stampers of the metal. The manufacture of dies for the cutlery and silver trades expanded enormously at the end of the eighteenth century, with the introduction of good quality crucible steel for the dies and the use of sheet metal for handles and other items of tableware. Diesinkers and engravers were required and engravers were also concerned in the decoration of cutlery and flatware. Again, the Cutlers' Company records have some of these trades in its apprenticeship lists, again after the 1780s:

    1 turner of wood knife handles
    5 knife handle makers
    1 haft presser
    1 bone cutter
    1 ivory turner
    5 die sinkers
    1 mark maker

Because of this increasing complexity of the manufacture of cutlery and flatware in the nineteenth century, and the rising influence of the unions, attempts were made to establish standards, at least in the payment of wages for work.

'Statements' – negotiated price lists of payment

Throughout the nineteenth century and beyond, unions, workmen and employers tried to maintain a set of prices for all aspects of cutlery manufacture. The printed Price Lists or 'statements' are an underused and undervalued resource, being hard to find since they were produced in very small numbers and were restricted to the men in the trade. Not only do they provide information about the money paid to grinders, forgers etc. but they are also essential for the reconstruction of manufacturing processes. Because they are contemporary documents, the 'statements' use the correct terminology for processes, unlike the words and phrases used by observers, which might be drawn from other related trades, but are often found to be incorrect – at least for the Sheffield trades. However, because of changes in materials and designs of knives and the greater use of machines, many of the terms used in the nineteenth century are now obsolete.

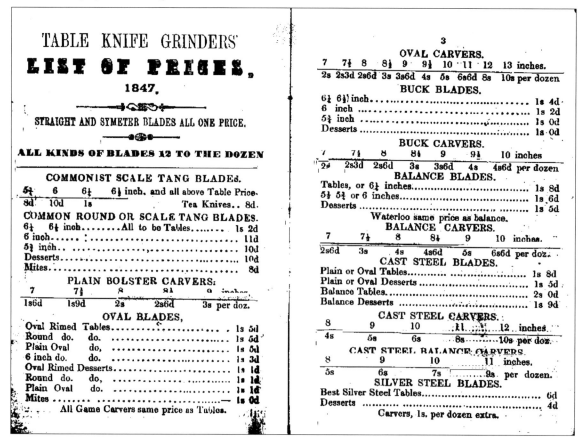

Figure 24 A page from the table knife grinders price list, 1847

The statements were produced through negotiation between the unions and the employers and cover specific trades and processes. In the present context, examples will be drawn from the statements for table knife grinders (1847) and table knife hafters (1844)[6].

The table knife grinders' list of prices begins with the declaration that 'straight' and 'scimitar' blades were to be ground at the same price and that all kinds of blades were to be 12 to the dozen. The number of items 'to the dozen' had long been a contentious issue and in the 1780s, Joseph Mather, a filegrinder, wrote a scurrilous poem about Jonathan Watkinson, who became Master Cutler in 1784, entitled 'Watkinson and his Thirteens'. This poem used the common practice of insisting on more than 12 knives to the dozen to express strong radical and revolutionary ideas.

The pages reveal the ranges of table cutlery as well as specific designs of blade and bolster as the prices are broken down into types of knives, length of blades and any specified further treatment required. From these prices, it is possible to see which designs were of better quality. For instance, common scale tang blades, six inches long, were to be ground for 10d. per dozen, while balanced table blades of cast steel cost two shillings per dozen. Carving knives, having larger blades, naturally cost more to grind. Buck carvers with ten-inch blades cost 4s.6d. per dozen, while the same sized cast steel balanced carvers cost 7s. However, there are many terms for processes and styles of knives which are incomprehensible, for example 'knobbed and wigged carvers'. This price list details the following designs:

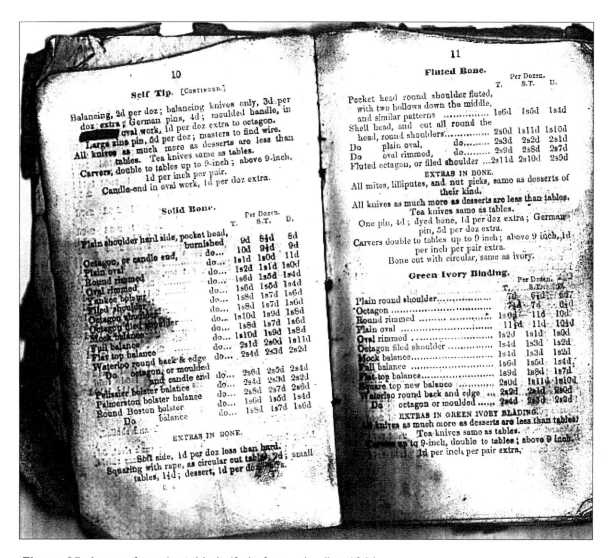

Figure 25 A page from the table knife hafters price list, 1844

common fish blades
American fish blade
Russia carvers
bread blades,
basket blades

The price list for the table-knife hafters is much more complex, because of the almost endless variations of materials and designs. The hafting materials listed include:

soft wood
cocoa (cocobola)
bone
solid bone
fluted bone
whole bone
sheep bone
ivory (also for dyeing)
white ivory
buffalo
buck
stag
pressed
shams
forbuck

The prices of working with the above materials vary, with extra costs being given for additional work, such as attaching ferrules, balancing the handle and pinning through the tang.

These price lists detail every aspect of work in manufacturing table knives, breaking down the processes and providing information about the range of work carried out. Unfortunately, they do not say *how* they did this work. These price lists must be viewed in conjunction with actual knives or at least with the trade catalogues, in order to appreciate the effort and skill which has gone into making a table knife. There were similar lists for other edge tool and cutlery processes.

The products

It is not intended that there should be here an exhaustive listing of all the types of tableware produced in the eighteenth and nineteenth century, but an overview of basic designs and the production implications is given. In the mid eighteenth century, there was a limited array of knives, forks and spoons, the main differences being the quality of materials used. People might have one type of knives, forks and spoons for eating, a pair of carvers, plus food

preparation knives. Documentary evidence, listed below, seems to suggest there were few designs and varieties of tableware. A century later, there was an increased range of cutlery and flatware, specifically for different foods and courses. Cutlers lavished decoration on dessert knives, which were often made of more costly materials, such as silver blades with pearl handles. Shapes and sizes of blades varied and, with the range of handle materials, bolster shapes, ferrules and endcaps, a manufacturer could have a range of dozens of designs.

Elizabeth Parkin's inventory, 1760s

Surviving examples of eighteenth century table knives show them to have curved, spatulate blades often described as 'scimitar'. They were quite large compared to present day knives, often being 27cm in overall length. In the mid eighteenth century, a new blade style called 'French' was introduced, which had straight parallel sides and the end was rounded or slightly pointed. Forks tended to have two tines, with a long shank to the bolster and handle, and were made to match the knives. Silver and pewter spoons were similar in shape and size to present-day spoons, but varying in decoration.

Our knowledge of the table cutlery and flatware depends on the surviving examples, from archaeological excavations, contemporary illustrations and finally a few documentary sources linked to their production. One important source is the inventory of Elizabeth Parkin or, more correctly, records of her hardware business which she passed on to Walter Oborne when she retired[7]. Elizabeth Parkin was the heiress of a substantial family business, built up by her grandfather, Thomas Parkin[8]. The records relate to the stock of the ironmongery business from the late 1750s, when Elizabeth Parkin retired to an estate at Ravensfield, near Rotherham, leaving her distant relative, Walter Oborne, in charge. Elizabeth died in 1766. The records show her business to have been one of buying and selling iron and steel; buying finished cutlery; an import/export business dealing in a variety of commodities and finally, money lending.

The stocktaking and day-to-day dealings show that many Sheffield cutlers depended on this business to buy their finished goods and to lend them money. There are long lists of names and details of loans to cutlers and tradesmen, often quite small amounts. From the lists, it is possible to appreciate the variety of knives made in Sheffield. Unfortunately, many of the descriptive names do not convey very much.

A list beginning in January 1758 shows the amounts of goods being brought in by the cutlers. The following table (Table 1) gives the entries for the men who brought in table cutlery in January.

Bone scale table knives appear to have been the most common pattern and the business was holding 238 dozen, priced at two shillings per dozen. Forks were listed with knives, suggesting matching pairs. Sham buck and sham stag refers to pressed horn imitating the more expensive handle material. In the stock list in 1766, there was only one entry for spoons: 1 gross of pewter teaspoons at six shillings a gross.

Table 1

date	name	goods	value
Jan 25	Ben Mellor	70 doz spotted French knives	£5.5.0
Jan 26	Wm Ashforth	6 doz square tipped knives and forks	7/-
Jan 26 & Feb 1	Jno Ibberson	4 gross spotted table knives 2 gross spotted table knives	£3.12.0 £1.12.0
Jan 28	Jo Stringer	4 gross spotted table knives 2 gross spotted French knives	£4.0.0 £2.0.0
Jan 28	Jno Ashforth	2 gross spotted table knives	£2.0.0
Jan 30	T Marshall	18 doz. spotted table knives 21 doz. spotted table knives	£1.12.3 £2.2.0
Jan 31	Geo Fox	6 doz. silver knives and forks	£1.15.0

'Spotted' knives were those having a cheap handle material of horn, stained to imitate tortoiseshell. The value varied but was approximately £1 per gross, though a discount system seems to have been operating so the men got less than the stated value. This list demonstrates the large numbers of knives and forks being produced, especially as John Ibberson takes in four gross of knives and the following week takes in a further two gross. No one man could have made that number of knives, working on his own and completing all stages in the production.

In 1766 the shop held £635 worth of cutlery and some flatware. The following is a list of some of the descriptions and prices of table knives:

```
4 doz. sham buck tab[le knive]s and 3
prong forks          [at] 2/-    8/-
4 doz. do. capt   [capped]
                     [at] 2/6   10/-
4 doz. sham stag do.
                     [at] 2/8   10/8
43 doz. bone scale tab[le] kn[ive]s and
f[or]ks              [at] 2/-  £4.6.-
1 doz pair fine pearl kn[ive]s and f[or]ks
                            £4.-.-
```

The records of Elizabeth Parkin's business provide a useful picture of the amounts of knives and forks being made and their values. The terms used are also useful in identifying the different styles and materials.

Museums and collections

Knives and flatware, which survive in collections, are often a poor representation of the Sheffield trades since museums tend to concentrate on the costly, most decorative and top-of-the-range items. This presentation by museums of such up-market cutlery leaves the 'ordinary' items of everyday cutlery and flatware appearing dull, boring and unsophisticated. In addition, by concentrating on stylistic developments and the decorative workmanship on exotic handle materials, there is often a lack of understanding of the basic manufacturing processes. Except in the change of shape over time, hardly any notice is taken of the knife blade itself and in the technical developments in the production of an effective cutting edge. Without an appreciation of work practices and manufacturing processes, descriptions of surviving examples of knives have often included inaccuracies and a misuse of trade terms. Even the words 'iron' and 'steel' are used as though they were the same thing[9].

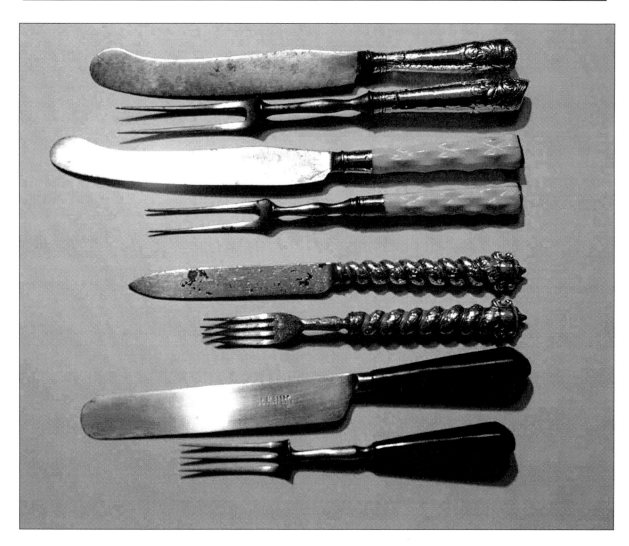

Figure 26 Examples of late eighteenth century and nineteenth century table cutlery and flatware

The best indication of the cutlery and flatware available in the nineteenth century is the illustrations in the catalogues of the manufacturers. From the middle of the nineteenth century, trade catalogues were being produced by manufacturers to show the range of goods to customers. Prior to this, pattern cards and rolls of cutlery would be taken or sent round to shopkeepers and buyers. The trade catalogues track the changes over time in styles, new items and the disappearance of some product lines. They can also identify the takeovers of firms and often have historical details in them – medals gained at exhibitions, indication of overseas customers and sometimes, photographs of work processes.

The Great Exhibition

The Great Exhibition in London in 1851 provided Sheffield manufacturers with an opportunity to demonstrate their skills. Many of the larger firms had specially made items such as the Norfolk Knife, a large spring knife with 75 blades, which is now displayed at the Cutlers' Hall. Rodgers had an enviable reputation for quality and was considered the world's leading cutlers. Together with some of Sheffield's silver firms, they had very large factories and, like James Dixon and William Hutton, they employed hundreds of people. These firms all had prestige works and their showrooms were tourist attractions.

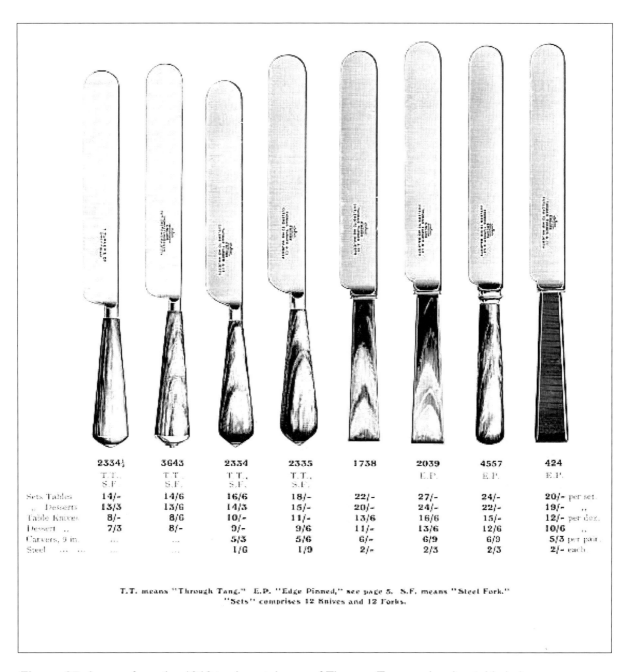

Figure 27 A page from the 1910 trade catalogue of Thomas Turner, showing table knives

In the guide to the exhibitors at the Great Exhibition[10], the following examples are firms which displayed table cutlery, with descriptions of new processes and special designs, indicating what was innovative at the time

William Brooks and Sons and George Wostenholme are described as simply showing an 'assortment of table cutlery'.

William Hargreaves and Co displayed 'a coromandel-wood case, lined with red silk velvet containing 12 table knives, 12 dessert knives and 1 pair of carvers – all with carved ivory handles, silver ferrules and highly-polished steel blades.' The firm also exhibited table knives with fancy wood handles 'made for the North American market', as well as round-of-beef and game carvers and bread knives.

Thomas Turner and Co had made a six-foot long exhibition pair of 'Albert venison carvers'. The firm also had other carvers; ivory handled table cutlery, some with close plated blades. The description of their stand also mentions vegetable forks and cheese scoops, plus butchers' and cooks' knives.

Parkin and Marshall had table cutlery with fluted pearl handles; fish carvers, the blade having open-work decoration with 'appropriate emblems'; a case of fish carvers in a shark design; a pair of melon carvers, with a newly designed blade. Many of their dessert knives were close plated, with ivory and pearl handles.

Thomas Ellin & Co displayed a table knife with an ox-bone handle and a common point to the blade 'being the shape used fifty years ago'. They too had several examples of carving knives, forks and steels, plus table cutlery with handles made from ivory, pearl, ebony, horn, cocoa and bone.

William Oliver chose to make a set of minute cutlery, less than 4in long. They too showed tables knives with an 1800 style, with green stained ivory handles and a round point blade, and an undetailed example of a 1750's knife. They had a pair Jones' patent carvers and steel, set in fawns' feet.

These exhibitors had immense pride in their work, and took pleasure in showing the world what they could do in manufacturing a knife, fork and spoon. From the brief descriptions given in the guide, the manufacturers made table cutlery, dessert knives, fish knives and forks, carvers for a variety of meats, bread knives with a few examples of other cutlery relating to food preparation. The paper on the manufacture of steel articles, particularly cutlery was presented to the Society of Arts five years after the Great Exhibition. In the discussion which followed, several comments were made about the relative quality Sheffield and foreign manufacturers especially those displayed the Paris Exhibition in 1855. Thomas Moulson, an ex Master Cutler had been a juror at the Paris Exhibition in 1855, and was concerned that Sheffield manufacturers had not improved over the previous thirty years. The French were held up as being able to produce well made and well designed cutlery and the Prussians were improving in leaps and bounds. Moulson appeared to consider that the decline was the result of way the Sheffield trades had been organised. This was a point of view not totally accepted in the discussion, but the various remarks show that there was a general feeling of self-satisfaction and that continental manufacturers had poorer quality of steel and lower labour costs.

The criticism that cutlery from France was better designed was absorbed by several people who aimed to improve the skills of Sheffield craftsmen. The School of Art had been founded in Sheffield in 1843 and later in the century, two museums and an art gallery were opened in the city where cutlers could see inspirational objects. The Ruskin Museum and the City Museum had both opened in 1875, the Mappin Gallery opened in 1887. Of these three, the Ruskin Museum had been established in 1875 in Sheffield primarily to educate the artisan. John Ruskin had amassed an enormous collection including paintings, drawings, rare books, geological specimens and plaster copies of architectural features. This collection was housed in a museum at Walkley, Sheffield and drew in hundreds of people. It moved to larger premises at Meersbrook, Sheffield in 1890, and attracted 60,000 visitors a year.

It is difficult to know the extent to which manufacturers employed trained designers to work on their range of goods. Pattern books for manufacturers survive and do not give details of how such patterns were developed, though some men have been identified as being involved with firms. Christopher Dresser was employed at James Dixon, silver manufacturers, though worked on holloware designs.

Notes

[1] The Jolly Grinder.

[2] Children's Employment Commission, report, 1842, p 49.

[3] S Harrison 1864 *A Complete History of the Great Flood at Sheffield*, (Sheffield, republished, 1974) p 31.

[4] Cutlers' Company archives, C6/2.

[5] Sheffield Archives,Tibbett Collection 762.

[6] Hawley Collection, reference numbers, eph.cut.47, 63.

[7] Sheffield Archives, reference number OR2.

[8] BA Holderness 1973 'Elizabeth Parkin and her investments, 1733-66, aspects of the Sheffield money market in the eighteenth century' in *Transactions of the Hunter Archaeological Society*, Vol.10, p 81–87.

[9] P Brown (ed) 2001 *British Cutlery an illustrated history of design, evolution and use* (York) Illustrations of 18th century Sheffield knives are labelled as having iron blades, e.g. p 110 and those from the nineteenth century, p 126 are described as having 'steel' blades.

[10] *Official Descriptive and Illustrated Catalogue of the Great Exhibition, 1851*, Vol. II, p 605–608.

Chapter 6

Summary

The period 1750–1900 in Sheffield was an interesting time in the development of the cutlery industry. The technological developments were impressive:

- expansion in the capacity of the waterpowered grinding between 1730–1770

- invention of crucible steel in the 1740s, which allowed better quality dies to be made

- introduction from the 1780s of steam power for driving the presses, stamps and grinding

- development of processes for bulk steel manufacture in the 1860s, bringing down the price of steel

- invention of plastics in the second half of the nineteenth century, for cheaper alternative to natural materials

These improvements in the raw materials for cutlers and power sources were coupled with an increased demand for tableware and more variation in cutlery for the wider range of foods being eaten, especially in middle-class homes. However, none of these factors seems to have impinged on the traditional organisation of the industry. The established order of the master, his journeyman and apprentice working in a confined workshop continued right through this period. Although several firms expanded to be employers of thousands, the bulk of the industry was still made up of small production units of a master and a few employees. The principal difference was perhaps the increasing fragmentation and specialisation of the trades.

From the seventeenth century a cutler, controlled by the regulations of the Cutlers' Company had made table knives and forks. There is evidence to show that by the end of the century, some men were specialising in one aspect of production – forging, grinding or hafting – though this was not universal. By the end of the eighteenth century, not only were some men specialising in one or more processes, but many concentrated on one type of product, become table knife makers, fork makers or fork grinders. They obviously benefited or perhaps drove, the diversification of designs and styles of products. As well as the forgers, grinders and cutlers (who were concentrating on the hafting), there were the subsidiary supply trades. Ivory carving, scale pressing, pearl cutters etc expanded and showed tremendous skill and craftsmanship in their work. All these people provided an ever-increasing range of tableware through the nineteenth century.

It has not been possible here to give an extensive account of all stages in the production of every type of knife fork and spoon, nor to give a stylistic dictionary of features found on Sheffield manufactured cutlery and flatware. The growing interest in the material culture and particularly the production methods in urban centres from the eighteenth century and the concomitant social implications are worthy of consideration. Increasing archaeological work prior to the redevelopment of town centres and brownfield sites has focused attention on the need to understand the work processes of particular industries and therefore an overview of work practices and products for this particular industry highlight the information available. Only by utilising all sources of information is it possible to reconstruct cutlery manufacturing sites and indeed, other industrial sites.

The relevant points can be summarised as:

- Cutlers, from at least 1624, manufactured table knives and later, also made forks. They were initially trained to perform all the processes in manufacture.

- Men, still being trained as cutlers, began to specialise in the different stages –

forging, grinding and hafting and by the end of the eighteenth century, specialised in different products

- The Cutlers' Company has resulted in a wealth of documentary evidence, especially the mark books

- The Cutlers' Company control perpetuated an industry of hundreds of small-scale manufacturing units which continued long after lost many of its powers in 1814

- Knives, forks and spoons can be made successfully by hand – forging, grinding and hafting – but the increasing availability of power assisted first the grinders and then forgers by allowing blades and blanks to be produced by machines

- The names for parts of knives, processes and tools are often specific to Sheffield.

Recently excavated sites in Sheffield city centre have shown the types of finds which might be expected from cutlery factories and other buildings in a city which had such a pervasive industry reaching from the large factories to the backstreet workshops and even into domestic properties.

The excavations of industrial sites have revealed tools, part-finished goods and a few completed objects. It is therefore necessary to be able to distinguish between the tools which were being used, those objects which were being made and other items which had been brought to the site for other reasons. Sheffield craftsmen were notorious for accumulating tools, raw materials, etc. from retiring workmen or redundant factories, on the off chance they might 'come in useful for something'.

While there is immediate appreciation of the beauty of a well-made knife, it is enhanced by an understanding of the processes involved. In highlighting the skills and craftsmanship of Sheffield cutlers, some explanation is offered as to the diversity and specialisation of the cutlery trade and the people who contributed to it.

Figure 28 Part-made knives from the excavation of Riverside Exchange, Sheffield (courtesy of ARCUS)

THE WORKSHOPS OF THE CUTLERY AND TABLEWARE INDUSTRY OF SHEFFIELD

—————————

VICTORIA BEAUCHAMP

Chapter 7

The cutlery and tableware industry: geographical development

Why did Sheffield develop as a centre for cutlery?

It has long been established that the accessibility of raw materials such as iron ore, coal, charcoal, and stone suitable for making grindstones were fundamental to the growth of Sheffield's cutlery and tableware industry. One reason it became a major centre for the industry rather than declining, as had other early centres such as York, Thaxted, Salisbury, Hereford and Chester[1], was due to the accessibility of waterpower[2]. Samuel and Nathaniel Buck in 1736 attached the following note to their engraving of 'The East Prospect of Sheffield'

'This town was anciently famous for making iron heads of arrows ... by degrees it has much improved in all manner of cutlery ware. Its situation is delightful and somewhat uncommon, it being situated on a round hill in the midst of a valley which is surrounded by much higher hills. This supplies it with many valuable falls of water necessary for carrying on the manufacture of the place. This advantage of streams to turn their mills, together with great plenty of coal in its neighbourhood render this perhaps the finest place in the Kingdom for the business which is here carried on'[3].

The late eighteenth century

Even before 1750 Defoe had described Sheffield (1724) as 'very populous and large, the streets narrow, and the houses dark and black, occasioned by the continued smoke of the forges, which are always at work. Here they make all sorts of cutlery ware'[4]. In 1750 the population of Sheffield was about 20,000[5] and the town had begun to expand into the Hollis Croft area to the north west of the town centre. It is unsurprising therefore that this new area of growth attracted the expanding cutlery industry.

The Fairbank papers[6], from their start in the 1750s, show a concentration of workshops in the Hollis Croft district.

The built up area of the town is believed to have doubled in size between 1736 and 1808[7]. The major landholdings of the Duke of Norfolk, Earl Fitzwilliam and the property of the Church Burgesses, were well placed to take advantage of this growth. Indeed building land seems to have been let 'by the estate as it was needed'[8]. Certainly there seems to have been no restriction on the location of industry nor any attempt to inhibit its spread. The wealth created by the tableware and cutlery, Sheffield plate, iron making and finishing, and merchanting trades allowed the extension of the town and further development of the isolated suburban tenements so characteristic of the region[9].

In 1770 the grid-iron street pattern was laid out on Alsop fields, formerly part of the Duke of Norfolk's deer park: this became the Arundel Street district, with a street plan which still exists today[10]. This was the first serious attempt at town planning in Sheffield and was designed as a middle-class residential area. By the end of the eighteenth century the district had failed to develop and became a mixture of domestic and industrial property in the nineteenth century. The 1787 directory shows workshops still clustered in the Hollis Croft and central areas (Fig 29).

In the valleys the number of waterpowered 'wheels', for which most evidence exists, increased from 36 sites in 1700 to 97 by 1800. All but seven of the sites predate 1775. The 1794 survey list[11] of Sheffield indicates that the sites connected with the metal trades also included eleven tilts, six forges, seven rolling mills and a furnace. The grinding 'hulls'[12] listed

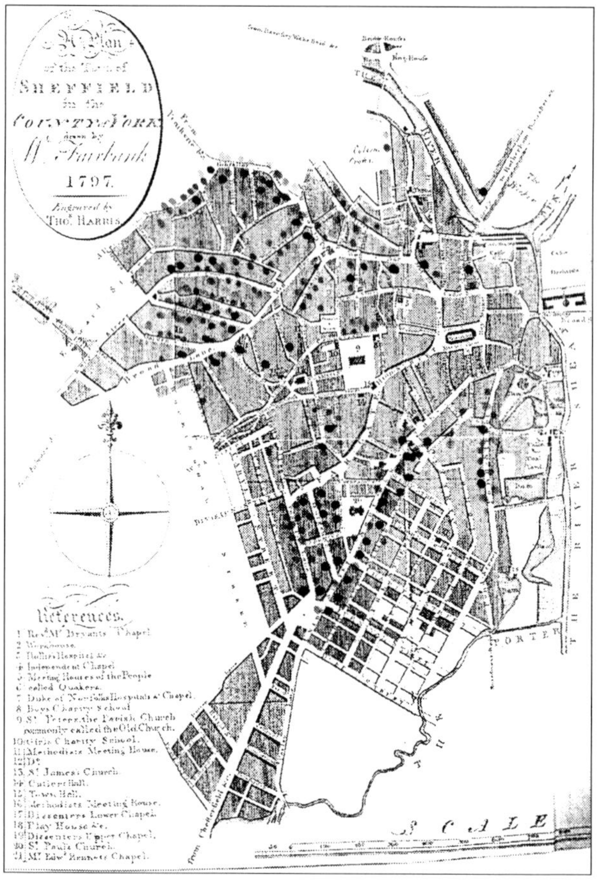

Figure 29 The location of the cutlery industry in 1787. Note the concentration in the Hollis Croft area to the north west of the town centre

contained 1029 trows or grinding troughs, which employed at least 1077 people.

The location of workshops across the town

The eighteenth century saw changes in the organization of the tableware and cutlery trades. Originally, the process of making a blade, from forging to hafting, would be carried out by one person. Prior to the incorporation of the Cutlers' Company in 1624 there had been almost a 'complete absence of differentiation or specialisation'[13]. By 1748 however, the grinders were sufficiently distinct to have formed their own sick club, but the combinations of forger-grinder or forger-cutler did not vanish completely[14]. The principal effect of this separation of processes was that each 'little mester' (see page 19) became dependent on at least one other. Production units had to be close

together if cutlery was to continue to be made economically and thus workshops in the town developed in groups 'held together as functional and spatial entities'[15].

In the eighteenth century therefore the workshops of the industry were located near to the workers' housing, dispersing only to locations near waterpowered sites for grinding. Specialisms also developed in several villages that surround Sheffield.

The nineteenth century

In 1801 there were 46,000 people living in Sheffield, the population more than doubling in the 50 years after 1750. In the next 50 years it was to more than triple, for by 1851 the population was 135,000 and by 1901 it stood at 409,000. Of the 65,000 people recorded in 1821[16] around 8500 were involved in the cutlery trades, as identified by a survey in 1824 carried out by a Sheffield Local Register. This figure, accounting for 97% of all of Britain's cutlers[17], included 2240 table knife manufacturers, 2190 spring knife manufacturers, 478 craftsmen involved in the making of razors, 806 in the scissor trade, 1284 involved with file manufacture, 400 saw manufactures, 541 edge tool makers and 480 fork makers, as well as 130 rural workers of various branches of the trade[18]. As Trinder writes:

> 'Industrial enterprise could be self-stimulating. The establishment of a successful concern could demonstrate that a particular activity was successful in a certain area, it could create a skilled labour force; make available products for the finishing trades, demand for raw materials, servicing skills and transport facilities'[19].

The effect of economic factors on the expansion and location of the industry

Development in the early part of the century was partly facilitated by the selling of Norfolk land in 1802, 1805, 1810 and 1814, which realised over £140,000 for the estate[20]. With each economic boom came a growth in the number of workshops and factories, helped by the increase in credit allowances for the larger firms by the newly established joint stock banks[21]. The largest boom in the first half of the nineteenth century came in the 1830s. In all, 156 new streets were proposed and created during this period. However, there continued to be a mix of residential and industrial properties.

The boom broke, however, and the 1840s proved to be a time of hardship, but Lloyd and Unwin have suggested that, far from being a period of contraction in the cutlery industry, the number of firms increased during times of depression; each man could set up on his own workshop for as little as £5[22]. The number of workshops did indeed continue to increase during periods of depression, in Hollis Croft, the areas around Devonshire Street and Rockingham Street[23], the newly developed Park area and by the Riverside.

The 1850s saw another building boom, especially in areas west and north of the town centre. In the centre 'the decline in the rateable value shown for large dwelling houses points to the conversion of many of them into factories and workshops. Almost every existing firm dating from those years has records showing conversion and adaptation'[24].

The 1860s continued to be prosperous, with only a minor slump in 1866. The rest of the decade was marked by a shortage of labour[25]. Severe depressions occurred between 1874–9, as elsewhere in the country, and although there was a brief period of relief they returned in 1883–1886 and in 1893. During the last forty years of the century there was a reduction in the numbers of cutlery workshops, especially in the Central and Park areas of the town.

Despite this reduction in workshop numbers by the end of the century, large firms remained the exception rather than the rule in Sheffield. The introduction of steam power did not have the significant effects seen elsewhere, in, for instance, the textile industry, where steam power had led to factory production in the conventional sense. Jones and Townsend wrote of Sheffield

'The nineteenth century factories were only such in the sense of being large buildings, containing up to 800 workers but more usually from 50–200 performing their tasks under the direction of individual management. In other respects the factories were compatible with the traditional handicraft system. The buildings were in fact aggregations of craftsmen's workshops'[26].

Of the 505 firms identified by the rate books as being in operation in 1891, 27 could be classified as 'large' or 'giant' using Lloyd-Jones and Lewis' classifications[27]. The others could be divided into 62 'medium' and 416 'small' firms, using the same classification.

Lloyd-Jones and Lewis' classification seemed the most appropriate to use here, as it was derived from the same data set, the Sheffield rate books, utilised for this research. Although the data may be skewed towards the larger firms because of the inclusion of the steel industry in the division of the rates, i.e. some of the medium-scale cutlery firms may have been large by the standards of the cutlery industry, the data set was considered sufficiently accurate to produce a picture of the scale of production in the cutlery industry throughout the nineteenth century. The terms of small, medium, large and giant throughout are therefore based on Lloyd-Jones and Lewis's classification.

Areas identified as centres of the cutlery and tableware trades in the nineteenth century

Six areas[28] (Fig 30) have been identified as having significant numbers of workshops related to the cutlery and tableware industry concentrated in them. Specific analysis of the rate books throughout the whole of the nineteenth century has allowed an assessment to be made of the location of the industry and its organization. Each of the six districts identified has unique characteristics. By plotting the data from the rate books, on reprints of the first edition OS maps, the development of each area was shown. Analysis of area-specific information through database manipulation has also provided a detailed image of the likely buildings that would have existed, whether small courtyard workshops or large tenement factories.

This enabled analysis of the spatial distribution of the industry, i.e. whether topography affected the types of buildings erected or whether there were other influences affecting the growth of each area.

The **Hollis Croft district**, already mentioned as being the first area of expansion outside the medieval boundaries of the town in the eighteenth century, had the most number of workshops by the 1820s and it maintained this

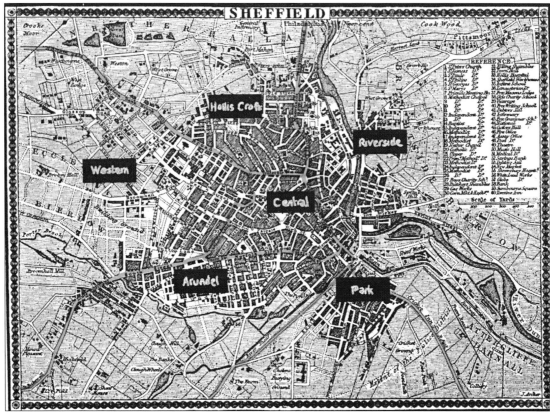

Figure 30 The six areas described in the text where the workshops of the industry and allied trades were located. Map by J Archer 1835 (Local Studies Library)

characteristic throughout the nineteenth century. In 1848, Haywood and Lee, Commissioners for a Sanitary Report for the Borough of Sheffield, described the area as 'a multitude of small workshops, mostly producing small items of cutlery, and a few larger cutlery-manufacturing establishments'[29]. By the end of the nineteenth century the rate book evidence shows that 30% of all 'cutlery'[30] manufacture took place within this area. In the years sampled, 1820 to 1891–92, in ten yearly intervals, a total[31] of 1057 entries relating to the cutlery trades in the district were recorded. Of these, 729 had a full address, including property numbers, amounting to a total of 544 different workshops[32]. However the rate books, cross-referenced with the trade directories, can only confirm 172 workshops in use by tableware, cutlery and the allied trades in 1891. This was about the average occupied in any year. By the end of the century owner occupation this area was about 25%.

The Hollis Croft area experienced greatest growth in the 1830s, when the number of

recorded workshops in the rate books more than doubled, from 88 to 183. In 1850 the maximum of 197 workshops in use by the cutlery trades was reached. Throughout the whole of the nineteenth century the area was dominated by small workshops. From the 1850s medium-scale works do appear but they number less than sixteen in total at the end of the century. Probably due to the gently sloping ground and the densely packed housing, only two large-scale works, situated on the outskirts of the area, were built in the nineteenth century. These were the workshops of J Askham in the 1870s at 57 Broad Lane and the works of Wade, Wingfield and Co, later Wingfield, Rowbotham and Co, cutlery manufacturers and general merchants of table and spring cutlery, razors, files, steels and saws, in the 1880s at 82 Tenter Street.

The **Arundel Street area** differs from Hollis Croft in a number of ways. The first planned development on Norfolk land had, by the middle of the nineteenth century, changed from being a residential area to an industrial one. Although today it is mainly the large works that remain, the rate books show that the majority of the workshops in the area in the nineteenth century could be classed as small. For example, at the end of the century only Joseph Rodgers' works in Norfolk Street could be regarded as giant, with a rateable value of £1484.10s.0d. and paying a rate of £111.6s.9d. Eight works could be classified as large; Bingham and Son, part of Walker and Hall's firm in Howard Street, and Thomas Turner and Co works in Suffolk Street, the group as a whole paying rates of between £33.3s.9d and £61.16s.10d. Twenty-eight works could be classed as medium, including the premises of Atkin Brothers in Matilda Street, Thomas Ellin and Co. in Sylvester Street and John Sellers and Son in Arundel Street. The other 241 small works recorded over the period, numbering just 78 by 1891–92, paid rates between 2s 3d and £9.18s.0d.

There appears to have been no specialisation in the Arundel Street area, workshops being evenly distributed throughout the cutlery and allied trades. Unlike the Hollis Croft area there was no rapid development in the 1840s and 1850s. The number of workshops slowly increases until the 1870s when 88 workshops are recorded as being in use and a final peak comes in the 1890s when there are a total of 99.

It is apparent therefore that, unlike the Hollis Croft district the Arundel area, in terms of the number of workshops in use by the cutlery industry, continued to expand, perhaps because of better access to communication routes, especially after 1870 when the nearby rail link to London was completed. Some clearance of smaller workshops may have taken place to make room for expansion of firms such as Thomas Turner's in Suffolk Street, W and S Butcher in Arundel Street, Gallimore and Co and Mappin and Webb, who all increased the sizes of their premises or moved into larger works during the course of the nineteenth century.

The **Western area** is located west of the modern Cambridge Street (formerly Coalpit Lane) between Broad Lane to the north and South Street (now The Moor) to the south. The district developed from the 1820s onwards, after the turnpiking of the Glossop Road. The streets west of Trafalgar Street were not developed until the 1830s, and the rapid expansion of this part of the town can be seen by comparing Tayler's 1832 map with White's 1841 map (Figs 31 and 32).

Growth continued at a steady rate until the 1850s, when a total of 119 workshops were recorded in use. Many of the workshops in this

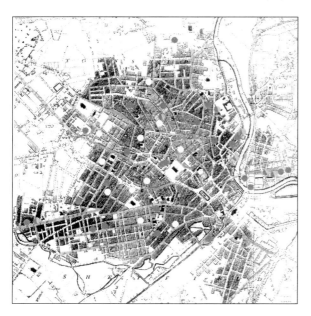

Figure 31 Tayler's map 1832. The concentration of the industry and allied trades is marked by dots. Note how the Western area has expanded by the 1840s by comparing this map with White's map of 1841

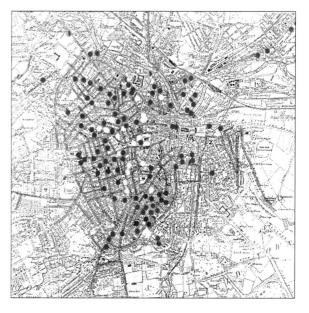

Figure 32 White's 1841 map. The location of the industry and allied trades for 1850 is shown by dots

area were taken over in the later part of the century by the packing and horn trades who moved into the area after the increase in rates in the central area from the middle part of the century. By 1891 over 50% of cutters and pressers of horn etc. were in the locality as were 38% of the city's edge tool trade. Also located here was 30% of the tableware and cutlery trade, the same proportion as the Hollis Croft area.

Like the Hollis Croft area the majority of the workshops in the area were small, accounting for 334 of the number recorded, although larger works did develop from the 1870s. Examples are Wm Hutton and Sons works in West Street and Ward and Payne at 106 West Street. In 1890 these firms paid rates of between £34 and £50.

Although the **Central area** declined as a centre for tableware and cutlery production after the 1840s, due to increases in rateable value, some firms remained. In Paradise Square, the frontages of the buildings (Fig 33) suggest an upper-class Georgian development, but a manufacturer of files, scythes, hay, machine and reaping knives, hoes, reaping hooks and sickles continued to work there in the 1870s. Workshop windows can be seen at the rear of some buildings in Paradise Square (Fig 34).

The main type of structure occupied by the cutlery industry was small but larger works did exist including worldwide exporters and 'Cutlers to the Queen' Joseph Rodgers.

By the end of the century (1891) there were just 21 tableware and cutlery workshops out of 123 in use. These included medium-scale works such as John Kirk of Townhead Street, manufacturer of spear point, table, butchers and dagger knives, spring cutlery, razors, scissors, edge tools, saws, files, steels etc. John Kirk had moved from the western area to the central area in the 1880s. There were also the large-scale works of Joseph Haywood and Co, Pond Street, Joseph Rodgers and Son, Pond Hill and the works of J Round and Son in Tudor Street. Like the larger works in the Hollis Croft area these larger workshops were located on the outskirts of the district on the boundaries with the Riverside and Arundel Street areas.

The last major area considered is that of the **Riverside** development along the Don. The majority of works here were on a larger scale than found elsewhere in the city. Like the steel works, the larger tableware and cutlery firms found this was the only land where they could build on any scale.

Of the 380 entries in the rate books over the nineteenth century 170 could be identified with

Figure 33 Paradise Square. A Georgian square with fine frontages. Workshop windows were found at the rear

Figure 34 Workshop windows at the back of Paradise Square

specific addresses, and from these at least 138 different properties could be identified. In total there were six works connected with the cutlery industry which could be classified as 'giant'. These were mainly those which were integrated with steel works, for example, Bury and Co on Penistone Road, Thomas Firth and Sons on Brightside Lane, the Hallamshire Steel and File company on Bardwell Road, Naylor Vickers and Co at Millsands and Thomas Turton and Sons at Sheaf Works, Maltravers Street. The exception was the works of Eadon and Son, file and edge tool manufacturers on Savile Street East. In addition to these there were eighteen 'large' works such as those of Ibbotson Brothers on Green Lane, merchants and manufacturers of steel, files, saws, railways springs and engineers tools, Moss and Gamble in Russell Street, manufacturers of steel, files, saws and edge tools, and Walters and Co on Penistone Road, merchants and manufacturers of table knives, shoe and bread knives, spear point knives, silver and plated dessert and fruit knives. These works paid between £30 and £77 towards the poor rate in 1890–91. 'Medium' sized works accounted for 21 premises, such as

Michael Hunter and Son on Andrew Street, who were merchants and manufacturers of table and spring cutlery, saws, files, edge tools, razors, scythes and skates and Wm Peace and Co in Mowbray Street, who manufactured steel, files, edge tools, scythes, machine knives and cast steel hammers. The rateable value of these properties was between £10.5s.8d and £30.6s.6d in 1891–92. However despite this area having the biggest percentage of large scale works there were 226 small workshops recorded. The major period of growth had been the 1830s, as in the Western and Hollis Croft areas, when the numbers increased from seventeen to 57, the peak coming in the 1850s when the workshops recorded in use by the rate books totalled 79. After that date the numbers settled around 60 until the end of the century.

The number of workshops located in the **Park** area expanded from the 1840s onwards, and reached their peak in the 1850s after which the area slowly declined. Like the Western and Hollis Croft districts, the tableware and cutlery industry and allied trades used small establishments. A total of 134 addresses relating to small workshops can be found in the rate books. Only five medium and one large works are recorded. The largest were the premises of Martin Hall and Co, manufacturers, silversmiths, electroplaters and cutlers in Broad Street, paying a rate in 1870 of £33.17s.6d.

In this area the tableware and cutlery industry predominates, but the small number of workshops in the area meant that it only contained 6.5% of the town's industry. The manufacture of tools was more significant, accounting for 16% of the total tool trade of the town.

In all the districts examined the number of addresses recorded and the number of those in use by the end of the century differ widely. Several factors may have led to this apparent overstocking of workshops:

a) *Trade directories are a notoriously unreliable source*[33].
As entries had to be paid for, workshops may have been in use by the trades even when not recorded as such; addresses may have changed as streets were renumbered, making the property number relate to a different building not previously used by the cutlery trades.

b) *Workshops were demolished and replaced by other structures or were designed as temporary structures.*

Powell argues that 'low incomes permitted only flimsy short-lived construction and materials ... making building replacements a perennial necessity'[34]. However, that workshops were short-lived structures and were likely to be demolished after a ten-year period is difficult to prove. In the Riverside area some may have been demolished to make way for larger works but in other districts a cycle of replacing old stock is a possible explanation. The workshops vacated by the cutlery trades are therefore most likely to have been reused by other trades, but no satisfactory answer can be found as to why so many buildings were made redundant during the course of the nineteenth century. Every thriving city has some vacant buildings; it is how long they stay empty, and whether their numbers are particularly high in slump periods that is important. This could be established only by assessing the rate books for each rate in every year.

c) *Workshops were not built for any particular trade and were therefore interchangeable between any of the Sheffield industries.*

The trade directories indicate that other trades reused many of the workshops. On five main streets, namely Garden Street[35], Arundel Street[36], Carver Street[37], Coalpit Lane[38] and Spring Street[39] the following conclusions could be drawn. In none of the streets do more than a few workshops remain empty. Those with no known used after they first appeared total four in Arundel Street; eight in Garden Street; four in Carver Street; five in Coalpit Lane (Cambridge Street) and six in Spring Street. Workshops in these five streets were converted to lodgings, beerhouses, an organ manufactory, workshops for painters and print makers, tailors, strop makers, surgeons, shoe makers, cabinet case makers and stores for builders and merchants, as well as shops[40]. Equally tableware and cutlery firms moved into workshops that had previously been occupied by other trades such as G Newbould, cutlery manufacturer who moved into a building that had once been occupied by J Roberts, a dyer, or William Straw, a scale maker who moved into a building once occupied by a G Taylor, strop manufacturer. George Ellis, manufacturer of joiners tools in Carver Street in the 1860s, from the evidence in the trade directories may have moved into the previous residence of B Rawlins, registrar.

The highly speculative nature of the workshops utilized by the industry can be illustrated by assessing the sources of finance available for erecting new structures[41]. The majority of the workshops identified by the Sheffield rate books were rented. On average, between 1820 and 1850, only 10% of the workshops were owner occupied[42]. After 1850 the percentage rises to an average of 35.5%. although in the Park, Riverside and Western areas, owner occupation accounts for up to 50% in some years (Fig 35) where larger firms occupying individually-designed structures are more widely represented. After 1850 there are growing numbers of partnerships which also correspond to the rise of owner occupation.

In large-scale works, for example Globe and Sheaf Works, which were built for the owners to occupy, space may have been rented out to the 'out-workers' of the firm. The speculative nature of many of the buildings, where the owner would hope to rent out each room, or in the case of 'wheels', each individual trough can be illustrated for example by Shepherd's Wheel, on the Porter. In 1801 it was owned by John Eyre in 1801 and operated by tenants such as Samuel Hind and Benjamin Wildgoose[43]. Fairbank estimated in c 1830 that in a 'wheel in Thomas Street, 120 troughs would produce an annual rental of nearly £610'[44]. In some cases there is evidence for the sub-letting of workbenches or 'sides' in small workshops such as Nook Lane, Stannington where the owner and his two brothers rented space to two other cutlers.

For the cutler establishing himself in business the outlay for rent, although it accounted on average for between a tenth and a fifth of his income[45], was a feasible possibility. The cutler would require between £3 and £4 to establish himself in business on his own account during the nineteenth century including the provision of tools and the renting of workshop space. Doris Walsh recalled that it could take 'two days work to pay the rent'[46] during the Second World War.

In comparison, the cost of erecting the typical small-scale workshop in Sheffield in the later part of the eighteenth century was between £24 and £50[47]. If 3.4% of a cutler's earnings were saved every week (c 9d) at 1850 prices, without taking any loans, it would take 35.9 years to pay for building a workshop, i.e. a working lifetime.[48] If the same amount was put away towards paying for renting a workshop, a cutler could

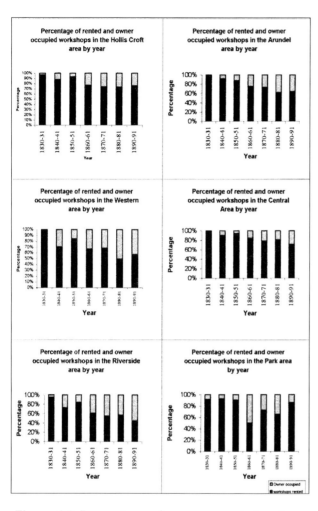

Figure 35 Percentage of owner occupied and rented workshops by area

take on a small workshop within a few weeks of starting work assuming that the rent was collected weekly (c 2 shillings per week). The question arises therefore as to who was erecting the workshops.

The building registers, introduced as a result of the local government regulations banning back-to-back housing, give details of the owners, their addresses, the proposed property and its location. Of the 73% of the 995 owners identified in the registers between 1865 and 1891 one third were cutlers (31%), 12% were in the building trades, including architects (1%)[49], and 8% were craftsmen[50]. The remaining 22% were spread between professional[51] (6%), commercial[52] (5%), food[53] (4%), manufacturers[54], minerals, agriculture, executors of wills and other categories (8%). These patterns support Chalklin's theory for an earlier period that in 'Sheffield and Birmingham

construction was mainly financed by undertakers outside the (building) trade'[55]. It can therefore be concluded that speculators were the main driving force behind the erection of many of the building utilized by the industry in the eighteenth and nineteenth centuries.

d) *The number of empty workshops may reflect a movement in the location of the trade.*
This may be relevant where firms wanted to expand and needed larger sites available in areas such as Arundel Street and the Riverside. By extracting data on all those firms that appear to have changed areas during the course of the nineteenth century, the following conclusions can be drawn[56].

In total 118 firms are known to have moved. The areas that showed the greatest loss of firms were the Central, Arundel and Park districts, while the Western and Riverside areas gained the most. Hollis Croft remained reasonably static; firms moved within the area with only minor loss to other districts (Fig 36). That the Riverside area gained the most firms can be explained by the availability of land on which to expand. Of the 23 firms that moved in from elsewhere, a quarter used their transfer to the district to expand. These included Michael Hunter, table knife manufacturer; Spear and Jackson, saw and steel manufacturers; Ibbotson Brothers, steel converters, refiners, merchants and manufacturers of fenders, grates, saws and files, William Brookes and Son, manufacturer of table knives, scissors, snuffers etc. and Unwin and Rodgers, manufacturers of pistol knives, pen and pocket knives, desk and fruit knives and scissors.

The principal reason for movement to the Western area was the increase in rateable values in other areas, especially in the Central area. From 1850 to 1890 the rateable value increased in the Central area by 1324% and the Arundel area by 570% compared to 354% in the Western district. Figure 36 shows substantial losses by these two districts to the Western area. The move to the west from Hollis Croft cannot however be explained by an increase in rateable value, as rates in the latter rose by only 284%. Those that removed from Hollis Croft to the Western district did not belong to a single branch of the tableware and cutlery trade, nor did they expand. Their relocation may have been due to personal preference for which there is no historical, geographical or economic explanation. An almost equal number of firms moved from the Western District to the Hollis Croft area[57]. Only three firms expanded as a result of relocating to the district. These were John Wilson, table, shoe and butchers knife manufacturer, and Atkinson Brothers, manufacturers of table, butchers, pen and pocket knives, razors, scissors, files and edge tools, both of whom moved from the Arundel Street area and Turner, Naylor and Marples from the Park District. All increased the rateable value of their works from small to medium between 1870 and 1891.

Although the data confirms that firms did move between areas for a variety of reasons, the numbers involved are unlikely to have contributed to the 'surplus' of workshops within each area. The total number of 118 traced as relocating is less than the numbers of vacated workshops in each of the areas by the end of the century, so with the exception of the Park district, the relocation theory can be discounted as a reasonable explanation. In reality a combination of firms moving, other industries taking their place, firms expanding and the demolition of old workshops are likely to explain the apparent surplus of tableware and cutlery workshops in the urban landscape.

In conclusion, the workshops of the industry had reached their peak number by 1850 in most areas. This corresponds with few workshops known to have been located outside the main built-up areas of the town in the 1850s (Fig 37).

Within this area their numbers continued to fluctuate however, although in constantly declining numbers, until the 1940s.

Distance between home and workplace

The distribution of workshops suggests factors such as location near the workforce. What must be stressed in all areas is the integration of workshops and dwellings. Until the nineteenth century the majority of workers in the tableware and cutlery trades are likely to have lived very close to the places where they worked. In Hollis Croft for example workshops and houses are to be found in the same courtyards. However as the town expanded to the west, and areas such as Walkley and Crookes were built up, the mixing of workshops and houses became less frequent. Areas such as Walkley in particular were developed by freehold land societies who placed limitations on the types of structures that could be built, and in this way these local societies proved to be more restrictive to the expansion of industry than the larger landlords of the town centre. Better communication routes throughout the city, in particular the tram system, made it easier for the general workforce[58] to travel further to work. However there is no evidence in Sheffield for the provision of workers housing on a large scale as in the textile industry.

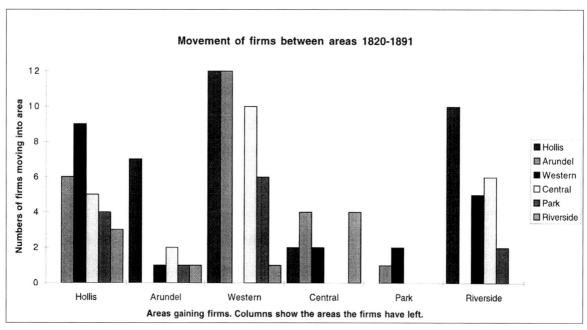

Figure 36 Movement of firms between areas 1820–1891

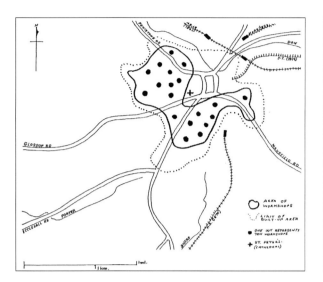

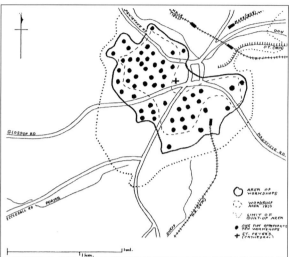

Figure 37a Sheffield 1820. The area of the workshops and extent of the built-up area

Figure 37b Sheffield's expansion between 1820 and 1850. The area of the workshops and the extent of the built-up area

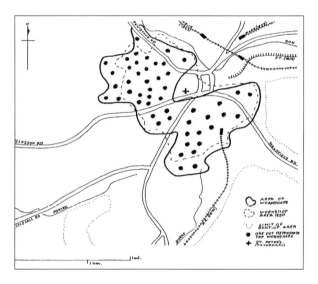

cause instigated by the local mill owners who were mindful of the collapse in 1852 of the Bilberry Dam at Holmfirth'[59].

The details provided include names and addresses of those affected, their occupation and places of work, as well as 'loss of time.' Although those affected mainly worked in the larger factories and tenement works, a picture of how far some of the workforce travelled can be established. The majority of workers who were affected by the flood travelled between a quarter and three quarters of a mile to work in 1864, with nearly a quarter of the workmen travelling between one and two miles, mainly from the newly developing residential areas in Crookes, Walkley, Broomhall and Sharrow as well as the expanding Park area to the east.

Figure 37c Sheffield expansion between 1850 and 1890. The area of the workshops and the extent of the built-up area. Note that the area of workshops has expanded little beyond the limit of the 1850 built up area

With the exception of grinders therefore, who still travelled to sources of waterpower, the majority of people in the nineteenth century still lived near to their place of work, sometimes within a few metres.

The 'flood claims' of 1864 (see page 41) provide a unique picture of how far people in the tableware and cutlery trades were willing to travel to work, as well as recording the devastation in the Loxley and Don Valleys after the breaking of the Dale Dyke Dam:

In the twentieth century the characteristics of the districts examined here were changed. The bombing of the Arundel area during the Second World War, the slum clearances of the 1950s in the Hollis Croft district and the decline of the other areas considered here as industrial centres mean that very few of the small-scale workshops that once formed the backbone of the tableware and cutlery industry survive today.

'The directors were aware that they could not escape paying compensation because the enabling act of 1853 had contained a protective

The few remaining are at risk of disappearing completely and it is vital they are investigated before this happens.

Workshops in the villages

The hearth tax returns for Lady Day 1672 show that only 38% of metalworking craftsmen resided in the township of Sheffield[60], suggesting that rural areas played an important role in the industry at this time. By 1750 many of the villages surrounding Sheffield had established themselves as specialists in various branches of the tableware and cutlery trades. The knowledge that local variations existed, even though the location of specific workshops are not known, helps to create a better understanding of the regional economy as a whole. Norton for example, lying to the south east of Sheffield 'had a virtual monopoly on scythes and sickles from at least the sixteenth century onwards'[61]. Eckington specialised in the sickle trade and by the end of the seventeenth century the industry in this area was largely a family trade carried on by the Staniforths, Booths and Huttons[62]. To the north of Sheffield, Shiregreen produced table forks, Ecclesfield made files and forks and Wadsley common penknives.

By the nineteenth century craftsmen began work as specialists in these areas rather than in connection with any agricultural pursuit. Examples are the workshops at Nook Lane[63] or James Vickers's razor scale pressers workshop, both at Stannington; files cutters' workshops at 1 Stepping Lane, or 9 Woodside Lane, in Grenoside, and Cross Hill, Ecclesfield. In the majority of cases these craftsmen were outworkers for larger firms who found it convenient to employ people to supply goods at times of peak demand and for small runs of specialised goods. However, the output of these rural areas was considered inferior to that produced in the town[64].

Throughout the century up to 33 villages are listed in the trade directories as having connections with the cutlery trades (Table 2). However, just the name of the craftsman is usually given and when there is an address it is not certain if this is relates to his home address or place of business. Villages to the north of Sheffield specialised in fork and file manufacture while those to the south made sickles and scythes. Nearly all the villages lay near river valleys, and could take advantage of waterpower to grind their products as well as sources of charcoal and sandstone.

From the information in the trade directories it is possible to see that in some villages the majority of the workers associated with the cutlery trades worked in the 'wheels' in the valleys, as at Ecclesfield where the majority of the fork makers worked at Oliver's Wheel. A large number would also have been outworkers, although it is difficult to trace the firms that they worked for.

Documents relating to specific firms usually only give details of names and the amount paid, rather than the quantity of the product produced and the place where it was made. For the early twentieth century, oral evidence is therefore the key to identifying the location of outworkers. Mr. Ellison at Grenoside remembers his father, a file cutter, and Mr Day recollects a neighbour, who was a small cutler at Sandygate, taking finished goods to town on a Saturday and collecting the 'blanks'[65] for the following week's work. The owner at Crown Works in Ecclesfield, a file manufactory, remembers women of the village cutting files for larger Sheffield firms in rooms in their own homes known as 'bottom shops'[66]. Dennis Smith interviewed Collin Goodison in the 1970s, and at Stannington references were made to a workshop in Nook Lane where the three Wragg Brothers worked for Wostenholme's, while two others worked for a different firm. Those who worked at the larger Alpha Works, employing 24 people in 1914, were making knives for the Spanish and Irish markets of Harrison Brothers and Howson, Thomas Turner, and Humphries.

Why did outworking continue for so long? Large manufacturers such as those mentioned above found it convenient, as they did not have to find workshop accommodation, nor did they have to provide heating or light. This was in common with many other sweated trades of the period, such as the textile and boot and shoe industries[67]. Those who remained outworkers did so largely through choice and in some cases the whole family was employed. Mr Ellison's father for example employed his sisters as file cutters and packers. At Crown Works, the present owner's brothers were employed ashardeners and forgers as well as file cutters, while his sisters were employed in the warehouse. Where work in the trades was carried out to supplement the family's income, it provided a welcome boost in the winter months

Table 2 The villages listed in the White's 1841 General Directory of Sheffield and the number of craftsmen in each trade

Village	Cutlery	File makers	Fork makers	Scythe and Sickle makers	Scissor makers	Tool makers	Scale pressers
Attercliffe	2	1			1	1	4
Brightholmelee	4	7					
Brightside Bierlow	4		22				
Catcliffe							1
Coal Aston						1	
Darnall	7				1		
Dore				4			
Dronfield	2			11		5	
Ecclesall Bierlow	10	1				4	
Ecclesfield	2	19	11				
Eckington	1			1		1	
Grenoside	1	3	12				
Hackenthorpe				2			
Heeley	1						1
Holmesfield				2			
Kimberworth			16				
Midhope and Bolsterstone	1						
Mosbrough	2			5			
Nether Hallam	15	1					
Norton	2			14		3	
Owlerton	4						
Shiregreen	1	1	32				
Stannington	26	1	1			2	8
Totley		1		1			
Treeton	1						
Troway				19			
Ughill and Dungworth	7						
Unstone		1					
Upper Hallam	5	3	1		3		
Wadsley	29	2					1
Wincobank			7				
Woodhouse	1						
Worrall		2					1

when no work could be done around the farm. It also provided employment to family members who were not needed to, or could not, work on the land. So long as there was a labour supply and prices remained competitive 'manufacturers had little incentive to turn to alternative means of production and every encouragement to go on relying on a 'system' that worked so obviously to their advantage'[68]

Now, little evidence remains in the villages of the industries that were once carried on there. In Grenoside just four workshops have been identified as having been associated with the industry, in addition to two sites associated with the production of crucible steel. In Ecclesfield only three workshops were identified, with a fourth site that has possible associations with the file cutting trade. In Stannington three sites have been surveyed out of a total of five workshops identified, and workshops have also been identified in Dungworth and Storrs and at Syke Bottom[69]. One fork maker's workshop survives at Shire Green and to the south scythe and sickle works survive at Norton, Birley Hay and Ford.

Allied industries

From the evidence above the landscape of the tableware and cutlery industry can be portrayed as one cluttered with mainly small workshops in the urban areas with some dispersal of processes, such as grinding and by the end of the nineteenth century forging, along the river valleys. However the industry needed materials such as steel for blades and horn for handles. As the cutlery industry grew it attracted and promoted the growth these trades within the region.

Steel
From 1624 all those trades governed by the Cutlers' Company had to have a steel edge and thus the production of steel was of vital importance to the cutlery industry. Some of the earliest known steel makers in the area were the Fells and their partners, who had works at 'Chapeltown, Wadsley, Attercliffe, Roche Abbey and Staveley'[70]. Other steel making facilities can also be identified at Richmond, Ballifield, Darnall, Rotherham and in some of the villages to the south east of Sheffield.

In 1742 Benjamin Huntsman developed the crucible method of steel production for a more uniform product. Samuel Walker was one of the first to make crucible steel commercially in the Sheffield region. Originally from Grenoside, he

moved to Masbrough (Rotherham) in 1746. The Tingle family took over Walkers' Grenoside buildings. The remains of the ash pits in a cellar beneath a crucible furnace, possibly belonging to the Tingles, are still visible under a garage in Back Lane.

The cutlery and steel industries continued to grow rapidly in the second half of the century. Even the Cutlers' Company entered the steel making business between 1759 and 1772, setting up a furnace in Scotland Street using Swedish iron. However it was not until the last quarter of the century that other steel manufacturers are identified in the trade directories and even then the scale of their business cannot be determined. Foreign visitors to the town such as Robsahm and Jars, in 1761 and 1766 respectively, mention the use of relatively small single-chest cementation furnaces. In general these eighteenth-century steel manufacturers located themselves in areas where the cutlery industry had developed, for example in Hollis Croft, Millsands and Norfolk Street.

The steel industry continued to expand throughout the nineteenth century, adding a completely new 'industrial sector on the east'[72] side of the town. Some steel works however remained within the existing industrial areas, as Figures 31 and 32 show. Those firms who wanted to expand looked for sites on the large areas of flat land with good transport facilities in the lower Don Valley.

In 1810 Barraclough records nine steel producing firms and 21 furnaces in operation in the Sheffield region. The largest producers were the Walkers at Masbrough, a possible reflection of the works' close connection to the canal[73]. There were 56 cementation furnaces in Sheffield in 1835; by 1863 this had increased to 205 furnaces, producing 78,270 tons of blister steel.

The first large scale integrated steel and cutlery works, Sheaf Works, was built by William Greaves adjacent to the canal basin just four years after the basin was opened. Gatty reported that when the works became fully operational in 1826 'it gave a new impulse to the system of our local manufacture'[74].

The largest producers of steel by 1851 were Naylor Vickers and Co at Millsands, Turton and Matthews at Sheaf Works, William Jessop's, Sanderson's and Doncaster's. However the cementation method of producing steel was becoming outdated. The process took too long (more than 8 days) and two of the largest crucible melting shops built after 1850 at River Don Works and Toledo Works no longer had cementation furnaces attached. It had been discovered that if Swedish Bar iron was melted together with a suitable proportion of cast iron, directly in the crucible, steel of appropriate carbon content would result. Thus the cementation process was omitted in all but the very finest steel.

Increased use of crucible steel meant that by 1842 each furnace was usually constructed with rectangular furnace holes which held two crucibles each of approximately 28–36lbs. In 1858 Siemens' development of the gas-fired furnace meant that furnaces could hold up to 30 crucibles in each hole as there was no problem over the maintenance of heat. The first furnace of this type in Sheffield is believed to have been used by Marriott and Atkinson and after 1868 it was used by the River Don works of Naylor, Vickers and Company[75]. Sandersons installed one in 1872 and William Jessop in 1897. Like all other innovations, Sheffield was slow to recognise the advantages of such a system and so it was not widely adopted as it was in America.

Steel production nearing the scale at which it was carried out in the twentieth century was made possible by the development of the Bessemer converter from 1856 and Siemens' Open Hearth method by the end of the century. However the steel produced by these processes was not used to any great extent in the tableware and cutlery trades but more as a replacement for wrought iron in railway rails, boilers, springs, railway tyres, gun forgings and shells[76].

Tweedale suggests that some steel manufacturers specialised in tableware and cutlery steel, in particular William Jessop and Sons, S and C Wardlow and Kayser, Ellison and Co. In the later nineteenth century George Wostenholm, one of the largest knife producers in the city, often brought steel from Thomas Firth. Some tableware and cutlery firms produced their own steel, such as Thomas Turner at Suffolk Works, and Joseph Rodgers eventually made its own crucible steel[77] at Norfolk works.

Analysis of the ratebooks for the nineteenth century shows that 134 other firms also produced their own steel on a small scale. Of these 38% were located in the Riverside area, 27% in the Hollis Croft area, 17% in the Western area, 13% in the Arundel area and 3% in the Central and Park areas. The majority of firms only had one cementation furnace.

The largest firms, not surprisingly, were located in the Riverside area and included George Barnsley and Son, W and S Butcher, Wheatman and Smith, S Osborn and Son, J Bedford and Son and William Brookes and Son. The smaller firms, found in all six areas, rarely described themselves as steel producers in the trade directories. The 46 firms that did were either refiners only or converters and refiners emphasising that by the nineteenth century crucible steel was used far more within the tableware and cutlery trades than blister steel. Today little evidence remains for these small-scale furnaces, as like the workshops which they serviced they have been demolished.

The horn industry

The provision of horn and bone developed in response to the demand for handles and scales. Although the horn industry is known to have existed at least since the seventeenth century it was not until the beginning of the nineteenth century that the trade experienced a rapid growth. The trade was centred in the heart of Sheffield, especially in areas such as the High Street, Change Alley, Fargate, Queen Street, Barker's Pool and Paradise Square[78]. By 1850 a total of 145 firms relating to the horn trade existed, employing 'well over 1000 hands'[79]. During the second half of the nineteenth century there was a move away from the central area of the town to the western districts possibly taking over some of the buildings that are known to have been vacated by the tableware and cutlery trades. This movement was probably due to the increasing rates that were applied to the commercial central area of town. Between 1850 and 1890 the rates in the central area rose by 1324% compared with 354% in the western area (Figures 31 and 32).

Printing and packing

Firms' catalogues needed to be regularly updated and printed, and the products needed labelling after they had been packaged in papers specially produced by other Sheffield firms. Schmoller recorded 29 paper mills that existed in the Sheffield area between the seventeenth and twentieth centuries, such as Olive Wheel on the Loxley, rebuilt as a paper mill by John and Abraham Webster in 1832[80].

Paper mills were located in the river valleys adjacent to the cutlery grinding wheels. Wherever possible they were located at the tops of the valleys, where the water was cleaner. During the nineteenth century, some of the grinding wheels on the Rivelin and Loxley were converted to paper mills, perhaps reflecting the slow movement away from water to steam power by the grinding trades during this period. Sheffield firms specialised in the production of rope paper which was acid free and therefore suitable for the packaging of iron and steel blades. By 1884 the numbers in the printing trades had risen to 216, including 72 letterpress printers, 35 lithographers and 109 engravers. One of largest catalogue printing firms in Sheffield in the nineteenth century was Pawson and Brailsford.

Goods being sent over long distances were packed in wooden boxes. The 1797 trade directory lists eight case makers situated in the Hollis Croft area, in Bailey Fields, Peacroft, Radford Street, Townhead Street, Westbar and West Street. By 1841 there were 25 listed under the heading of cabinet, razor scale and strop manufacturers, as well as 14 coopers. These firms continued to be located around Hollis Croft but had some were situated on the western side of town around Rockingham Street, and in the Arundel Street area so that they could be near to the cutlery workshops that they served. In 1884 there were 76 firms in these areas.

Quarrying for grindstones
Towards the end of the seventeenth century, the Cutlers' Company, recognising the growth that had taken place within the industry, began to rent grindstone quarries, which they sublet to tenants at Crookesmoor, Swinehead Hill and Brincliffe Edge[81]. These quarries were to remain an important source for grindstones until the nineteenth century, not just for the Cutlers' Company. In addition, stones came from Wickersley, Beeley Moor and Ashurst, and, further afield, from 'Thrybergh Barnsley, Hathersage, Grenoside and Bakewell'[82] Wickersley, near Rotherham, was said to produce 5000 grindstones per annum at the beginning of the nineteenth century[83].

From the evidence above, the tableware and cutlery industry significantly stimulated the growth of other trades in the area. Today however, the only survivors alongside the industry are the steel manufacturers, and those firms involved in printing and packing. The

paper makers have all disappeared, with the exception of British Tissues at Oughtibridge who no longer have any connection with the tableware and cutlery trades. The horn trade has also disappeared after the invention of synthetic handles and as a result of changing public and political attitudes.

Reference to these industries here is essential if the location of the workshops of the tableware and cutlery industry is to be understood in the context in which they were built. While the steel industry needed more specialised buildings, it is likely that those who provided the materials for handles and those in the printing and packing trades may have taken over buildings that had once been occupied by the cutlery industry.

Conclusion

The landscape of the tableware and cutlery industry became more complex as the trade expanded, based on the inter-relationship of the specialisms within the industry and the allied trades such as steel, horn and bone, the packing industry and the quarrying of grindstones.

In the eighteenth century the reliance on waterpower for grinding dictated that the majority of this work was carried out in the river-valleys upstream of the urban centre. In the nineteenth century steam power freed the grinders from this constraint although many continued to use waterpower until the twentieth century. Some large-scale works did develop with the advent of steam power, especially tenement works whose workspace was rented out mainly to individuals. The large integrated multi-storeyed works that became characteristic of the textile industry during the period were a rare sight in Sheffield even at the end of the nineteenth century[84]. However, it is these sites that survive today and they give a distorted view of the organization of the industry.

The economic development of the town influenced the location of the industry based on the need for expansion. The speculative nature of many building projects meant that dwellings and workshops were often built in close proximity. The industry often expanded into areas of new growth, firstly into the Hollis Croft area, and later the Arundel, Western, Riverside and Park areas. Economic data provides evidence for a thriving industry that expanded rapidly throughout the period. However the rate books suggest that there were a large number of workshops used by the tableware and cutlery industry that were either not used again or only periodically. This cannot yet be explained fully, although the workshops appear to have been taken over by other trades once they had been abandoned by the cutlery industry. This stresses the integration Sheffield's industries, many of which grew as a result of the successful cutlery trade.

Topography appears to have little influence on the location of the industry. The exceptions to this are waterpowered sites and the large-scale works that were mainly limited to the Riverside area where land was available for expansion.

The industrial landscape of Sheffield was therefore formed mainly by the organisational needs of the industry, rather than topographical features and geological resources.

Notes

[1] Lloyd, G I H 1968 reprint of 1913 edition *The Cutlery Trades* Cass Library of Industrial Classics London p 89 (hereafter Lloyd G I H 1968).

[2] Hunter, J revised by Gatty, A 1869 Hallamshire, *The History and Topography of the Parish of Sheffield* Pawson and Brailsford Sheffield p 6; Abercrombie, p 1924 *Sheffield a civic survey and suggestions towards a Development Plan* Liverpool University Press p 7; Linton, M 1956 *Sheffield and it's Region* p 230; Hey, D 1991 *The Fiery Blades of Hallamshire* Leicester University Press p 8, Tweedale, G 1996 *The Sheffield Knife Book* p 16.

[3] Quoted in 'A Study of Sheffield' read Feb 11th 1939 to the Manchester Geographical Society.

[4] Quoted in Tweedale, G 1993 *Stan Shaw, Master Cutler: The Story of a Sheffield Craftsman* Cromwell Press Wiltshire p 7.

[5] For difficulties in estimating the population of Sheffield in the eighteenth century see Flavell, N 1996 *The Economic Development of Sheffield and the Growth of the Town c1740–1820* Unpublished PhD Thesis University of Sheffield.

[6] The Fairbank Collection consists of a unique collection of surveyors papers covering the period 1739–1833. Work carried out by J Unwin, funded by The Leverhulme Trust, revealed that no other collection survives elsewhere in the country. The collection consists of field and building books, account books and correspondence papers relating to building property and work on turnpike roads, railways, canals, enclosures and advice on investments in the Sheffield area. A research group at the University of Sheffield is producing a detailed catalogue of the collection's contents.

[7] Nunn, P 1985 *The management of some S. Yorkshire Landed Estates in the 18th and 19th centuries, linked with the central economic development of the area (1700-1850)* PhD University of Sheffield p 334.

[8] Chalklin, C W 1974 *The Provincial Towns of Georgian England: A Study of the Building Process 1740-1820* Arnold London p 72.

[9] Nunn, P 1985 op cit. p 336.

[10] Figures 31 and 32 show the area's development.

[11] Fairbank Collection Cp26/90 Sheffield Archives.

[12] Name of a workshop where grinding takes place.

[13] Lloyd, G I H 1968 op cit. p 174.

[14] ibid pp 177–8.

[15] Gad, G 1994 Location patterns of Manufacture in Toronto in the early 1880s *Urban History Review XXII* no 2 p 114.

[16] All census data for 19th century from Lloyd, G.I.H. 1968 op cit. p 152.

[17] Taylor, S.A. 1993 The Cutlery Trades in *A History of Sheffield 1843-1993:Society* Sheffield Academic Press p 194.

[18] Lloyd, G I H 1968 op cit. p 445–6 Appendix V

[19] Trinder, B. 1982 *The Making of the Industrial Landscape* Dent p 7.

[20] Nunn, P. 1985 op cit. p 339.

[21] The financing of construction of workshops will be considered further.

[22] Lloyd, G I H 1968 op cit. p 193 and Unwin M J 1988 *The Pen and Pocket Knife Industry, an investigation into the historical tradition of working practices and trade organisation.* MA thesis University of Sheffield (CECTAL).

[23] Classed as the Western Area for this analysis.

[24] Pollard, S 1959 *A History of Labour in Sheffield.* Liverpool University Press p 5.

[25] Pollard, S. 1959 op cit. p 127.

[26] Jones, G.P. and Townsend, H. 1953 The Rise and Present Prospects of the cutlery trades *International Cutler Vol. 3 no 1* p 18.

[27] Lloyd-Jones, R and Lewis, M J 1983 Industrial Structure and firm growth: the Sheffield iron and Steel Industry 1880-1901 *Business History 25* p. 60–63 Using the rateable value (RV) of property, Jones and Lewis's Classification was: Small = RV of £1-150, Medium £151-500, Large = £501-1500 and Giant = £1501+. Using the Rates paid, Small = £1-10, Medium = £11-30, Large = £31-80 and Giant £81+.

[28] All information in this section comes from the work carried out by the author on the rate books for Sheffield 1820–1891, in conjunction with the trade directories.

[29] Haywood, J and Lee, W *Report on the Sanitary Conditions of the Borough of Sheffield in 1848* Local History Pamphlets Sheffield Local Studies Library.

[30] Cutlery here is used in the specific sense rather than to mean the cutlery and allied trades.

[31] That is the number of entries in the Hollis Croft areas that had accumulated by 1891.

[32] 92 workshops in 1890–91 had no address and therefore cannot be confirmed as being different from previous entries.

[33] Series of Articles in the *Local History Magazine* 1994 April (vol.44): Shaw, G *The evolution and availability of directories* p 14–17; July (vol.45): Shaw, G and Coles, T *Methods of compilation and the work of large-scale publishers* p 10-14; Sept. (Vol.46): *Directories as Sources in Local History* p 12-17.

[34] Powell, C.G. 1980 *An Economic History of the British Building Industry 1850–1979* Architectural Press London p 6-7. In later chapters the poor quality of the buildings used by the cutlery industry in this area will be discussed.

[35] Hollis Croft Area.

[36] Arundel Street Area.

[37] Western District.

[38] Central Area.

[39] Riverside.

[40] In the traditional sense i.e. for the buying of provisions.

[41] Beauchamp V A 1996 *The workshops of the Cutlery*

Industry in Hallamshire 1750–1900 Unpublished PhD Thesis 9067 University of Sheffield, Chapter 2 looks in detail at the sources of finance available to speculators, the percentage of owner occupation in each of the six areas discussed here in relationship to the cost of living, building costs and income of the cutlers.

[42] The reliability of the data can however be called into question as the owner is not always recorded.

[43] Crossley, D *et al* 1989 *Waterpower on the Sheffield Rivers* STHS and University of Sheffield. Printed by Charlesworth and Co Huddersfield p 74.

[44] CP2 (132) Fairbank Collection.

[45] Based on S Pollard's 1959 op cit. p 60 average of c 30s a week for a grinder, for a cutler the average was c 20s.

[46] Doris Walsh quoted in Jenkins, C and McClarence, S *On a Knife Edge* SCL Publishing Sheffield p 31.

[47] Beauchamp V A 1996 *The workshops of the Cutlery Industry in Hallamshire 1750–1900* Unpublished PhD Thesis 9067 University of Sheffield Chapter 2 on the Financing of the cutlery workshops.

[48] Beauchamp V A 1996 *The workshops of the Cutlery Industry in Hallamshire 1750–1900* Unpublished PhD Thesis 9067 University of Sheffield p 90–97.

[49] 1% of total, 10% of building occupations.

[50] Craftsmen include, button makers, cabinet case makers, carvers and gilders, comb makers, coopers, cordwainers, dressmakers, engineers, French polishers, hosiers, pianoforte tuners, straw hat manufacturers, tailors, watch makers, wood engravers, painters, founders, and wheelwrights.

[51] Includes accountants, appraisers, estate agents, bankers, brokers, auctioneers, clerks, land owners, dentists, doctors, gentlemen, incumbents, justices of the peace, surgeons and teachers.

[52] Includes, beerhouse keepers, carriers, chemists, omnibus operators, drapers, earthenware dealers, glass dealers, ironmongers, grinderly and leather dealers, milliners, toy dealers and shop keepers.

[53] Includes grocers, fish dealers, wine and spirit merchants, grocers, butchers, and restaurant owners.

[54] not related to cutlery.

[55] Chalklin, C.W. 1974 *The Provincial Towns of Georgian England: A Study of building process 1740–1820* Arnold London p 282.

[56] Rate books were sampled at 10 yearly periods throughout the nineteenth century by assessing the first rate for each year from 1820–1891. They provided information on the location of workshops, the owner and the occupier. All entries were cross-referenced to corresponding trade directories for the period. The figures given in this section relate to the total number of firms found throughout the century.

[57] 12 moved from Hollis Croft to the Western Area, 9 moved from Western to Hollis.

[58] Grinders who worked at the water-powered sites had always travelled long distances to work.

[59] Cass, J 1989 The Flood Claims a Post Script to the Sheffield Flood of March 11th and 12th 18C4. *Transactions of the Hunter Archaeological Journal vol. 15*

[60] Hey, D 1972 op cit. p 11.

[61] ibid. p 10.

[62] Hey, D 1994 Lecture given at the Cutlers' Hall on Scythesmiths and Sicklesmiths: the origin of local crafts.

[63] See Appendix for a list of grid references

[64] Pollard, S 1959 op cit. p 61.

[65] Rough unworked stamped or forged metal in the shape of any article. (Dyson, R 1979 reprint of 1936 ed. *A Glossary of Old Sheffield trade words and dialect.* University Printing Unit Sheffield p 11).

[66] Informal interview carried out in February 1995. The 'bottom shop' was so called because it was on the ground floor and was probably the kitchen. He noted that it was the men that collected the work for their wives every Saturday.

[67] Bythell, D. 1987 *The Sweated Trades* Batsford Academic, London p 181.

[68] ibid. P 177.

[69] See list of sites.

[70] Barraclough, K C 1984 *Steel making before Bessemer: Volume 1 Blister Steel the Birth of an Industry* The Metals Society London p 70.

[71] Barraclough K C 1984 op cit. p 91.

[72] Linton, M. 1956 op cit. p 234.

[73] Barraclough, K C 1984 op cit. p103–4.

[74] Tweedale, G. 1996 op cit. p 29.

[75] Barraclough, K C 1990 *Steel making 1850–1900* The Institute of Metals p 24.

[76] Simons, E. and Gregory, E. 1940 *Steel making simply explained* Pitman and Sons ltd London p 74 and p 108.

[77] Tweedale, G. 1996 op cit. p 21.

[78] Taylor, W. 1927 *The Sheffield Horn Trade* J W Northend Ltd Sheffield p 6.

[79] ibid. p 8.

[80] Crossley, D *et al* 1985 op cit. p 34.

[81] Hatfield, J and J 1974 *The Oldest Sheffield Plater* Advertiser Press Huddersfield p 62.

[82] Hunter, J and Gatty, A 1869 op cit. p 171.

[83] Hey, D. 1980 *Packmen, Carriers and Packhorse Roads* Leicester University Press p 142.

[84] Sheffield Independent 15/4/1854.

Chapter 8

Architects, buildings and building materials

Introduction

In endeavouring to understand the structures housing the tableware and cutlery industry, a review of the designers and construction materials for the actual buildings used by the tableware and cutlery industry is essential. Buildings had to incorporate specific characteristics relating to the needs of the trades. Studies of eighteenth and nineteenth century English architecture have largely ignored industrial buildings, especially the small and more mundane workshops of the period.

The architect

Architecture as a profession did not emerge until the middle of the nineteenth century. In the later part of the eighteenth and early nineteenth centuries the majority of the buildings erected for the tableware and cutlery industry would have been of vernacular design, the builders following traditional patterns. Engineers were occasionally used to design larger buildings, as were surveyors such as the Fairbank family[1], who also costed the work to be carried out.

In assessing the emergence of architects and the architectural profession in this instance, it is necessary to examine their association with the workshops of the industry and consider how much industrial building design they did. Did they apply the styles of the day to their buildings? Did speculative building hinder or aid the architect in his work?

In 1834 the Institute of British Architects was founded, and in 1837 became the Royal Institute of British Architects (RIBA) when it received its royal charter[2]. By the middle of the nineteenth century the architect was recognised as the designer and supervisor of a building project, who relied on the quantity surveyor to supply him with figures so that the builder could tender for work. The Sheffield Society of Architects and Surveyors was established in 1887. The membership list records three fellows and two associate members of RIBA, including J B Mitchell Withers, Charles Hadfield, J D Webster, C J Innocent and A F Watson. Two of these were connected with the design of industrial premises, but only C J Innocent can be identified as designing buildings specifically related to the cutlery trades. For example in 1865 he designed a mark maker's shop for George Maltby to be built on Albert Road, Carbrook[3]. Fellows of the Institute of Surveyors who joined the Sheffield Society included T J Flockton and F Fowler[4]. These men are not recorded as having designed any workshops for the cutlery trades.

In the majority of cases, architects did not receive any formal training. In the eighteenth century, William Fairbank I and II had both been schoolteachers with a mathematical training. By the middle of the nineteenth century however the trade directories show that this was not the case, architects associated with designing workshops for the cutlery industry usually appearing for the first time in the trade directories as architects. There is no evidence that A Appleby, E Falding, George Foster or J Lister[5] were ever master craftsmen, but John Clark and James Hall are known to have had some formal training, in Clark's case, as a surveyor.

In 1868 John Clark is recorded as being an assistant surveyor at 109 Nottingham Street. During this time he designed nine properties connected with the cutlery trades, including seven workshops[6], a warehouse[7] and the works[8] of Henry Holdsworth, Britannia metal manufacturer, in Bramall Lane. In 1871 he is recorded for the first time as an architect in the trade directory. James Hall was recorded as an assistant to an architect at Don Terrace, Penistone Road before he established himself on his own account at 18 Bank Street in 1862. No record survives of any work which he carried out before that date[9]. These two architects were the most successful of those identified during the period. In six sample years[10] they secured in total 585 jobs between them[11].

Only William Flockton (1804–1864) emerged from a building background. The son of Thomas Flockton, carpenter, joiner and builder, William appears in the 1833, 1837 and 1841 directories as an architect, joiner and builder. The largest industrial premise he designed was Castle Grinding Mill on Blonk Street.

The number of architects in Sheffield rose steadily throughout the nineteenth century (Table 3) and by 1864, when the building registers begin, the profession was well established. The rise in the number of architects can be explained by the establishment of building regulations in the second half of the nineteenth century.

Table 3 Number of architects recorded in the trade directories throughout the nineteenth century

Year of trade directory	Number of architects
1822	4
1833	13
1841	14
1852	14
1862	23
1868	18
1879	57
1888	42
1893	47

'Always tiresome to conform to, and the pride of the architect to evade, bye-laws also required literacy to understand and interpret...[Architects] were therefore well placed to tussle with the increasing complexity of Victorian building law, on behalf both of clients who naturally lacked the requisite knowledge, and of builders, who often lacked literacy.'[12]

The 1853 Smoke Bye-Laws were the earliest in Sheffield associated with industrial building design. These stated that 'every fire-place or furnace employed or to be employed, within the Borough of Sheffield, in the working of an engine or engines by steam, shall be constructed so as to consume or burn all the smoke arising from such fire-place or furnace'.[13]

In 1858 the Local Government Act Office issued guidelines to the Public Health Act of 1848. These allowed municipal corporations to issue bye-laws relating to the width and construction of streets, the structure and stability of buildings, the prevention of fire and the provision for ventilation, drainage and conveniences. The 1864 bye-laws raised the minimum room height from 8ft to 8ft 6in but the thickness of the timbers on the inside face of flues was reduced from 9 to 4½ inches. 'Party walls were not required to rise through the roof as this was not in accordance with local building practices!'[14] The majority of these bye-laws were aimed at domestic buildings and in particular at banning the erection of back to back houses. Few of the regulations were applied to industrial premises except those relating to sanitary conditions.

The introduction of the 1875 Public Health Act is reflected in the building registers by the increase in the number of plans rejected at the first application for planning permission. James Hall and John Clark between 1870 and 1871 had nine out of 204 plans rejected at the first submission. Between 1875 and 1876 this had risen to 27 out of 109 plans or a quarter of all their work. The principal change in the regulations concerned the ventilation space around the building. On some plans a note was attached indicating that if a building was 'set back to the new improved line'[15] it would be accepted. The 72 bye-laws introduced into Sheffield in 1889 were based on the provisions made by the 1875 Public Health Act[16]. These, for the first time since 1853, set down specific laws regulating industrial buildings. The warehouse class, which included warehouses, factories, manufactories, breweries and distilleries, stipulated structural measurements for each size of building. For example the external and party walls had to be constructed so that:

'where the wall does not exceed 25ft in height it shall be 13.5ins thick at its base. If the wall does not exceed 45ft in length (up to 30ft high) it shall be thirteen and a half inches thick at its base .... if it exceeds 45ft in length (up to 40ft high) it shall be 22 ins thick at its base ...Where the wall exceeds 70ft but does not exceed 80ft in height: if the wall exceeds 45ft in length it shall be increased in thickness from the base up to within 16ft of the top of the wall by 4.5 ins (from 22ins).'[17]

Specific regulation relating to ventilation, windows and drainage still only applied to domestic and public buildings.

The 1878 Factory and Workshop Act[18] did not contain any regulations regarding the structure of buildings. The regulations calling for fencing, sanitary provision and cleanliness were aimed at the owners of the workshops rather than the architect.

It can therefore be concluded that due to the increase in the complexity of building regulation at the end of the nineteenth century, the need for a professional architect increased if planning permission for new buildings was being sought. Of the 995 applications for planning permission relating to workshops, between 1864 and 1891, a quarter were submitted by professional architects and there may be other cases where an architect was used but not recorded.

The role of architects in the design of industrial buildings

A key question is whether architects played a major role in the design of industrial buildings or did the vernacular maintained its dominance throughout the nineteenth century. Of the architectural firms identified in the building registers connected with workshops of the tableware and cutlery industry, few have left any records relating to their businesses. The plans and designs deposited in the Sheffield Archives

relate to churches, schools and public buildings, rather than industrial buildings connected with the Sheffield trades, so that none compare with the Fairbank collection of the eighteenth and early nineteenth century. Alfred Appleby and Son is the only firm which has left any record of the work they carried out, between 1879 and 1900[19]. This included the Norfolk Lane warehouse for Walker and Hall in 1879, that of William Fearnclough, blade manufacturer in Garden Street in 1884 and alterations to the works of Needham, Veall and Tyzack in Milton Street in 1891[20].

Architectural styles

Works in Sheffield that can clearly be identified as having been designed with architectural style in mind were usually medium or large scale structures such as Sheaf Works, erected in 1823; Globe Works (1825); Castle Grinding Mills (1830s); Eye Witness Works, Milton Street (started c 1852); Victoria Works in Gell Street (1868); and Elliott's in Sylvester Street, the frontage for which was erected in 1875.

Sheaf Works, erected for William Greaves in 1823, may have been designed by an engineer 'ingrained with the Georgian vernacular'[21] rather than by an architect *per se*. It was the first integrated factory in Sheffield, but its main block, a pedimented ashlar building, resembles a small country house[22] (Fig 38).

Figure 38 Sheaf Works, the first integrated factory in Sheffield where steel and cutlery were made on a large scale (Local Studies Library G1/10)

The architectural style is that of the 'classical revival' which was popular throughout the Georgian period as it conveyed a 'hierarchy of decorum: it meant that the degree of stateliness and the amount of decoration should reflect the status of the client ... It came to stand for ideas of order and harmony in general, which were thought to be derived from nature, God and the Universe.'[23]

Globe Works also reflected the popularity of classical detailing for larger works[24]. Designed by Messrs G A Wall[25] for Ibbotson Brothers as an integrated house and works and erected between 1825 and 1830, the appearance once again resembles that of a stately home (Fig 39a). The frontage is ashlar, the first floor having Ionic pilasters in pairs on either side of the windows. At the back, however, a vernacular style was retained for the workshop buildings (Fig 39b).

Buildings erected in the last quarter of the nineteenth century also retained classical proportions. The offices and warehouses designed for Elliot's at Sylvester Works for example, had Georgian characteristics although some attempt was made at incorporating the 'constructional polychromy' style of William Butterfield[28]. This is the introduction of an ashlar course running at the top of each storey (Fig 40).

The Italianate style, popular with buildings connected with the textile trades, was not used in cutlery workshops and factories. Unlike the textile mills further north, the cutlery industry had no impressively high chimneys to decorate such as Manningham Mills at Bradford with its campanile design. In Sheffield, chimneys, such as those at Butcher's Wheel and Cornish Place, retained a functional simplicity which went with the rest of the building (Fig 41a and b).

Figure 39a Globe Works, Penistone Road. Note the first floor Ionic pilasters either side of the windows (1995)

Figure 39b Globe Works. The workshops behind the main frontage retain some of the vernacular tradition (1995)

The appreciation of the classical style continued throughout the nineteenth century. 'Classical proportioning was very widely used because of its monumental and imposing appearance.'[26] It did not however retain the stateliness of the first quarter of the century and pillars and decoration disappeared. This scaled-down version was termed the 'neo-classical' and because it was much cheaper to build, was applied to more moderate industrial buildings of the period. Frequently it resembled the style used for the town houses of the Georgian period. In some cases these were converted in the nineteenth century to workshops, providing a ready styled frontage for the firm[27].

Industrial premises were rarely constructed in the Victorian Gothic style, and the workshops of the cutlery industry are no exception. This could be seen as somewhat surprising as one of the great advocates of the 'moral' style was John Ruskin, an admirer of the Sheffield craft tradition. However the working conditions of the cutlery trades were far from 'moral' or 'divine'[29], with the average life span of a grinder in 1870 being 44 years and a hafter 49 years[30]. The only example of the use of the gothic style was for Castle Grinding Mills, designed by William Flockton[31] and built in the 1830s, was intended as a tenement factory, to be rented out for the grinding and polishing of cutlery. Edgar Jones argues however that this structure was not

Figure 40 Elliot's Sylvester Works, Arundel Street. One of the few examples of 'constructional polychromy' used on an industrial building in Sheffield. Note the ashlar course at the top of each storey and the use of layers of bricks to create different textures

Figure 41a Chimney at Butcher's Wheel, Arundel Street. Like that at Cornish Place it has retained its functional simplicity

Figure 41b Chimney at Cornish Place

really Gothic but of a Palladian origin with turrets added to give it a medieval gloss[32]. It was not the Gothic form advocated by Pugin, who believed that if ornament was used it should be appropriate to the form and meaning of the building.

'There should be no features about a building which are not necessary for convenience, construction or propriety; second, that all ornament should consist of enrichment of the essential construction of the building'[33].

That non-vernacular styling does not seem to have been applied to the majority of the workshops connected with the tableware and cutlery industry can be explained by the organization of the trade and the speculative nature of the building undertaken. It has been shown that architects were only employed to design integrated works such as Globe Works, Sheaf Works or Eye Witness Works. In the nineteenth century, frontages were used as publicity, fine frontages portraying the success of the firm to the customer. Advertisements appearing in the trade directories often include an image of the works, or as the owner wished the premises to look (Fig 42).

Figure 42 Globe Works. (Pawson and Brailsford p 143). Here the Works is seen in a rural setting and the frontage stretched to give it an image of grandeur

Tenement factories and the small courtyard workshops usually had no styling incorporated into their design. 'Little Mesters' (see page 19) required the cheapest workspace available if they were to set up business on their own account[34]. Those who owned the tenement factories were reported in 1897 to be 'persons who never see them, who recognise no obligations and who are represented locally by an agent who remits the rent and an engine

tender.'[35] In these instances the owners and instigators of the building would be looking for maximum profit and did not have an image to portray.

In summary therefore, the lack of large integrated firms and the large degree of speculative building for the tableware, cutlery and related trades, stifled the possibility of architectural design for the majority of buildings. The vernacular characteristics remained, and it is by these that the buildings of the industry can be identified. Vernacular design was the 'builders' domain.

What percentage of a builder's work involved industrial structures?

Data in the field and building books allows an analysis of the number of building jobs done in association with the Fairbank firm. Table 4 shows the results.

The data shows that industrial structures did not make up more than a quarter of the craftsmen's work recorded by Fairbank over an average of 25 years. In a similar way to the architects, the majority of the 'builders' work carried out was connected with domestic and other structures. Typical examples of the latter are Fenton's painting work at N Stead's house, or E Parker junior's head board[38], James Frith's garden wall by A Chapman[39], or J Wheat's joiner work by J Badger at tenements in Paradise Square[40].

Builders in the nineteenth century

An increase in the numbers of building craftsmen during the nineteenth century can be identified in the trade directories (Table 5), reflecting the rapid growth of the town. In 1850 the population of Sheffield was 135,300; by 1891 it had grown to 324,000, an increase of 239%[41]. Correspondingly, between 1864 and 1891, 23,306 new houses were built[42]. However, despite knowing the names of those connected with the building trades the types of jobs which they carried out cannot be fully analysed as no builders' records survive.

The building registers can identify some builders who were involved with the erection of new workshops if they were the owners or depositors of plans. William Kirk, builder, was associated with seven jobs connected with workshops or shops. This is in comparison with 49 applications

Table 4 Number of jobs carried out in each category by the major craftsmen identified in the Fairbank Field and Building Book and the dates which they worked

Craftsman	Years worked	Industrial[36]	Commercial	Domestic	Public	Other[37]	Total
A Chapman	1760–1786	27	4	29	9	134	203
B Ball	1753–1781	4	0	4	3	19	30
E Needham	1753–1777	6	0	3	0	17	26
J Stacey	1771–1798	30	6	19	21	52	128
J Badger	1770–1811	24	4	23	0	39	33
T Jackson	1756–1775	12	0	1	1	19	33
S Jackson	1778–1800	4	1	6	0	5	16
F Fenton	1753–1781	12	3	32	11	68	126
J Rhodes	1761–1800	1	1	8	4	27	41
T Rodgers	1774–1794	5	0	6	2	9	22
H Atkin	1772–1785	4	2	3	0	11	20

Table 5 The number of craftsmen in each trade listed in the directories, and the total listed for the building trades

Year	Builder/joiners/ carpenters	Plumber and glaziers	Masons and bricklayers	Slaters	Total
1833	93	22	66	16	197
1841	122	40	88	22	272
1852	163	42	88	12	305
1862	184	55	134	16	389
1868	199	66	136	20	421
1879	808	169	333	24	1334
1893	628	106	127	45	906

for houses and seven for commercial property. Kirk however was not the owner but the depositor of these plans. He seems to have had an association with Nathaniel Hodgson, owner and builder, in seven of the applications that possibly suggests that Kirk was a designer and Hodgson put up the money for the buildings. It is clear from the trade directories that Kirk was not a craftsman, but a manager of speculative ventures, as he does not appear under the trade lists, but only with the individual names and addresses. In comparison, David Kaye was the owner as well as the depositor of 90% of the plans associated with him, and industrial buildings appear to have formed a significant part of his work. Between 1874 and 1877 the building registers show him to be involved with four jobs connected with houses and commercial property and three with industrial premises. In all cases the applications for workshops were in conjunction with houses[43]. In total he applied for planning permission for 70 houses, three shops, three workshops and a file shop.

Building materials for the workshops

The bulk of raw materials used in the construction of the workshops came from local sources. Stone was excavated from nearby quarries situated in what were then rural areas on the edge of the town. Bricks and lime were often produced on the site of the actual buildings and this can be seen in some of the early buildings in the irregularity of the shape and colour of the bricks[44]. Although there was an abundance of woodland in the surrounding area, timber was probably largely imported from Scandinavia once the Don Navigation and canal had been built. Glass came from outside Sheffield for the most part, with only two glassmakers being recorded within the limits of the town in the nineteenth century, the furthest suppliers being located in Lancashire. These were material factors in producing a local style of building, considered in more details in the following chapter.

Conclusion

The above shows the limited extent of the information available on the builders of the tableware and cutlery workshops, especially after 1848 when building information in the Fairbank archive ceases. It is therefore impossible to build an accurate picture of the working patterns of mid to late nineteenth-century builders, although the building registers do give some information. The role of the 'builder' appears to have developed by the end of the nineteenth century from that of craftsman such as mason, bricklayer, joiner or carpenter, to a manager of projects, sub-contracting work to the individual craftsman. The builder would frequently be listed with the carpenters and joiners in the trade directories, suggesting that it is from these trades that the more entrepreneurial builder emerged.

The number of industrial buildings in the work of the builders identified was usually small, most of their work being connected with domestic dwellings. It has also been shown that the builders would have designed the majority of the industrial buildings in the vernacular, especially since identified architects carried out only a small percentage of industrial work.

Notes

[1] See Ebu references. There are numerous designs including Greys Malt house, warehouse, workshops along with toll houses, fire offices and schools.

[2] Linstrum, D. 1978 *West Yorkshire Architects and Architecture* Lund Humphries London p 25.

[3] 5/12/1865 Building Register CA205, Sheffield Archives.

[4] C J Innocent was also a member. The Institute of Surveyors was formed in 1868 and put surveyors on the same professional footing as architects.

[5] These names were identified in the building registers 1864-1891. In total they were responsible for the design of at least 61 workshops in the 33 years sampled. The search was carried out on the term 'workshop' alone as by the end of the nineteenth century the term 'shop' was more likely to refer to commercial premises.

[6] 3/51866, 17/8/1866, 13/2/1867, 29/5/1867, 26/7/1867 and 25/10/1866, building registers CA 205.

[7] 7/3/1866 and resubmitted 16/3/1866.

[8] 6/12/1866 and additions to them 13/2/1867and 21/3/1867.

[9] The building registers commence in 1864.

[10] 1865-66, 1870-71 and 1875-6.

[11] Includes all types of work not just industrial.

[12] Saint A 1983 op cit p 67.

[13] Smoke Bye Laws 12/10/1853 in pursuance of the Municipal Corporation Act, printed by Richard Smith and Co 1871, Sheffield p 1.

[14] Gaskell, S M 1983 *National Statues and the Local Community: Building Control by National Legislation and the Introduction of Local Bye-Laws in Victorian England.* British Association for Local History p 34.

[15] For example 26/5/1875, Building Registers CA 205, Sheffield Archives.

[16] Marshall, R.J. 1993 *Town Planning* in *A History of the City of Sheffield: Society* Sheffield Academic Press p 20.

[17] Bye-laws with regard to the new streets and buildings and drainage thereof 11/9/1889, p 15-16.

[18] Vict.41 1878 ch 16, p 102-140.

[19] 91/B1/1 is a list of clients and work carried out by the Appleby firm. Sheffield Archives.

[20] The present day 'Eyewitness Works'.

[21] Brockman, H.A.N. 1974 op cit. p 17.

[22] *Statutory List of Buildings and Special Architectural or Historical Interest* English heritage 1995 p 449 and Beauchamp, V A 1995 in *Industrial History of South Yorkshire* edited by D Bayliss for the Association for Industrial Archaeology, Redruth, p 45.

[23] Dixon, R and Muthesius, S 1993 op cit. p 17.

[24] English Heritage and Sheffield City Council 1995 *Historic Buildings in Sheffield: Understanding Listing* EH and SCC p 12.

[25] Parry, D 1984 *Victorian Sheffield in Advertisements* Moss Valley Heritage Publications p 15.

[26] English Heritage 1995 *Statutory List of buildings of Special Architectural or Historic Interest* EH p 163.

[27] At Venture Works, 103 Arundel Street for example, the house, probably designed by the architects James Paine and Thomas Atkinson, was converted to offices and a workshop block was attached behind. In the second half of the century simple variants on classical lines.

[28] Butterfield had first used this style at All Saints, Margaret Street, London between 1850 and 1860. Pragnell, H 1995 *Britain: A Guide to Architectural Styles from 1066 to the Present Day* Ellipsis London, London p 258.

[29] The gothic style was to become the established architecture of churches, Ruskin and Pugin advocating that it was the most constructionally truthful.

[30] Pollard, S 1959 *A History of Labour in Sheffield* Liverpool University Press p 331.

[31] Flockton also designed much of the High Street in Sheffield.

[32] Jones, E 1985 *Industrial Architecture in Britain 1750-1939* Batsford, London p 111-112.

[33] Quoted in Jones, E op cit p113.

[34] Hattersley, R. 1990 *The Makers Mark* Pan Books, London p 45. Describes how his great grandfather Frederick Hattersley had rented a 'dingy room in a desperate and impecunious attempt to be his own master'.

[35] British Parliamentary Papers *Industrial Revolution: Factories Session 1897-99* vol. 26 IUP.

[36] This included workshops, breweries, malthouses and warehouses.

[37] Other reflects stables, barns etc. and those titles which had no mention of a structure.

[38] 1762-11-23-FB23-90 and 1781-2-2-BB64-186 respectively. Fairbank Collection.

[39] 1764-11-07-FB28-08 ibid.

[40] 1778-04-18-BB60-197 ibid.

[41] Pollard, S 1959 op cit. p 89.

[42] Pollard, S 1959 p 337.

[43] See building registers CA 205 13/2/1874, 30/9/1875, 11/6/1875, 13/10/1875, 14/6/1876, 29/6/1876, 13/6/1877

[44] Beauchamp V A 1996 *The workshops of the Cutlery Industry in Hallamshire 1750-1900* Ph.D. Thesis 9067 University of Sheffield p 177-190.

Chapter 9

The structural and external characteristics of the workshops

Introduction

In this chapter, the use of documentary sources is combined with fieldwork examples to show the structural and external characteristics of the tableware and cutlery workshops. This does not however include detailed assessments of individual structures or company histories but draws on information from a variety of sites to create a greater understanding of the relationship between the processes and the building. Key questions are whether the tableware and cutlery workshops can be identified from external characteristics alone and if the choice of materials and structural features was dictated by the function of the building.

Size

The first impression of any building is its size. In order to consider this in a meaningful way the buildings are divided into general divisions of 'small', 'medium' and 'large'.

Small scale
Small-scale workshops usually consist either of a single room in a single-storey building (Fig 43) or up to four rooms in a two-storey structure such as the courtyard workshops to be found in

the town, for example Stan Shaw's workshop in Garden Street. (Fig 44). Externally, fieldwork and map evidence has demonstrated that these buildings usually measure between 5 ½ and 11 yards (5–10m) in length and 3 to 5½ yards (3–5m) wide.

Figure 44 Two-storey courtyard workshop. Stan Shaw's Garden Street workshop (1994)

Medium scale
The second type of building is the small-scale 'works'. Examples of these are Kendal Works (tenanted), A Wright and Son, Sidney Street (Fig 45) and Victoria Works, Gell Street. Externally they measure between 11 and 20 yards (10–18m) long and 3 and 6 yards wide (2.74–5.5m). The width of the building was restricted by the need to use natural light for illumination of the workshops. These buildings have two to three storeys and sometimes a cellar.

Waterpowered sites can also be considered as medium-scale works although these are usually single storey and can be divided into 'ends' or separate grinding 'hulls' (Fig 46).

Large scale
Examples of large integrated structures are James Dixon's Cornish Place (Fig 47) and Butcher's Works (Fig 48), and tenement wheels

Figure 43 Single storey workshop at Nook Lane, Stannington (1995)

Figure 45 A Wright and Son, Sidney Street (two-storey works)

Figure 47 Cornish Place. The buildings in this complex range between three and five storeys. The frontage is only three storeys

Figure 46 Shepherd's Wheel, River Porter. Note the two 'ends' which were sub-let

Figure 48 Butcher's Wheel, Arundel Street has a four-storey front elevation

such as Union Wheel and Soho Wheel. Large-scale sites consist of buildings greater than 20 yards in length, although their width may not be significantly different from medium scale structures. The maximum width recorded is 8.3 yards wide (7.59m)[1], restricted by the problems of internal lighting. Large-scale works can also consist of ranges of buildings, usually between two and five storeys in height, accommodating a larger workforce or, if tenanted, a number of small firms.

The three scales of building identified reflect the changing nature of the accommodation used by the tableware, cutlery and related trades throughout the period studied. The larger scale works do not appear until the advent of steam power that made the grouping of workshops necessary, in order to make the best use of the power source. While these buildings have become the prominent survivors of the industry

of the nineteenth century, the small and medium scale workshops were more numerous[2].

Structural considerations

The examination of structural features during the course of fieldwork has shown that no specific elements point to the use of a building by the tableware and cutlery industry. Structurally, basic building principles applied to all the workshops examined emphasising the speculative nature of their erection. If the industry moved out of a building, it was easily adapted for other uses and vice versa.

Brick and stone were the primary building materials as elsewhere in the country, although stronger bonds within large complexes used by the tableware and cutlery industry may indicate some buildings were used as warehouses[3]. To add strength and fireproofing to large-scale works, cast iron columns and brick jack arches were introduced. The use of such columns can be seen clearly in the upper storeys of Butcher's Wheel and in Cornish Place. Unlike the decorative columns found in some of the textile mills recorded by Giles and Goodall[4] those that remain in the cutlery workshops are purely functional.

Floor structures and coverings varied according to the size of the building. Single-storey buildings usually had stone or dirt floors; the majority of multi-storeyed premises had timber floors, although the ground floors were sometimes flagged[5]. Floors in multi-storeyed buildings were usually supported by a wooden joist system, resting on the internal skin of the wall, on which wooden planking was laid. These were often patched over time. Willie Kugler recalled that at his father's workshop c 1920 was 'there were great gaps in the floor so that if he dropped any tools there was a good chance that he would have to fetch them from the 'chasers' downstairs.'[6]

The joists were supported by the external walls. They were not always visible, and the ceilings that were directly attached to the joists, were a mixture of plaster and grinding swarf, as at Kendal Works. In the Fairbank Field and Building books most of the carpentry jobs relating to smithies contain details of the cost of floor framing, the number of joists required and the cost of laying the floor boards. At John Pitt's workshop and warehouse in Trafalgar Street, the floor joists were to be 6½ by 2½ inches size and laid at a distance of 18 inch centres[7]. According to Ching's estimations this would carry a live load of less than 40lbs per square foot[8]. The floor covering in the warehouse and shop were to be boards 1 inch thick and 9 inch wide, grooved and tongued.

Where heavy work was carried out the floors were of concrete[9]. Timber floors would not have supported the grinding troughs in the upper storeys of Butcher's Wheel. Concrete floors supported on brick jack arches also added strength to the structure.

It is possible to conclude therefore, that the weight of the machinery associated with certain processes carried on within a structure dictated the type of floor, i.e. if grinding was to take place in the upper storeys of buildings the floors had to be strengthened. In single storeyed buildings the floor covering was dictated by cost in addition to the needs of the industry. However, neither of these factors was unique to the tableware and cutlery trade.

The presence of chimneys can indicate a fireplace, a hearth or a steam engine, depending on type. It can be difficult to distinguish between a fireplace chimney and a hearth chimney, as they look the same although illustrations show that hearth chimneys within the town could be taller to increase the draught[10].

Groups of chimneys are also significant. On Ball Street for example, the number of chimneys, situated on the edge of the building, suggest that this part of Alfred Beckett's works was used for forging (Fig 49).

Figure 49 Hearth chimneys, at Alfred Beckett's, Ball Street

One significant chimney type that should not be confused with the tableware and cutlery industry specifically is the crucible stack (Fig 50). They did occur, however at integrated works such Well Meadow Street where Samuel Peace made steel and files and Michelthwaite and Co, manufacturers of steel, files and saws, Malinda Street[11].

Figure 50 Crucible stack, Malinda Street

Chimneys connected with the use of a steam engine may be located centrally within a yard or integrated into the building structure, for example at Eye Witness Works (Fig 51a). In 1896 the chimney at Butcher's Wheel stood at 120ft[12] (36.58 metres) (Fig 51b). This was used by three engines located in the main buildings at opposite corners of the yard and one in a temporary wooden structure attached to the southern block. Goad's fire plans indicate that the bases of the chimneys were mainly square in section[12].

Figure 51 a and b Chimneys for engines at Eye Witness Works (left) and Butcher's Wheel (right)

Chimneys however rarely survive. Due to the danger of high chimneys collapsing and those situated within buildings seriously damaging the rest of the structure, many have been removed. Even those that were for fireplaces have become redundant with the introduction of portable electric heaters and the installation of central heating in some of the larger works[13].

External or 'envelope'[14] features

External or envelope features provide far more characteristic evidence of a workshop's use by the tableware and cutlery industry, in particular the windows and entrances suggest different functions and branches of the cutlery trades[15].

Entrances
Entrances to the workshops varied according to the size of building and whether it was a tenement factory or an integrated works. If the building was owner occupied the entrance was more elaborate than those of the courtyard workshops and tenement factories.

Fieldwork has indicated that where the original frame exists, entrances to forges can be identified by the stable or 'dutch' doors[16]. These had the advantage of letting air circulate while restricting floor-level draughts (Fig 52). Batten doors were used to access the small-scale workshops, and by other branches of the tableware, cutlery and related trades. These 'consisted of vertical boards nailed at right angles to cross strips.'[17] These doors were also used as entrances to workshop blocks in larger factories, whether single occupancy or tenement.

Figure 52 Example of a stable or dutch door at forge in Garden Street

Doors to the main offices were of better quality. At Sylvester Works for example there is a panelled door consisting of stiles and muntins (Fig 53 a to c)[18] as at Burgon and Ball and at Globe Works.

Goods entering larger works would usually pass through the cart entrance to the courtyard. These entrances would invariably be detailed in stone and sometimes the name of the firm or works would appear (Fig 54 a and b). Cart entrances in rows of terraced houses usually indicate the presence of an industrial building

Figure 53 a to c Doors to the offices of larger works were of better quality than those to the work-shops and usually had decorative surrounds. Sylvester Works (Elliot's) (top left) Burgon and Ball (top right) and Globe Works

behind. These however are not characteristic of the tableware and cutlery workshops, being more likely to represent builders' premises.

One feature which is lacking from the majority of tableware and cutlery workshops and factories is the 'taking-in door' on the upper storeys as found in the boot and shoe and textile industries. From fieldwork and documentary evidence the majority of raw material and finished work appears to have been taken in and out through the main entrance to the building. With tenement factories in particular, it would not have been structurally feasible for every workshop to have a taking-in door. Another reason for their scarcity may be connected with the small quantity of goods handled by firms making a taking-in door and crane unnecessary.

Where taking-in doors in the conventional sense do exist, they are located in the warehouses of

Figure 54 a and b Courtyard entrances often displayed the name of the firm or works top: Beehive Works, Milton Street, bottom: Challenge Works, Arundel Street

the larger works. Fieldwork has also identified their use at Butcher's Wheel (Fig 55) and in a small two-storey file cutters workshop at 132 Cross Hill Ecclesfield. Other works have ground floor loading doors as at Eye Witness Works (Fig 56), Kendal Works, Butcher's Wheel and Victoria Works.

It can be concluded that taking-in doors were not a characteristic feature of the buildings of the Sheffield trades. Structural considerations and the organisation of the tenement factories meant that they could not be provided to all the workshops. Staircases, both internal and external were the alternative way of getting raw materials and goods to the upper stories. Loading doors were sometimes used by the larger firms at ground floor level.

Windows

The most characteristic external feature of the workshops associated with the cutlery trades is

Figure 55 Taking in doors are rarely seen on cutlery workshops. Where they do occur they are usually located in the packing shops and warehouses as at Butcher's Wheel

Figure 56 Ground floor loading doors are a more common feature than taking in doors. Shown here is Kendal Works

the windows. Four types of fenestration, used to light workshops of the tableware, cutlery and related trades have been identified. Of these only two can be said to indicate a particular trade, i.e. those lighting workshops used for file cutting and grinding. This however does not rule out the use of buildings with different fenestration by those trades. The type of windows merely shows the use for which the building was originally designed.

Typical windows
The most common form of window type was made up of casements consisting of 6 or 8 (10

in x 8 in) small panes. Two or three casements are set in wooden frames with either a horizontal slide opening (Fig 57) or a hinged outward opening.

Figure 57 Traditional cutlery workshop windows with a horizontal slide opening

The windows are grouped together in long ranges across the top stories of the building. They are not found on the ground floor, as they were not deep enough to provide sufficient light especially when the building was situated in a crowded courtyard where little light could penetrate. These windows are found on most of the small-scale workshops.

The size of these windows was between 41 in x 36 in and 41 in x 54 in. Very little decoration is found around these windows. Often they are just let into the brickwork but occasionally lintels may be visually articulated with a soldier course as in the workshops on Egerton Street (Fig 58a). On rare occasions a slight camber is imposed such as on the upper storey at Morton's (Fig 58b). This type of window is usually found on both sides of the workshop unlike the other types that are usually only found let into one wall.

The typical Sheffield type of window have not been seen on workshops of the Prescot watch or file trades, the Leicestershire boot and shoe industry, or the textile workshops of the period, with the exception of Carlton Mill, Sowerby Bridge[18] where identical windows are found but are set in stone jambs and mullions rather than wooden frames. These windows can therefore be identified as being characteristic of the tableware and cutlery workshops in this region.

'Low shop' windows
These are much larger than the typical windows but are still made up of small panes. On the average window these number 30. The panes are grouped in pairs in wooden frames. This

window type is found on the ground floor of buildings used by the Sheffield trades to maximise the amount of light in these shops (Fig 59). In size these windows are c 54 inches square and often the more typical windows will appear above the 'low shop', so called because these workshops carried the lowest rateable

Figure 58a Decoration is rarely found above the typical windows of the cutlery workshop. The example above shows vertical bricks above windows in Egerton Street

Figure 58b Above the windows at Morton's cambered arches have been used to add simple decoration to the upper storey windows

value in the rate books, and they were situated on the ground floor. Today few survive, belonging to the poorest type of workshop they have usually been demolished along with the courtyards and the back-to-back houses of the workers.

Grinders' windows

This type of fenestration occurs in the grinding wheels. These windows have no glass but have iron bars on to which oiled cloth could be placed in the winter months. They are most commonly found at the waterpowered sites in rural settings, although they occasionally occurred in the smaller scale grinding hulls within the town such as Mr Gaunt's Grinding Wheel and Cutlers' Shop in Cambridge Street (see Fig 74, page 101)[19].

Figure 59 To the right, 'Low shop' windows at Cross Rockingham Street, Sheffield (D Crossley, slide collection). Note the more typical windows above to the left

The advantage of this type of window for the trade was that it allowed the dust to escape while also keeping the grinding hulls cool. It is recorded in the Children's Employment Commission reports of 1865 that even in winter a grinder could work up a sweat. In the larger wheel these windows were not used and the grinders, it is reported, smashed the glass out of the windows in order to improve the atmosphere within the workroom[20].

Office and frontage windows

The windows of this type are to be found in the manager's offices, warehouses and packing rooms of the larger firms. Usually they are Georgian windows with vertical sashes. Sometimes they may be round-headed as in Taylor's Eye Witness Works offices or Kutrite Works (Fig 60). This type of fenestration adds distinction to the frontage of the building and promotes the image of success, a building

Figure 60 Eye Witness Works, Milton Street. Note the fine Georgian styling of the manager's office (1995)

designed by an architect rather than following the vernacular. This type of fenestration can therefore be said to be common with nearly all polite Georgian architecture of the period and is therefore not a particular characteristic of the cutlery industry.

In summary, the first three window types are characteristic of the tableware and cutlery industry. Workshops can thus be identified in the field despite similarities with types elsewhere in the country. In some cases they can define the branch of the trade for which the building was intended. Where the more general window types are found other evidence has to be used to confirm the purpose of the building, for example documentary records, oral testimony or internal characteristics.

Conclusion

The structure and external features of the buildings of the cutlery industry were not particularly characteristic of the trade with the exception of window types. From these the

various branches of the trade could be identified, although not conclusively, as building functions varied over time. Clearly there were other factors involved and in the following chapter the processes themselves and how they may have affected the internal layout of buildings are examined.

Notes

[1] Plan number CA206/ 2284 Mr Gaunt's Grinding Wheel.
[2] For further details see Beauchamp, V A 1996 *The workshops of the Industry in Hallamshire 1750-1900* Unpublished PhD Thesis 9067 University of Sheffield Chapters 1 and 2 on the location and financing of the buildings of the cutlery industry.
[3] Ibid p 177-190 considers in detail the bricks and brickwork used in buildings associated with the cutlery industry.
[4] Giles, C and Goodall, I 1992 *Yorkshire Textile Mills 1770-1930* RCHME London p 68-69.
[5] See Figure 3, Chapter 5.
[6] Willie Krugler, engraver, Notes about his life and family, Hawley Collection, University of Sheffield.
[7] CP3-32 Fairbank Collection, Sheffield Archives.
[8] Ching, F D K 1991 op cit. 4.5 This assumes that the joists have simple spans. Today the minimum requirement for a manufacturing establishment is 125 lbs per square foot (Ching ibid. p A6).
[9] Lime ash may have been used at an earlier date for the same purpose.
[10] Topham's View of Sheffield from the site of the Midland Station 1866 shows the tall hearth chimneys to be found attached to some workshops in the town. (see Beauchamp V A 1996 chapter 4 figure 18).
[11] Bayliss, D et al 1995 *A Guide to the Industrial History of South Yorkshire* Association for Industrial Archaeology p 28.
[12] Goad's Fire Plans 1896 Sheet 23 674/B1/24 Sheffield Archives.
[13] Giles, C and Goodall, I 1992 op cit. p 150.
[14] Plans for Howson Bros and Harrison 1905 AP85 1-9 Sheffield Archives.
[15] Ching, F D K 1991 op cit. p 2.8.
[16] ibid p 2.8.
[17] Ching, F D K 1991 op cit. p 7.3.
[18] ibid p 7.5.
[19] Building Registers plan no 2284 CA 206. Sheffield Archives.
[20] Appendix to the Fourth Report Mr. J.E.White's Report p 42.

Chapter 10

The internal characteristics of the buildings

Introduction

In order to clarify the use of the buildings, internal features must also be examined. It has been established that external appearance alone is not enough to assign a specific function to the workshops of the tableware and cutlery industry, in the absence of documentary evidence. Internal evidence and spatial organisation are therefore vital if the processes carried out within a building are to be identified and working practices understood.

Several studies have been made which assess the processes and working conditions within the industry. The Royal Commissions of the nineteenth century[1] investigated children's employment in order to make recommendations for the Factory Acts. G I H Lloyd's *The Cutlery Trades*[2] examined the processes involved in making cutlery as well as the economic and social background to it. More recent studies have included *On a Knife Edge*, which records workers' memories of the industry[3] and Sally Ann Taylor's thesis *Tradition and Change, the Sheffield Cutlery Trades 1870–1914*[4] which evaluated the evolution of processes in the period studied and their social effects. Ruth Grayson's *Industrial Organisation in Nineteenth Century Sheffield* and paper on the *Independent Artisan in Sheffield* both emphasised the continuity of methods used within the industry[5]. Joan Unwin's thesis on the pen and pocket-knife industry examined that particular aspect in detail[6]. Colin Turner has briefly assessed the workshops and requirements of each trade[7] but none has looked in depth at the equipment needed or the layout of the workshops in relation to the methods of production.

The features likely to survive in the archaeological record from each process are discussed below. In addition, whether or not a buildings function can be identified from the internal organisation of workrooms and if this had any effect on the processes carried out.

Forging

The first process in the production of a knife is the forging of the blade from a steel bar or rod. For larger blades, as found on table knives and tools, the forger is assisted by the striker. This is known as double-handed forging. Small blades, for example those found on pen or pocket knives could be hammered out by the forger alone. This was termed 'single-handed forging'.

The needs of the forger were few, 'a small reheating hearth, hand bellows, fuel and anvil (stiddy), and hammers'[8]. The forger's workshop usually has an internal area of 10 yards square (9.14m). In the centre of the shop was placed the stock (a block of stone or wood) and the stiddy. There were differently shaped anvils for the various branches of the trades[9]. Figures 61 and 62 show butcher blade and file forging respectively. The different types of anvils are clearly visible. In these figures the 'aggon' or upturned chisel for cutting off the 'mood' can be seen. Today forging is rarely carried out by hand, the blades being stamped or 'flied out'. For hardening, in addition to the equipment mentioned above, the forger or hardener would require tongs for holding the blades and a vat for water or oil for cooling or quenching the blade[10].

In the archaeological record little evidence survives for the processes carried out. The stock, being of sufficient weight that it did not need to be attached to the floor, is likely to have been removed together with the stiddy. All tools used by the forger, such as the tongs seen hanging above the hearth in Figures 61 and 62, and the forger's characteristic hammer with the bent head, which improved the efficiency of the swing, will have been taken away. The vat for the water or oil used for cooling in the hardening process, often only an old oil drum or bucket, is unlikely to remain. Hammer scale[11] may survive and can be analysed by specialists with the aid of electron microscopes and mass spectrometers. The only clear evidence to remain is the forgers' hearths which form part of the structure of the workshop.

Figure 61
Double handed forging of butcher's blades at Thomas Turner's c 1901. Note at A1 the 'aggon' or upturned chisel used for cutting off the 'mood'. The spike at B2 is used to guide the forger when placing the blade over the aggon. To the right of the photograph is the forger's hearth with its stepped chimneybreast and the forger's tongs hang from it. The forger's hammers, weighing between four and twelve pounds have characteristically bent heads which made the swing more efficient. The same shape is also used for file cutters' hammers. Note that the floor of the workshop is flagged. (Photograph from the Hawley Collection, University of Sheffield. Originally produced in *Handicrafts that survive* p 20)

Figure 62
File forging, Thomas Turner's 1902. Note the aggon (A1) and the difference in the shape of the anvil when compared to the blade forger's anvil. Note the stepped breast of the forger's hearth and the shape of the hammer and the handle of the hammer worn after years of use thus marking clearly where the hammer was held. ((Photograph from the Hawley Collection, University of Sheffield. Originally produced in *Handicrafts that Survive* p 55)

Hearths

Forgers' hearths

The forger's hearth is similar to any blacksmith's hearth and would be found in most of the workshops termed as smithies. Hearths of this type remain in forgers' workshops, for example in the courtyard of 52 Garden Street. Other examples can be found in scissor forgers' workshops and file cutters' workshops, where they were used for making file blanks and the file cutters' chisels (Fig 63 a and b).

Figure 63b File forger's hearth, Stepping Lane, Grenoside. Note that the chimney-breast is stepped and constructed of brick, whilst the base is of stone. It is also possible to see the ash hole (A1) and hole for tuyere (B2) indicating that the bellows were situated to the left of the hearth. On the right is a bowl under which a fire could be lit. This may have been used for melting lead used to make the beds on which the files were cut

Figure 63a Scissor forger's workshop, Bingley Cottage, Stannington. This hearth has a stone breast and lintel. Note the hole for the tuyere at A1. The space on the right-hand side of the hearth may have been used for tempering the blades

Within the town, hearths are usually constructed of refractory brick, stone, or have a stone lintel in rural areas. The chimneybreast is usually stepped. The hearth is positioned at waist height with a depth of between 80–100cm (31.5–39.4ins). The width of the hearths at Nook Lane[12], and Bingley cottage were between 1.25m and 1.5m (1.37–1.64 yards).

Below the main hearth is a second smaller hole or 'ass hoil or nook'[13] where the ashes and clinker could be raked out. In the urban workshops the hearths that survive have been whitewashed while in the rural workshops the brick and stonework retains its natural state. This possibly reflects the greater influence of the 1878 Factory Acts in urban areas.

In order to increase heat within the hearth, bellows would be required. The most commonly used were the Double Blast Bellows costing between £5-15-0d and £20. In size these ranged from 16 to 36ins (40.6–91.4cm) in diameter and stood about 4ft high (122cm).

As the hearth extended into the room the bellows could be placed at the side (Fig 64) thus

Figure 64 Single-handed forging at Thomas Turner's. Note how the bellows are placed at the side of the hearth to minimise the amount of room they took up. The extended handle (A1) was used to make it more convenient for the forger to use whilst watching the metal. The skill of the forger was to know exactly when to remove the metal from the heat. This was usually done by observing the change in colour. Also seen in the photograph is the hearth and the water vat. By 1901 gas was being used to fuel the hearths as demonstrated by the pipes at C3. (Hawley Collection)

not compromising the workspace. Figure 64 also shows an extended handle allowing a single forgeman to operate the bellows while observing the metal being heated. Careful inspection of the hearth, if in good condition, will however reveal the 'tuyere' hole into which tuyere irons were inserted. These can be seen in Figure 4.4. 'Tue' irons were 'metal nozzles protecting the pipe of the bellows where it enters the forger's hearth'[14]. The major manufacturers of bellows in Sheffield were Absalom, Harrop and Pearson who were located at Fitzroy Bellows Works on Ecclesall Road in 1883.

Cutlers' hearths

Forging hearths are very characteristic but to avoid confusion the cutler's hearth is considered

in detail. The cutler's hearth (Fig 65) was rectangular in plan with stepped sides and containing two to three openings.

One opening, usually the largest, served the purpose of heating the room by means of an open grate. Adjacent to this was a small opening placed at about waist height that was used in a similar way to a forger's hearth for hardening and tempering blades once they had been finished. A comparison of the openings shows that the aperture used for hardening is much smaller than the others. An example of this type of hearth can be seen at Kelham Island Museum. These hearths were approximately 1½m wide and 80cm deep. 'Long shape bellows' would have been used to operate these types of hearths as shown at Kelham Island.

Figure 65 Cutler's hearth, Kelham Island. Note the three openings for hardening (A1), the ash hole (B2) and the fireplace (C3). The 'long shaped bellows' are mounted on a wooden frame to which an extended handle is attached so that the cutler could observe the heat in the hearth and the metal. With thanks to Sheffield Industrial Museums Trust

These would have been mounted in a homemade wooden stand. They could be compressed by means of a wooden handle in a similar way to the forgers bellows. The 1864 Sheffield List priced these bellows at between £1-6s-0d and £16-10s-0d depending on size. Once again they would have been placed at the side of the hearth to minimise the space they took up and a 'tuyere' used to maximise their efficiency.

Grinding

After forging the blade of a knife is sent to the grinder to give it an edge. The grinding wheel, for wet grinding, is mounted in a trough made of wood, stone or concrete (as at Butcher's Wheel) or iron as described in the *Workshops of England*[15] at Mappin Brothers. The water in the trough covers a 2in segment of the wheel. Wet grinding was used for all 'heavy' work and from at least the 1840s for pen and pocket knives[16]. For a table knife grinder the wheel was usually 4ft to 4ft 6in (122–145cm) in diameter which

would be worn down to about 21in (53cm) and then be passed on to a pocket knife grinder who could use it until it measured fifteen inches in diameter[17]. The smallest types of grinding stone, as small as 1 or 2in in diameter (2.5–5cm), were used for hollow-grinding open razors (Fig 66). At the end of the century, sandstone wheels were replaced by artificial or emery wheels. These were regarded as being safer as they did not contain flaws and 'there would be no grit flying around.'[18] The wheels were fixed on to the axles using wooden wedges, although in some instances iron plates were noticed by the Children's Employment Commission. The latter method was considered to be much safer as it added strength to the centre of the stone and reduced the risk of breakage[19]. As a result of the variation in sizes of grindstones the troughs also varied. The German Wilson papers give the size of a 'Blade grinders Trow':

'Wood ... sides 3in thick bottom 4in thick ends $2^{1}/_{2}$ in thick 2ft 2in deep inside, 5ft long at top 5ft long at bottom inside width 14in at bottom, 15in at top with one end 21in deep with three bolts through one end and four at other'[20].

A pocket-knife grinders trough was stated as being:

'42in long by 12in wide by 1ft 6in deep. Axle trees for razor grinders when new 32in long to make three deep framing not less than 9 feet long.'[21]

The grinder sits on his horsing, a wooden saddle which is attached to the floor by means of large chains. On average the horsing is 14 inches wide[22] and may be raised or lowered by adding or removing wooden packs so that it is always level with the top of the wheel. Bricks, stones, or blocks of wood were placed under the feet so that the elbows could be rested on the knees. This produced the effect of ensuring that every blade was placed on the wheel in the same way thus introducing an element of consistency. To apply a large blade to the wheel a 'flatstick' was used. In front of the grindstone was placed the swarf board which caught all the swarf (or muck) off the blade and wheel as it is ground. The grinders 'kit' consisted of a bucket of water in which blades were cooled after grinding[23] and which could be used to keep the water in the trough at the right level.

Grinding wheels may be set individually or up to three deep. This can be clearly seen in the

Figure 66 Hollow razor grinding at John Clark's Mowbray Street c 1921 (Photo from Hawley Collection). Note the size of the grindstone (A1). Also seen in the photograph is the grinders' kit (B2). Behind the grinder the blades are being polished. The glazing wheels, covered in glue and emery, can be seen hanging on the wall in a wooden rack. The wooden drums from which power is transmitted from the main shaft can be seen at the back of the workshop (C3)

second floor hull at Butcher's Wheel (Fig 67a), in the Pawson and Brailsford illustration, (Fig 67b)[24]. This illustration shows that for saw grinding the grinder stood up so that his whole weight could be used to hold the blade against the wheel.

The evidence that remains for grinding varies according to the condition of the building. The horsing, like the blocks on which the feet were placed, has in most cases been removed, however the hooks for the chains may still exist as at Butcher's Wheel. The swarf board was usually made of wood and once again will not survive once the building has gone out of use. The grinders 'kit' will have disappeared. Occasionally grinding wheels and mounting blocks may be found, especially in rural areas, scattered around the remains of the building, but in the towns they have usually been disposed of, often by being sold on as garden ornaments.

Swarf is evidence for wet grinding but its presence in a building is not necessarily proof of grinding at that particular site. It has been shown that swarf could be incorporated into plaster for ceilings and Alan Day recalls fetching swarf from Swann's, saw grinders, to clean the emery and glue from glazing wheels[25].

Fans
The use of extractor fans was not widespread within the industry although it had been demonstrated that they helped to improve the air quality within the workshops[26]. However in White's report there are many interviews which give details of the absence of fans in the grinding hulls and workshops and the reasons why. In his introduction to the report White states in paragraph 43[27]:

'The great benefit of fans in protecting the workers from dust in dry grinding of every kind, indeed the absolute necessity of them for the preservation of health, is universally

Figure 67a Grinding hull, Butcher's Wheel, Arundel Street. Note the wooden troughs on brick bases set three deep and the hooks with once held down the chains attached to the horsing (A1)

Figure 67b Illustration from Pawson and Brailsford of a grinder's hull. Here the setting of wheels three deep is clearly seen. Note also the swarf board (A1). Blocks were often placed under the grinder's feet to support the arms (B2). It is common in grinding hulls to see glazing wheels suspended on racks on the wall and ceiling. In this illustration the use of brick jack arches and cast iron columns can be clearly seen and the presence of the overseer (C3) suggests that this is an integrated works

admitted. In many places fans are put up and used, but numbers of dry grinders, particularly fork grinders, who need them most, are without them, and some neglect to use them even where they are out up, thus injuring others, who work in the same hull, as well as themselves. I have not been able to ascertain the proportion of workers who do not use them at grinding dry, but from the evidence and from what I have myself seen, it is considerable. The expense alone cannot, or at any rate should not, be the cause of the neglect. A fan may be put up so as to protect several workers at the cost of a few pounds eg from £5 to £10, or for much less, eg from 30s to £3, for only one. Where there are fans they are sometimes used by glaziers and polishers as well as grinders.'

The reasons quoted by the men and women interviewed by White for not installing fans, or if they were installed prohibiting them being used, ranged from too much noise to 'the trade was bad enough as it was; and if the men lived longer it would be so over full there would be no such thing as getting a living.'[28] Another reason for not using a fan in the polishing processes was given at Joseph Rodgers and Son, Norfolk Street as 'the draught cools the metal and prevents it from polishing so easily'[29].

From the documentation above it is not surprising that very little evidence survives for

the use of extractor fans within the workshops and grinding hulls of the cutlery trades. In the grinding hulls, such as Butcher's Wheel, there was no evidence for their use but this was probably because wet grinding was taking place here and the dust would be kept down to some extent by the water. Grinders' dust can still be sensed in many of the buildings visited today. In rural areas fans were not used because the grinding hull windows were not glazed and therefore the dust could escape easily.

The only archaeological evidence for the use of fans is connected not with grinding but with the polishing and glazing of goods, for example at Kirkanson's, 50 Garden Street. The extractor fan has a hood which is positioned on the workbench over the grinding and polishing machinery (Fig 68a). From here pipework would take the dust to the outside. The fans would be powered from a line shaft, creating a vacuum that sucked the dust into the pipes. At Kirkanson's it was said that huge clouds of dust could be seen emerging from the flue into which all the pipes fed (Fig 68b).

Figure 68a Extractor fans used with polishing machinery at A Wright and Son, set into the middle of the bench

Figure 68b
The external evidence for extractor fans at Kirkanson's, 50 Garden Street. The yard used to be covered in dust which was extracted by the fans from the workshops. This was collected and sold, to be incorporated into mortar

The cutler

From the grinder the blade would be passed on to the cutler who assembled the knife and put the handle on. Traditionally the handles or outer scales of the knife would be pearl, tortoise shell, abalone[30], stag, ivory, bone, or buffalo horn. From the 1860s new materials were introduced such as celluloid and from the 1880s products with handles made from vulcanite, xylonite and ebonite became available. Evidence of these materials can often be found in the workshops either in their raw state or partially worked. The inner scales of pocket knives were made of iron, brass or steel.

In 1843 *The Penny Magazine* described the cutler as working at:

'a small bench near a window, and is provided with a number of tools to facilitate his operations – such as a vice, a small anvil, several files, steel burnishers, a drill-bow and drills for boring holes, a glazer coated with emery, a polisher coated with oil and rotten-stone, steel plates to act as gauges in making holes through the various parts of the knife, and numerous other appliances which we cannot

enumerate. With the aid of these he shapes and adjusts his various pieces, fastens them with pins or rivets, files down these pins to give them a neat and level appearance, polishers every part after it is fixed; and, in short, he does to a pen knife what every watchmaker does to a watch – he makes very few of the parts, but he adjusts them all'[31].

The most important part of any cutler's workshop was the workbench. This was usually made up of two or three lengths of timber (Fig 69a). Other examples can be seen at Kendal Works (Fig 69b) and Kirkanson's. Any workbench found less than 1in thick was probably not used for cutlery and may have been a warehouse bench, such as can be seen in Butcher's Wheel and Kendal Works (Figs 70a and b).

The cutler would keep his tools on the workbench. These included as the quote in *The Penny Post* illustrates, a vice, a small stiddy or anvil, files and a bow-drill or parser. Hammers were also used and their weight depended on the type of hafting materials being used. Sometimes files and hammers were kept in wooden racking mounted on the walls above the bench. The various wheels required for finishing

Figure 69a Cutler's workbench, Kelham Island. Note the thickness of the timber. With thanks to Sheffield Industrial Museums Trust

Figure 69b Workbench at Kendal Works, made up of short lengths of timber. Note line shaft under bench. (Photo: Sanella, 1994)

Figure 70a Packing shop benches at Butcher's Wheel

Figure 70b Packing shop bench at Kirkanson's Garden Street

the knife were usually made from wood and would be covered in emery for glazing or made from soft calico for polishing. Often the final finishing would be sent to specialists, usually women, for buffing. The vice that the cutler usually had was termed a leg vice. Sometimes they were mounted on wooden blocks to adjust the height to a comfortable working position. They were used in preference to bench vices because, until casting was perfected, they were easier to make[32]. In size the leg vice was approximately 39–41 inches[33] (1m–1.05m) in length from the jaws to the bottom of the shank. They were made of iron, sometimes with steel jaws. The jaws themselves were $4^1/_4$ins (11cm) long and ½in (1cm) in thickness.

The tools rarely survive in the workshops. Even the racking on which they were kept, as shown in Baker's 'The Cutler's Shop in Uproar' (Fig 71), have usually disappeared. The only evidence for the tools, if the work bench itself survives, are a small square hole where the shank of the stiddy had been fastened or bolt holes for a vice.

Buffing and polishing

To polish up the knives before the advent of steam power treadle glazers (or leg frames) would be used. These consisted of two uprights supporting a glazing wheel and placed on a small bench (Fig 72). Below the bench was a large wheel through which an iron crankshaft was placed and to which a wooden treadle was attached. A leather belt connected the wheel and the spindle of the glazing wheel. By treadling the pedal the glazing wheel was turned and the blades could be polished. Treadle

Figure 71 The Cutler's Shop In Uproar (Baker, W E Kelham Island K1919.20). Note the racking for the Tools (A1), the Treadle Glazer (B2), the Parser or Bow Drill (C3) and the Leg Vice (D4)

Figure 72 a) Buffing and polishing used to be carried out on a treadle glazer or leg frame, b) today it is carried out on machines to which different head can be attached and which have integrated electric motors. Polishing machines driven by shafting however are still considered superior by some as they ran at a faster speed giving a higher quality finish. (pers comm. silver worker, Leah's Yard)

power left the hands entirely free to apply the blade to the wheel. Even young children could use these, as a block of stone could be placed at the side of the treadle to stand on.

Steam power meant that more advanced glazing and buffing machines came into use. These machines and wheels could be brought from firms such as Farrer and Son on Division Street. Once again no evidence would be left for this type of machine other than the bolt holes which attached it to the bench. Once the firm had closed the machines could be sold on for use elsewhere or for scrap value. The racking on which the wooden glazing and polishing wheels were suspended will also have disappeared although some wheels may remain.

Evidence for steam powered machinery

As much of the cutler's work was done at workbenches placed against the windows, overhead line shafting in steam powered workshops rarely appears to be centrally located within the rooms; thus there are few brackets on cast iron columns as found in the textile mills, where the rooms were much wider, to accommodate the looms. Any line shafting brackets were usually attached to the wall. This is particularly noticeable at Cornish Place (Fig 73).

However as many of the processes described here did not require powered machinery, it is only in the large scale works that any evidence for it exists.

Notes

[1] Parliamentary Papers 1887 Workshops and Factories and the Children Employment Papers 1843, 1864 and 1865. Irish University Press.
[2] Lloyd, G I H 1968 reprint of 1913 *The Cutlery Trades* Cass and Co. Ltd. London.
[3] Jenkins, C and McClarence, S 1989 *On a Knife Edge* Sheffield Libraries and Information Services, SCL Publishing Sheffield.
[4] Taylor, S A 1988 *Tradition and Change, the Sheffield Cutlery Trades 1870-1914* Unpublished PhD Thesis University of Sheffield.
[5] Unpublished papers 1993-4.
[6] Unwin, M J 1989 *The Pen and Pocket Knife Industry, an investigation into the historical tradition basis of working practices and trade organisation.* Unpublished MA Thesis University of Sheffield.
[7] Turner, C A1986 *A Sheffield Heritage: An*

Figure 73 Wall brackets for line shafting at Cornish Place

Anthology of Photographs and Words of the Cutlery Craftsmen. Division of Continuing Education, University of Sheffield and Sheffield Trades Historical Society Sheffield.
[8] Turner, C A 1986 op cit. p 9.
[9] See Sheffield Illustrated List for example of 1864 Hawley Collection, University of Sheffield.
[10] Turner, C A 1986 p 16 Oil is better as it reduces the risk of cracking the blade.
[11] Tiny pieces of metal which are detached during the forging process from the heated rod.
[12] The author wishes to thank V Seddon for assisting with fieldwork and drawing up the plans to the workshop in Nook Lane belonging to Franklin Cottage.
[12] Dyson, R 1979 reprint *A Glossary of Words and Dialect formerly used in the Sheffield Trades* STHS, University of Sheffield p 10.
[13] ibid. p 40.
[14] Strass, G L M et al 1864 *Workshops of England* Groombridge and Sons, London p 112.
[15] Lloyd, G I H 1968 p 46
[16] Turner, C A op cit., p 19.
[17] Bill Hukin in *On the Knife Edge* 1989 p 64.
[18] White, J E 1865 Appendix to the Fourth Report op cit., p 9 para 92.
[19] PhC 530/1 p 15 Sheffield Archives.
[20] PhC530/1 p 21.
[21] White, J E1865 op cit., para 48 p 5.
[22] Present day grinders also add a wetting agent.

[23] Taylor, J 1879 *The Illustrated Guide to Sheffield and the Surrounding District* Pawson and Brailsford, Sheffield, p 136.

[24] Interview with Alan Day 16/4/1995.

[25] See the evidence produced in White's report to the Children's' Employment Commission 1865 Appendix to the Fourth Report. Evidence.

[26] White, J E 1865 op cit., p 4 para 43.

[27] From J C Hall's treatise on the Sheffield Grinders Disease, quoted by White in his report op cit. p 13-14 For failure to install fan due to noise see also no 26 op cit. p 18 the evidence of Edward Sotheran.

[28] Paragraph 31 White's Report 1865 op cit. p 19.

[29] Any mollusc of the genus *Haliotis*, with a shallow ear-shaped shell having repertory holes, and lined with mother of pearl. (O.E.D. 1990).

[30] Pollard, S 1959 *A History of Labour in Sheffield* Liverpool University Press p 129.

[31] Quoted in Tweedale, G 1993 *Stan Shaw, Master Cutler: The Story of a Sheffield Craftsman.* Hallamshire Press p 62.

[32] Pers. comm. Ken Hawley May 1996.

[33] Vices in the Ken Hawley Collection.

Chapter 11

Internal layout of the cutlery workshops

Introduction

The present-day evidence that survives in workshops, once used by the cutlery industry, shows little detail of the processes of manufacture. Only where permanent features still exist, such as hearths, will it be possible to reach any firm conclusions about the use of the building. To determine how a building functioned, spatial analysis can assist in the interpretation of the inter-relationship of the workspaces.

Rapoport remarked, while commenting on the cultural determinants of form, that vernacular architecture was 'accepted and adjusted to specific requirements ... [making] it very specific to its context and place.[1]' The work of Hillier and Hanson in their *Social Logic of Space*[2] was fundamental in taking Rapoport's ideas and creating an easily understood mapping system to document the internal organisation of structures both buried and standing. Like Rapoport they stated that buildings could be analysed as organisers of space rather than just objects:

> 'Buildings may be comparable to other artefacts in that they assemble elements into a physical object with a certain form; but they are incomparable in that they also create and order the empty volumes of space resulting from that object into a pattern. It is this ordering of space that is the purpose of the building, the physical object itself ... In so far as they are purposeful, buildings are not just objects, but transformations of space through objects.[3]'

Workshop size

Information relating to size has been derived from the field and building books of the Fairbank Collection, from architects plans drawn for the planning office since 1864, from maps and from the author's own surveys[4].

Small-scale buildings

The single-roomed workshops found in these buildings usually had a working space of between 10 to 40 square yards (8–30m^2). They would have been occupied by between one and five or six men or women who either owned but more commonly rented the workspace. In some cases the workbenches were sub-let.

Medium-scale buildings

Included in this category are small-scale 'works' such as Kendal Works (a tenement works), A Wright and Son, Sidney Street and Victoria Works, Gell Street containing a number of rooms varying in size from 7 square yards (6m^2) to 63 square yards (53m^2). They could be occupied by a single firm or let out as separate workshops. This type of building, if occupied by a single firm, may also include some office space which is not seen in the small workshop building.

Waterpowered sites, although externally the same size, would have had one workroom or 'hull', or have been divided into two parts called 'ends' which were then sub-let, as at Shepherd's Wheel. These would have been between 100 square yards and 200 square yards (91.44–182.8m^2) in size. These would be occupied by between 9 and 20 grinders. Waterpowered sites did not contain offices within the hull. At larger works such as Abbeydale, a manager's office was often housed in a separate building.

Large-scale buildings

Large-scale works such as Dixon's Cornish Place, Butcher's Works and Soho Works, like medium scale premises, had a variety of workroom sizes. In the integrated works, office space, large warehouses and packing rooms up to 300 square yards (250m^2) in size can be found. The variety of room sizes reflected the number of processes carried out.

Changes in room sizes, for example the increasing floor space of packing shops in large scale works, however, do not reflect a general change in working conditions. These reflected changes in the marketing rather than the production of goods. It is therefore hypothesised that 'cells'[5] of production did not increase in size from 1750–1900.

Workspace size

The average area in the 1750s calculated from the Fairbank Field books was 42.36 square yards (35.42m^2). In the later building books covering the turn of the nineteenth century the average was 42.76 square yards (35.75m^2). The Fairbank evidence therefore supports the hypothesis that the areas of workspace did not change in the period 1750–1800.

The average 'cell'[6] in the later nineteenth century is 39.33 square yards (32.9m^2). Only the packing shop at Butcher's Wheel can be regarded as exceptionally large. The hypothesis holds true therefore that while structures in which the workshops are arranged become larger over the period, the individual 'cell' of production does not increase.

Room size indicates that the independence of the craftsman continued in the larger works and that larger rooms were likely to have been used as warehouses and for packing rather than for manufacturing goods within the cutlery industry.

Organisation of rooms in the workshops

By assessing the organisation of cells of production it is possible to determine if a building was designed as an integrated or tenement works. The simplest way of evaluating the layout of a building is to use Hillier and Hanson's model which created a systems diagram clearly showing the inter-relationship of 'cells' within a structure by the use of the 'gamma analysis.' These diagrams were called 'justified gamma maps'[7] and they provide a form by which hypotheses can be created about the internal and external relations of each cell 'as part of the general theory of the social logic of space[8]. They consist of circles which represented cells within a structure and lines representing the routeways to other cells. These maps are particularly useful for the analysing small- and medium-scale works and determining whether they were designed to be a tenement or integrated works.

A proposed three-storey grinding wheel in Cambridge Street for example, from the outside may appear to have been designed for one firm. Analysis of the floor plan however shows that (Fig 74) each of the workshops is independent of the others and can only be accessed from the outside.

A building of similar scale to Mr Gaunt's grinding wheel is that occupied by A Wright and Son at 16 Sidney Street (Fig 75). The floor plan shown on Goad's Fire Plans of 1893[9] and the present layout indicate that the building was never designed to be used by more than one firm. The gamma maps however do not indicate the sub-letting of the ground floor to Wilkinson Scissors which now takes place. The relationship between the two firms is complex, for while remaining an independent firm, all of Wilkinson's scissors are sold through A Wright and Son.

Gamma maps are most useful when analysing large and complex buildings. Union Wheel for example, 280ft long, would in other parts of the country such as Manchester[10] or Leicestershire[11] be considered as an integrated site. However on consideration of the floor plan (Fig 76) it is obvious that all the workshops are individual cells of production. Each storey is only accessible from the outside and the workshops have single entrances off a main corridor running through the centre of the building. The evidence for the individual firms comes from documentary evidence which details 24 firms on the first floor alone in the 1920s[12]. Firms also have workshops distributed throughout the building as in the case of Franklin's file cutting firm, Rutherford's cutlery manufactory, and J W Ward's tool manufactory. The variety of trades that were carried out within the building is also significant as it indicates, as suggested above, that there were very few distinguishing characteristics between the trades. Those features that were distinguishable were often portable such as stocks and stiddies, tools and machinery. Unfortunately this building was demolished in the 1970s.

At works such as Cornish Place, and Butcher's Wheel (Fig 77) the floor plans are arranged to benefit the integrated works, i.e. the workrooms are interconnected. In recent times parts of the buildings have been tenanted as the original firms have closed, moved sites or have been incorporated into conglomerates whose main operations lie elsewhere.

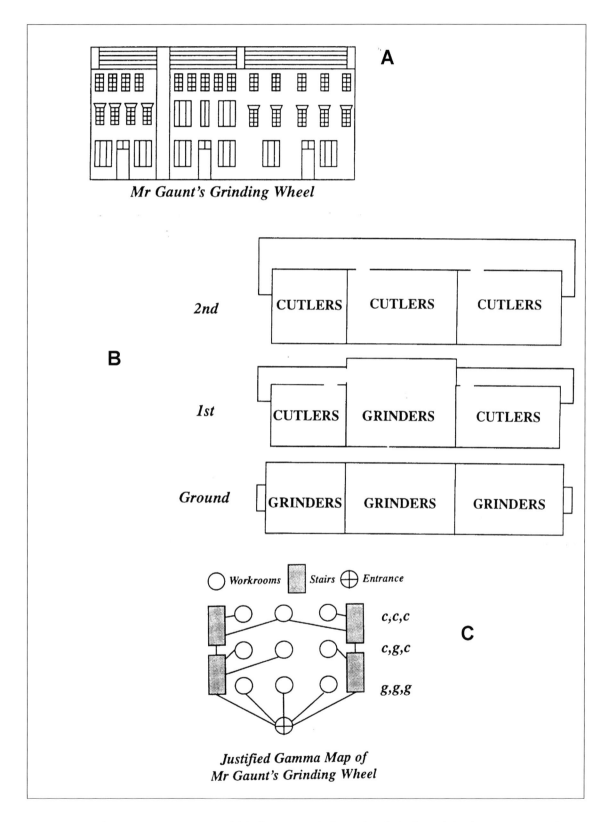

A

Mr Gaunt's Grinding Wheel

B

2nd — CUTLERS | CUTLERS | CUTLERS

1st — CUTLERS | GRINDERS | CUTLERS

Ground — GRINDERS | GRINDERS | GRINDERS

◯ *Workrooms* ▨ *Stairs* ⊕ *Entrance*

C

c,c,c

c,g,c

g,g,g

Justified Gamma Map of
Mr Gaunt's Grinding Wheel

Figure 74 a) Plan and elevation of Mr Gaunt's grinding wheel. At first sight this appears to be an integrated works but closer inspection reveals that each workshop has a separate entrance. b) This is more clearly shown with the aid of a flow diagram. c) A gamma map emphasises the point

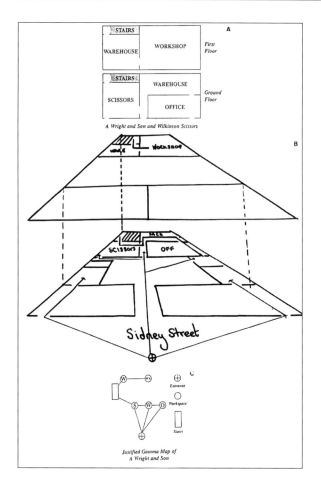

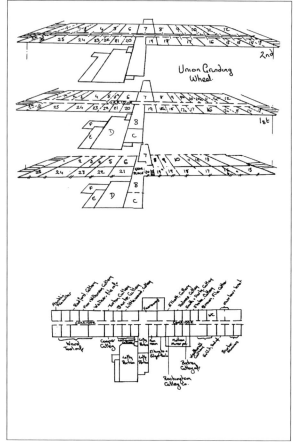

Figure 75 a) A Wright and Son, an integrated works now containing two firms, b) the flow diagram shows the possible movement of goods through the building, c) the gamma map shows clearly that this is an integrated works

Figure 76 The tenement nature of this building is emphasised by the number of firms recorded in the 1920s

Working conditions

Finally working conditions should be considered. To some extent these have already been summarised by looking at the processes and the evidence left behind in the archaeological record. However to understand them, if not to empathise with them, the combination of archaeology with the documentary evidence is essential.

The image that one gains from the documentary sources available is that the workshops were dirty, poorly lit and cold. In section five of the Second Report of the Commissioners on the Employment of Children, which describes the state of the place of work in 1843, paragraph 225 suggests that the:

'workshops require a through draft to carry off the dust, and much of the increased unhealthy nature of grinding [is] owing to the more crowded state of the rooms at the town wheels. Cleanliness is of course out of the question; and nearly equally so in all the Sheffield Trades. The hafting or cutlers shops are in general tolerably airy and healthy, and as coals are cheap, well enough protected from damp.[13,]

In 1865 the Appendix to the Fourth Report written by J E White concluded that little had changed since 1841 when Mr Symons had conducted the research for the 1843 report. He concluded that there had been an increase in the number of wheels within the town in which the workshops were built back to back, thus making the:

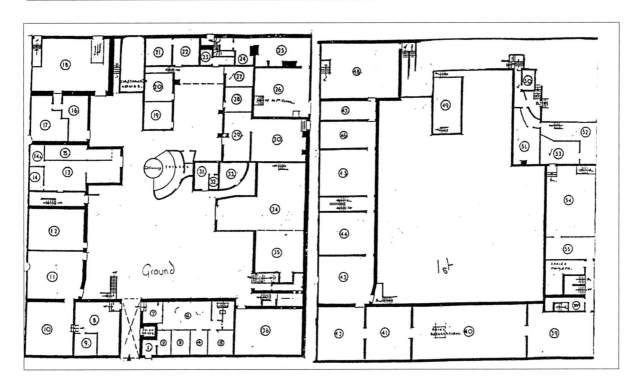

Figure 77 The floor plan of Butcher's Wheel shows that it was designed as an integrated works as the workshops are linked to one another

'rooms or hulls ill-lighted and gloomy; some which I have seen are quite unfit for use. In some the plaster is falling from the ceiling, in others wet is dripping from the floor above, and is sometimes caught by sheets of metal placed to protect the workers beneath. The glass is generally broken out of the windows, and purposely by the grinders to allow the dust to escape and to admit light, which the glass covered by the dirty spray from the grinding, keeps out. This subjects the workers to draughts, and in the winter to severe cold ... The dust is also blown back upon them ... The floor are often sloppy with wet.' [14]

White's portrayal of the other workshops used by the industry is equally damming, referring to them as, 'cramped and ill-arranged ... by all appearances the cleaning and whitewashing etc. are in general much neglected.'[15] Even in 1887 the Annual Report of Her Majesty's Chief Inspector reported that many of the workshops were 'dirty and discreditable' as 'what is every man's business is no man's business,'[16] referring to multi-tenanted workshops where no one took it upon themselves to clean up.

Conditions have not much changed over the past 140 years, for 'little mesters' and 'outworkers'. In Jenkins and McClarence's work those interviewed said that the workshops were 'death traps, with walls, floors, benches and tools thick with grime.'[17] Doris Walsh, who had worked as an acid etcher at Butcher's Wheel, reported that it was 'cold'[18], noisy and dirty[19] and Billy Hukin, an open razor grinder, said that 'the usual workshops you couldn't keep clean. They were draughty and not properly heated. A real muck heap, a lot of places. Oh, I've no time to clean it up, they used to say ...You couldn't keep a place like that clean because there was so much muck flying around, dust and grease. And the whitewashed walls would get filthy.'[20]

When on field visits to redundant buildings such as the upper storeys of Butcher's Wheel, Cornish Place, and Kendal Works and the workshops at 50 Garden Street, the smell of metal, grease and dust still lingers. This feature of the workshops is impossible to record.

Conclusion

The main characteristics seen in the buildings associated with the tableware and cutlery industry and allied trades have been identified here. By means of examples, found in the field and in the documentary evidence, detailed descriptions of these features and how they fitted into the processes involved in the various branches of the trades have been given. Analysis of spatial organisation, using gamma maps, has revealed little new evidence relating to the process of tableware and cutlery manufacture. However it can be used to determine whether larger workshops were designed as integrated or tenement works.

Notes

[1] Rapoport, A 1980 Cultural Determinants of form in King, A D eds *Buildings and Society* Routledge and Kegan London p 285.

[2] Hillier, B and Hanson, J 1984 *The Social Logic of Space* Cambridge.

[3] ibid. p 1.

[4] The definitions are based on those defined above, i.e. based on rateable value.

[5] A 'cell' is a room. The term is used by Hillier and Hanson when describing gamma maps and by the author later in this chapter.

[6] workshop or grinding hull.

[7] ibid. p 143.

[8] ibid. p 143.

[9] 674/B1/24 Sheffield Archives.

[10] Textile industry.

[11] Footwear industry.

[12] Insurance Plans UGW plan 27 Sheffield Archives.

[13] Second report of the Commissioners on the Employment of Children Sessions 1843-5 Vol. XIII IUP reprints, p 34.

[14] Appendix to the Fourth Report - Reports and Evidence of Assistant Commissioners: Report upon the metal manufactures of the Sheffield District by J E. White. 1865 para 42 p 4 IUP reprint.

[15] ibid para 45 p 4.

[16] British Parliamentary Papers Industrial Revolution, Factories, Report 31/10/1887 p 36.

[17] Jenkins, C and McClarence, S 1989 *On a Knife Edge* Sheffield Libraries and Information Services, SCL Publishing Sheffield p xii.

[18] ibid, p 27.

[19] ibid, p 32.

[20] ibid, p 62.

Chapter 12

Summary

The characteristics of the workshops of the tableware and cutlery industry have been considered by analysis of their location, design and internal features and are summarised here.

The predominant use of the vernacular style rather than architect designs for the majority of workshops emphasises the low cost and speculative nature of the buildings. Only the large integrated works have any form of architectural embellishment designed to impress clients, the local community, or in some cases retain the confidence of shareholders. However even these larger works often retain the vernacular style for workshops behind the frontage. This served to emphases the superior status of the manager compared with the workforce and is particularly noticeable at Eye Witness Works, Milton Street.

Structurally, the workshop buildings have little to distinguish them from other domestic or industrial buildings. This is another indication that many were speculatively built to suit the needs of a wide range of trades. However within the cutlery industry the use of particular 'cells' of production by branches of the trades maybe identified from the windows that can be found in the region. In particular buildings used for grinding and file cutting have distinguishing characteristics. The lack of taking-in doors, a common feature in the textile and boot and shoe industries, emphasises the small scale on which many firms worked.

Internally, the buildings can offer more information about the branch of the tableware and cutlery industry for which it was used and how the building was organised. Evidence for hearths, for example, suggests that a workshop has been used for forging, troughs or solid floor in an upper storey indicate grinding, while the lack of any of these features suggests that the finishing of cutlery took place. It is however unusual to find the characteristic tools of particular trades, such as the hammers, parsers and stiddies, leg frames and stocks which were usually removed when a firm closed.

By assessing the relationship of rooms within medium- and large-scale works it is possible to identify whether a building was designed as an integrated or tenement works. Where the rooms are interconnected it suggests that a building was erected for the use of one firm. If workshops can only be accessed from an external staircase or central corridor, a different firm is likely to have occupied each 'cell'. However, even in these larger works, whether integrated or tenement, the evidence suggests that individual workspaces were no larger than in the smaller workshop structures. Larger firms, taking charge of their own advertising and sales rather than using factors like the smaller firms, led to the development of larger workrooms such as warehouses and packing shops. Analysis of room size and organisation within a building can miss evidence for the complex sub-letting which took place of rooms and benches within the workshops and factories.

It can be concluded therefore that the majority of workshops utilised by the tableware and cutlery industry were speculatively built, suggesting that the specialist needs of the industry were few. The slow adoption of power by the industry suggests, that like many other industries, the Industrial Revolution was about slow development and continuity rather than rapid change.

This analysis has gone some way to making the identification of buildings used by the industry easier and has demonstrated that even where documentary evidence does not exist the structures themselves identify the branch of the trade which occupied the workshop and the type of firm, whether it be large-scale or an independent 'Little Mester'. Recent surveys carried out by English Heritage has added the detailed work required to analysis further the cutlery and related steel works possible in the near future[1]. Examples of recent reports are those for Truro Works, Cornish Place and Butcher's Wheel[2].

A future for the remaining cutlery workshops?

This analysis was carried out in the early 1990s and already some of the sites mentioned in the text have been demolished. Although demolition may at first sight seem the best possible option, improving skills in renovation, refurbishment and conversion means that conversion can be a profitable alternative, which also means some preservation of the historic environment.

In the future what remains of the workshops of the cutlery industry will be the 'product of the fashions prevailing ... arrived at by consensus, *but* a consensus of the taste forming elite which will vary over space and time'[3]. The future of Sheffield's workshops depends on heritage planning being 'proactive', making use of conserved buildings in a contemporary role. Allowing the 'pendulum [to] swing too far so that buildings of dubious value are being propped up at great expense'[4] should be guarded against. It should be remembered that what survives today is the result of constant evolution; no building has been frozen in time, although walking into the courtyard of Butcher's Wheel, one sometimes feels that here working practices have changed little over the last 100 years.

No city can be turned into a museum of its past; to suggest that all workshops connected to the tableware and cutlery industry need preserving so that Sheffield can remember its roots denies the continuity of the industry into the new millennium. Preserving the buildings will not preserve the trade. If the industry is to continue, it must adjust to current market forces, diversify its products, and maintain the quality for which it is renowned. However the name of 'Sheffield' alone will not sell goods, no matter how fiercely it is defended against fraudulent use. Tableware and cutlery firms currently in operation will have to continue to advertise and come up with innovative ideas.

Some buildings will be and should be retained to remind future generations of the past and help them to plan for a better future. The reuse of old buildings has in some cases helped to promote companies by giving them a distinctive image, rather than occupying a prefabricated building which blends in with the rest of late twentieth century industrial design. Inevitably some will become museums, but others will

continue to evolve through new uses as they have done for a century and a half. Planners should strive to encourage innovative uses that perhaps leave only the external characteristics intact. The workshops of the cutlery industry were largely built by speculators for a multiplicity of purposes and therefore there should be no problems, where they are still structurally sound, to find a useful purpose for the surviving buildings in the twenty-first century, especially as there is a return to the entrepreneurial small firm and in Sheffield a growing need for affordable and 'designer' accommodation close to the city centre.

To end on an optimistic note, the cutlery industry today continues to thrive with world leaders such as Richardson's and Taylor's Eye Witness still based in Sheffield. In total there are 110 firms recorded by the Cutlery and Allied Trades Research Association (CATRA), employing 5400 people[5]. Half of these firms continue to occupy the traditional buildings of the industry built in the nineteenth century.

Notes

[1] A summary of recent findings has been published by English Heritage 2001 '*One Great Workshop': The buildings of the Sheffield Metal Trades*. Plans and photographs are lodged with English Heritage National Monuments Record.

[2] RCHME reports 1995-1996.

[3] Ashworth, G J 1991 op cit p 8.

[4] Goody, B 1982 op cit p 8.

[5] Figures for Standard Industrial Classification 28.6 Cutlery, tools and general hardware, Annual Employment Survey September 1995, Office of National Statistics.

List of sites mentioned in the text

RURAL

Alpha Works, Stannington	SK301883
Cross Hill 132, Ecclesfield	SK361935
Crown Works, Ecclesfield	SK357937
James Vicker's Workshop 643 Stannington Road, Stannington	SK355868
Nook Lane, Franklin Cottage, Stannington	SK309886
9, Woodside Lane Grenoside	SK332943
Topside, Grenoside	SK329939
Back Lane, Grenoside	SK329939
Rock House, Nethergate, Stannington	SK301882
Scythe Works, Ford	SK441384
Syke Farm, Dungworth	SK288894

SHEFFIELD

A Wright and Son, Arundel Street	SK355867
Abbeydale Industrial Hamlet	SK326820
Aberdeen Works, Trafalgar Street	SK349872
Alpha Works (Harrison Bros and Howson), Carver Street	SK352873
Anglo Works, Trippet Lane	SK352874
Billy Thornton's Workshop, Canning Street	SK349872
Butcher's Wheel, Arundel Street	SK355868
Challenge Works, Arundel Street	SK355867
Cornish Place (Dixons), Green Lane	SK351883
Cutlers' Hall, Church Street	SK354876
Eye Witness Works, Milton Street	SK348867
Garden Street 52-54 (Stan Shaw's)	SK347876
Globe Works, Penistone Road	SK348883
Howard Hotel, Howard Street	SK357869
Hutton Buildings, West Street	SK348874
Kendal Works, Carver Street	SK352873
Kirkansons's, Garden Street	SK347876
Kutrite Works	SK351877
Leah's Yard, Cambridge Street	SK352872
Morton's, West Street	SK347873
Sheaf Works, Maltravers Street	SK361877
Sylvester Works (Elliotts), Sylvester Street	SK354865
Truro Works, Matilda Street	SK357867
Venture Works, Arundel Street	SK356869

WATERPOWERED SITES

Clough Wheels, Sheaf	SK356861
Frank Wheel, Rivelin	SK300874
Hind Wheel, Rivelin	SK309876
Holme Head Wheel, Rivelin	SK315881
Holme Wheel, Porter	SK327858
Ibbotson Wheel, Porter	SK319857
Kelham Island	SK352882
Little London Wheel, Rivelin	SK314880
Little London Wheel, Sheaf	SK347847
Malin Bridge Wheel, Loxley	SK325894
Moscar Wheel, Sheaf	SK339836
Mousehole Forge, Rivelin	SK325891
Plonk Wheel, Rivelin	SK307876
Pond Forge, Sheaf	SK359874
Rivelin Bridge Wheel, Rivelin	SK322885
Roscoe Wheel, Rivelin	SK317883
Second Coppice, Rivelin	SK294873
Shepherd's Wheel, Porter	SK317856
Third Coppice, Rivelin	SK295873
Upper Coppice, Rivelin	SK293873
Upper Cut Wheel, Rivelin	SK312878
Wadsley Forge, Don	SK336905
Walkley Bank Tilt, Rivelin	SK324888
Wolf Wheel, Rivelin	SK302875

POSTSCRIPT

COMMON PEOPLE: UNCOMMON SKILLS

JAMES SYMONDS

'It is now widely recognised that no history can be balanced if, in a concern with the mighty and the eminent, it neglects the common man. Since he himself rarely put pen to paper, this history must in the main be recovered by sifting traditions, passed on from one generation to another and by examining what others, with more or less fairness and understanding, have said or written about him...'

(Pollard 1959, vii)

In the forty-three years that have elapsed since the publication of Sidney Pollard's ground-breaking work, A *History of Labour in Sheffield* many changes have befallen the city and its people. As this volume goes to press the Heart of the City Project, a government inspired 'urban renaissance' initiative, is transforming the area surrounding the town hall. Elegant fountains now play on the site of the former Peace Gardens, the glass walls and wooden superstructure of a new Winter Gardens complex is slowly taking shape, resembling the skeleton of a strange prehistoric creature. All of this is a far cry from the smoke-wreathed skies and soot-stained facades that dominated the skyline of Sheffield as recently as the early 1960s.

The nature of work has also changed. Between Arundel Gate and the Midland Railway Station, Sheffield City Council has established a Cultural Industries Quarter. The quarter includes the famous Butcher Wheel, and several other buildings formerly used as cutlery workshops. New life is being breathed into these buildings by television production companies and other firms working in creative media. The way in which space is rented and used by these new industries in former industrial buildings stimulates an analogy. It has much in common with the way in which the 'Little Mesters' organised their trade: shared occupancy of tenement blocks by multiple tenants, flexible production methods geared to supplying several different clients, and a pattern of work determined by the length of contract and agreed deadline for completion. It may be that the

observance of 'Saint Monday' also persists within some of the smaller creative partnerships when a particularly lucrative or high status contract has been successfully completed.

Sidney Pollard relied upon the 'sifting of traditions' and the analysis of handwritten and published sources for the compilation of his history. In his day, the dialogue between archaeologists and documentary historians was minimal, and was often conducted with a feeling of antipathy. When they were not working abroad, in search of classical civilisations, British archaeologists were mostly concerned with problems relating to the prehistoric and Roman settlement of these islands. In 1959, the Society for Medieval Archaeology had only been established for a little over two years and the formation of a Society for Post-medieval Archaeology was almost nine years away. Even the very idea of studying the English urban past by means of archaeological techniques was in its infancy[1]. It is therefore not surprising, if somewhat regrettable, that the study of post-medieval urban artisans and workers, such as those employed in the Sheffield cutlery and tableware trades, excited no interest among contemporary archaeologists. We are at least fortunate that writers such as G I H Lloyd and J B Himsworth, who possessed an intimate knowledge of the cutlery and tableware industry, provided detailed descriptions of working practices in the first half of the twentieth century.

Lloyd and Himsworth were motivated by an intense pride in the achievements of Sheffield craftsmen and were also, in a sense, mourning the loss of traditional working methods, and the substitution of increasingly mechanised forms of production. Of course times change, and to modify Michel Foucault's famous phrase, every age has its *archaeology*. Today, historical archaeologists are fascinated by the creation of the modern world and frequently engage in the study of industrial processes. The impact of modernity upon material life is widely recognised as a significant area of archaeological research. In Sheffield, brownfield sites, the physical accumulation of more than two centuries of industrialisation, are now routinely investigated by archaeologists prior to redevelopment. Above ground, efforts are made to survey and photograph industrial buildings before they undergo a change of use.

The citizens of Sheffield retain a burning pride in the achievements of their cutlery and tableware industry, but as each year passes the memories and experiences of the individual workers who participated in the industry are being slowly eroded. It is still possible to see young children being shown exhibits relating to cutlery by older relatives at Kelham Island Museum. However, these days the relative will most likely be a grandparent rather than a parent. The contribution that can be made by historical archaeology in integrating all of the sources of evidence for this once great industry, and in maintaining a social memory, is therefore of growing importance.

This may imply that the industrial past has been forgotten. In recent years, however, there has been a proliferation of heritage attractions celebrating the former South Yorkshire metals trades. The Magna Centre at Rotherham takes steel manufacture as its theme, and the Millennium Galleries in central Sheffield display exquisite cutlery of world class quality. The industrial past has not been forgotten, it has simply been repackaged to attract a new generation of heritage tourists to the region. In many ways, this rebranding is part of a more general shift in Britain from manufacturing to service industries. The capacity for technological innovation and precision in metalwork that characterised Sheffield workshops in former years is, nevertheless, still in evidence. The latest manifestation of this is the selection of Sheffield as a centre for the manufacture of aerospace components in the twenty-first century.

It is hoped that this volume will serve as a worthy introductory guide to the historical archaeology of the Sheffield cutlery and tableware industry. As old buildings are refurbished, and in some cases cleared for new, a wealth of information on these trades is being steadily accumulated by archaeological investigations. Future volumes in this series will explore the above and below ground archaeology of Sheffield's industrial buildings, with case studies of archaeological excavations at Thomas Turner's Suffolk Road cutlery works and other sites. Steel will also figure prominently in this series. It is anticipated that volumes will be produced incorporating recent archaeological work on early steel cementation and crucible furnaces at Riverside Exchange, and the Jessops' Works at Brightside, Sheffield.

Notes

[1] Work had taken place in the 1940s and early 1950s on sites of Roman and post-Roman date in Canterbury., Cirencester and St Albans. The potential value of an archaeological approach had perhaps been most clearly demonstrated by Professor W F Grimes, who led a campaign of excavations on bomb-damaged sites in the City of London, commencing in 1947. See W F Grimes (1968) *The Excavation of Roman and Medieval London*, London.

BIBLIOGRAPHY

Abercrombie, P 1924. *Sheffield a civic survey and suggestions towards a Development Plan.* Liverpool: Liverpool University Press

Addy, S O 1888. *A Glossary of Words used in the Neighbourhood of Sheffield.* Sheffield.

Addy, S O 1925. Medieval English Cutlery. *Transactions of the Hunter Archaeological Society.* Vol. III, No. 1, 9–23

Agricola, G 1556 *De Re Metallica.* Hoover H C and L H Hoover (trans.) 1950. Facsimile. New York

Aldcroft, D H and M J Freeman 1983. *Transport in the Industrial Revolution.* Manchester: Manchester University Press

Alfrey, J and T Putman 1992 *The Industrial Heritage: Managing Resources and Uses.* London: Routledge

Allison, A 1946. Crucible Steel *Iron and Steel.* April, 135–138

Anon. 1897. The Architecture of our Large Provincial Towns: X Sheffield. *The Builder.* Vol. LXXIII. Oct, 273–280.

Anon. n.d. *The Company of Cutlers in Hallamshire in the County of York.* Sheffield: The Cutlers' Company

Anon. *A Study of Sheffield.* Read Feb 11th 1939 to the Manchester Geographical Society. Unpubl. *Art and Evolution of Cutlery*, A Goldsmiths'

Ashworth, G J 1991. *Heritage Planning.* Netherlands : Geo Pers

Aspinall, P 1977. *The size and structure of the house building industry in Victorian Sheffield.* Working Paper No 49. Centre for Urban and Regional Studies University of Birmingham

Balgarnie, R 1970. *Sir Titus Salt: Baronet*

Ball, C 1992. *Millwrights in Sheffield and South Yorkshire 1550–1900.* MA University of Sheffield Division of Adult Continuing Education. Unpubl.

Barker, T and D Gerhold 1993. *The rise and rise of Road Transport 1700–1990.* London: Macmillan

Barnes, J n.d. *Ruskin in Sheffield.* Sheffield

Barraclough, K C 1984. *Steel making before Bessemer: Volume 1 Blister Steel The Birth of an Industry.* London: The Metals Society

Barraclough, K C 1990. *Steel making 1850–1900.* The Institute of Metals

Barsby, P.1996. *The Quarrying and Use of Stone in the Sheffield Area from the 15th Century* MA University of Sheffield (D.A.C.E.). Unpubl.

Barton, K 1968. The origins of the Society for Post-medieval Archaeology. *Post-medieval Archaeology* I, p 102–103.

Bayliss, D 1995. The South Yorkshire Industrial History Society, *A Guide to the Industrial History of South Yorkshire* Association for Industrial Archaeology: Redruth

Beauchamp V A 1996. *The workshops of the Cutlery Industry in Hallamshire 1750–1900.* PhD Thesis 9067, University of Sheffield. Unpubl

Beaver, H 1936. The Localisation of Industry *Geography* 21, 191–196.

Beveridge, W et al 1968. *Prices and Wages in England from the twelfth to the nineteenth centuries.* London: Cass

Binfield Cyde et al. (eds) 1993. *The History of Sheffield 1843–1993.* Sheffield: Sheffield Academic Press

Binfield, C 1997. The Cutlers' company and the churches. In Binfield, C and Hey, D (eds) *Mesters to Masters: A History of the Company of Cutlers in Hallamshire.* Oxford: Oxford University Press, 284–311

Blackwell, D H 1973. *The Growth and Decline of the Scythe and Sickle Trades in Hallamshire.* PhD thesis University of Sheffield. Unpubl

Boland, P and P Collins 1994. A Strategy for Industrial Archaeology in the Black Country. *Industrial Archaeology Review.* Vol XVI no 2, 157–170

Bostwick, D 1985. *Sheffield in Tudor and Stuart Times.* Sheffield

Bostwick, D 1989. *The Great Sheffield Picture Show: Paintings of Sheffield and its People, 1800–1900.* Sheffield

Braverman, H 1974. *Labor and Monopoly Capital.* New York: Monthly Review Press

Brockman, H A N 1974. *The British Architect in Industry 1841–1940.* London: George Allen and Unwin

Brown, W. (ed.) 1894. Yorkshire Lay Subsidy 25 Edward I. *Yorkshire Archaeological Society Record Series* 16, 76

Brown, P (ed.) 2001. *British Cutlery: an illustrated history of design, evolution and use.* York.

Brunskill, R W 1990. *Brick Building in Britain.* London: Victor Gollancz

Buchanan, R A 1972. *Industrial Archaeology in Britain.* Harmondsworth: Penguin

Buckatzsch, E J 1976. Places of origin of a group of immigrants into Sheffield 1624–1799. In Clark, P (ed.) *The Early Modern Town: A Reader.* New York: Longman and the Open University Press, 292–296

Byrant, H 1930. *Modern Building Practice.* London: Caxton

Bythell, D 1987. *The Sweated Trades.* London: Batsford Academic

Caffyn, L 1986. *Workers housing in West Yorkshire 1750–1920.* London: RCHME Supplementary Series 9

Cass, J 1989. The Flood Claims: A Post Script to the Sheffield Flood of March 11th and 12th 1864. *Transactions of the Hunter Archaeological Society* 15, 29–37

Chalklin, C W 1974. *The Provincial Towns of Georgian England: A Study of the Building Process 1740–1820.* London: Arnold

Chapman, S D 1971. Fixed capital formation in the British Cotton manufacturing industry. In Higgins, J P P and S Pollard (eds) *Aspects of Capital Investment in Great Britain 1750–1850: Report of a Conference held at the University of Sheffield January 1969.* London: Methuen, 57–119

Ching, F D K 1991. *Building Construction Illustrated.* New York: Van Nostrand Reinhold

Ching, F D K 1995. *A Visual Dictionary of Architecture.* New York: Van Nostrand Reinhold

Clark, C 1994. Ticking Boxes or Telling Stories. In *Managing the Industrial Heritage.* London: Routledge, 45–49

Clarke, L 1992. *Building Capitalism.* London: Routledge

Coleman, D C 1975. *Industry in Tudor and Stuart England.* London: Collectors Books

Cooney, E W 1960. Long Waves in Building: The British Economy of the Nineteenth Century. *Economic History Review* XIII, 2

Cooper, C 1961. Sheffield Works: Steam engines in 1835. *The Hub* 10, 3, 19–23

County History*: Leicestershire* Vol. IV. Oxford: Oxford University Press

Cowgill, J M de Neergaard and N Griffiths 1987. *Knives and Scabbards.* London: HMSO

Craddock, P T and M L Wayman 2000. The Development of Ferrous Metallurgical Technology. In Waydon, M L (ed.) *The Ferrous Metallurgy of Early Clocks and Watches: Studies in Post Medieval Steel.* London

Cranstone, D 2001. Industrial Archaeology: Manufacturing a New Society. In Newman, R D Cranstone and C Howard-Davis. *The Historical Archaeology of Britain, c 1540–1900.* Stroud: Sutton Publishing, 183–211

Crocker, G 1991. The Godalming Knitting Industry and its workplaces. *Industrial Archaeology Review* XVI, 1, 33–54

Crossley, D et al 1985. *Water Power on the Sheffield Rivers.* Huddersfield: Charlesworth and Co

Crossley, D 1990 *Post Medieval Archaeology in Britain.* Leicester: Leicester University Press

Crouzet, F 1990. *Britain Ascendant: Comparative Studies in Franco-British Economic History.* Cambridge: Cambridge University Press

Cutlers' Company archive, C6/1 and C6/2, Apprenticeship and freedoms records

Cutlers' Company archive, D19/1-5, The Storehouse records, 1680s

Cutlers' Company archive, reference S1/1-3, Scissorsmiths' Covenant

Danile, R W 1934. A reproach to Sheffield: Deplorable Conditions in Factories and Workshops. Dimness Glare and Inefficiency. *The Electrician.* Nov. 23, 64–6

Davidoff, L and C Hall 1987. (reprinted 1994), *Family Fortunes: Men and Women of the English Middle Class 1780–1850.* London: Routledge

Davis, M 1989. The archaeology of standing structures. *The Australian Journal of Historical Archaeology* 5, 54–64

Davis, R 1972. *The Rise of the English Shipping Industry in the 17th and 18th centuries.* Newton Abbott: David and Charles

Department of National Heritage 1995. *Protecting Our Heritage: A consultation Document on the built heritage of England and Wales.* London: HMSO

Dept of Environment 1991. *Planning Policy Guidance Note 16.* London: HMSO

Dept of Environment 1994. *Planning Policy Guidance Note 15.* London: HMSO

Derry, J C 1914. *The Story of Sheffield.* London: Pitman and Sons

Dixon, R and S Muthesius 1993 *Victorian Architecture.* London: Thames and Hudson

Dodd, A E and E M Dodd 1980. *Peakland Roads and Trackways.* Moorland Publishing

Doughty, M (ed.) 1986. *Building the Industrial City.* Leicester: Leicester University Press

DuBoff, R 1967. The Introduction of Electric Power in American Manufactory. *Economic History Review* XX, 509–518

Dyson, B R 1936. *A Glossary of Words and Dialect Formerly Used in the Sheffield Trades.* Sheffield. (Reprinted 1979) Sheffield Trades Historical Society

Edgington, D 1996. *Old Stationary Engines.* Aylesbury: Shire Publications

Egan, G and R L Michael (eds) 1999. *Old and New Worlds.* Oxford: Oxbow Books

English Heritage 2001. Brighter Future for Sheffield's Historic Metal Trades Buildings. *English Heritage News Release* 943/11/01. 20th November 2001

English Heritage 1995. *Statutory List of buildings of Special Architectural or Historic Interest.* English Heritage

English Heritage 1995. *Conserving the inheritance of industry: English Heritage Grants for industrial archaeology 1984–1993.* London: English Heritage

English Heritage and Sheffield City Council 1995. *Historic Buildings in Sheffield: Understanding Listing.*

Faulkner, D 1991. *Chain-making and Nail-making: the domestic industries of the Black Country.* BA dissertation, University of Leicester. Unpubl

Favell, N 1996. *The Economic Development of Sheffield and the Growth of the Town c 1740–1820.* PhD, University of Sheffield. Unpubl

Fuller, T 1987 *The Worthies of England.* London: Folio Society. Cited in Hey, D The Establishment of the Cutlers' Company. In Binfield, C and D Hey (eds) 1997 *Mesters to Masters: A History of the Company of Cutlers in Hallamshire.* Oxford: Oxford University Press, 12–25

Funari, P P A M Hall and S Jones (eds) 1999. *Historical Archaeology: Back from the Edge.* London and New York: Routledge

Gaskell, S M 1983. *National Statues and the Local Community: Building Control by National Legislation and the Introduction of Local Bye-Laws in Victorian England.* British Association for Local History

Gatty, A 1873 *Sheffield Past and Present.* Sheffield

Gerhold, D 1993. Packhorses and wheeled vehicles. *Journal of Transport History* XIIII, 1, 1–26

Gerhold, D 1996. Productivity change in road transport before and after turn-piking 1690–1840 *Economic History Review,* XLIX, 3, 491–515

Giles, C 1996. *Historic Building Report: Butcher's Wheel, 72 Arundel Street, Sheffield.* London: RCHME

Giles, C and I Goodall 1992. *Yorkshire Textile Mills 1770–1930.* London: RCHME

Gille, B (trans. Greaves R) 1971. *The Fontana Economic History of Europe Vol. 3 Section 4: Banking and Industrialisation in Europe 1730–1914.* London: Fontana

Girtin, T 1975. *The Mark of the Sword.* London

Goodall, I 1996. *Historic Building Report: Cornish Place, Cornish Street Sheffield.* Swindon: RCHME

Goodfellow, A W 1942. Sheffield Turnpikes in the 18th century. *Transactions of the Hunter Archaeological Society,* V, 73. Cited in Lars Magnusson, 1994. *The Contest for Control: Metal Industries in Sheffield, Solingen, Remscheid and Eskilstuna during Indusrialisation.*Oxford, Providence, U.S.A.: Berg Publishers, 46

Goody, B 1982. *New Use for old stones.* Strasbourg: Council of Europe.

Gould, S 1995. Industrial Archaeology and the Neglect of Humanity. In Palmer, M and P Neverson (eds) *Managing the Industrial Heritage.* Leicester: Leicester Archaeological Monographs 2, University of Leicester, 49–54

Grayson, R 1994. *Industrial Organisation in Nineteenth Century Sheffield.* Unpubl

Grayson, R 1994. *More Myth than Reality: The independent artisan in nineteenth century Sheffield.* Unpubl

Grayson, R with Hawley, K 1995. *Knifemaking in Sheffield and the Hawley Collection.* Sheffield: PAVIC

Green, E 1989. *Banking: An Illustrated History.* Oxford: Phaidon

Gunter, G 1994. Location patterns of Manufacture in Toronto in the early 1880s. *Urban History Review* XXII, 2, 113–139

Hadfield, C 1972. *The Canals of Yorkshire and NE England.* Newton Abbot: David and Charles

Hall, T W 1928. *Descriptive Catalogue of Sheffield Manorial Records.* Vol.II. Sheffield

Hammond, M 1985. *Bricks and Brickmaking.* Aylesbury: Shire Publications Ltd

Harrison, S 1864. *A Complete History of the Great Flood at Sheffield.* Sheffield, republished 1974

Haslam, A P 1909. *Electricity in Factories and Workshops.* London: Crosby Lockwood and Son

Hatfield, J and J Hatfield 1974. *The Oldest Sheffield Plater.* Huddersfield: Advertiser Press

Hattersley, R 1990. *The Makers Mark.* London: Pan Books

Hawson, H K 1968. *Sheffield: The Growth of a City 1893–1926.* Sheffield: J W Northend

Hayes, G 1995. Reprint 2nd edition. *Stationary Steam Engines.* Aylesbury: Shire Publications Ltd

Hayward, J F 1956. *English Cutlery 16th-18th Century.* London: HMSO

Haywood, J and W Lee 1848. *Report on the Sanitary Conditions of the Borough of Sheffield.* Sheffield

Hey, D 1972. *The Rural Metalworkers of the Sheffield Region.* Leicester: Leicester University Press Dept of English Local History Occasional Paper 2nd series

Hey, D 1980. *Packmen, Carriers and Packhorse Roads.* Leicester: Leicester University Press

Hey, D 1990. The origins and growth of the Hallamshire Cutlery and Allied Trades. In Chartres, J and D Hey (eds) *English Rural Society: Essays in Honour of Joan Thirsk.* Cambridge: Cambridge University Press, 343–367

Hey, D 1991. *The Fiery Blades of Hallamshire.* Leicester: Leicester University Press

Hey, D 1994. *Scythesmiths and Sicklesmiths: the origin of local crafts.* Lecture given at the Cutlers' Hall. Unpubl

Hey, D 1998. *A History of Sheffield.* Lancaster: Carnegie Publishing

Hey, D 1997. The establishment of the Cutlers' Company. In Binfield, C and D Hey (eds.) *Mesters to Masters: A History of the Company of Cutlers in Hallamshire.* Oxford: Oxford University Press, 12–25

Hey, D and J Unwin 1993. *The Cutlers of Hallamshire 1624–1699.* Sheffield: University of Sheffield, Division of Adult Continuing Education

Hey, D et al (eds) 1993. *A History of Sheffield 1843–1993: Society.* Sheffield: Sheffield Academic Press

Higgins, D M 1997. Trade Marks and the Defence of Sheffield. In Binfield, C and D Hey, (eds) 1997. *Mesters to Masters: A History of the Company of Cutlers in Hallamshire.* Oxford: Oxford University Press, 85–114

Hillier, B and J Hanson 1984. *The Social Logic of Space.* Cambridge: Cambridge University Press

Himsworth, J 1953. *The Story of Cutlery.* London

Hogg, 1958. *Footwear Manufacture*

Holderness, B A 1976. Credit in English Rural Society before the nineteenth century with special reference to the period 1650–1720. *The Agricultural History Review.* 24, II, 97–109

Holderness, B A 1973. Elizabeth Parkin and her investments, 1733–66. Aspects of the Sheffield money market in the eighteenth *century. Transactions of the Hunter Archaeological Society,* 10, 81–87

Holland, G C 1843. *The Vital Statistics of Sheffield.* London: Tyas

Hudson, P 1983. *Landholding and organisation of Textile manufacture in Yorkshire Rural Townships 1660–1810.* In Berg, M (ed.) *Manufacture in Town and Country.* Cambridge: Cambridge University Press, 261–289

Hudson, P 1986. *The Genesis of Industrial Capita.* Cambridge:Cambridge University Press.

Hunter, J (revised by A Gatty) 1869. *Hallamshire the History and Topography of the Parish of Sheffield.* London

Hunter, J 1829. *The Hallamshire Glossary,* facsimile reprint, 1983 Sheffield

Hutton, W S 1900. *The Modernised Templeton.* London: Crosby Lockwood and Son

Jenkins, C and McClarence, S 1989. *On a Knife Edge.* Sheffield: SCL Publishing

Jenkins, D T 1975. *The West Riding Wool Textile Industry 1750–1835. A Study of Capital Formation.* Wiltshire: Pasold Research Fund

Johnson, M 1993. *Housing Culture.* London: UCL Press

Johnson, M 1996. *An Archaeology of Capitalism.* Oxford: Blackwells, 12

Jones, E 1985. *ndustrial Architecture in Britain 1750–1939.* London: Batsford

Jones, G P and Townsend, H 1953. The rise and present prospects of the Sheffield cutlery industry. *International Cutler.* Vol. 3/1 (March), 18–20

Jones, M (ed.) 1997. *Aspects of Sheffield: Discovering Local History.* Sheffield: Wharncliffe Publishing Limited

Jones, M 1993. *Sheffield's Woodland Heritage.* Rotherham: Green Tree Publications

Karskens, G 1999. *Inside the Rocks: The Archaeology of a Neighbourhood.* Alexandria, NSW: Hale & Ironmonge, 54

Kellet, J R 1958. Breakdown of Gild and Corporation Control over the Handicraft and Retail Trade in London. *Economic History Review, Second Series X, 3,* 381–394

Kerr, H and M Palmer 1994. *The nineteenth century silk-ribbon weaving industry of Coventry and North Warwickshire.* University of Leicester 3rd year dissertation. Unpubl

Lamb, J P 1936. *A Guide to the Fairbank Collection of Maps, Plans and Surveyors Books and Correspondence.* Sheffield City Libraries

Lancaster University Archaeological Unit 1995. *MPP Industrial Monuments Specification*

Leader, R E n.d. *A Century of Thrift: An Historical Sketch of the Sheffield Savings Bank 1819–1919.* Sheffield: Northend

Leader, R E 1901. *Sheffield in the Eighteenth Century.* Sheffield

Leader, R E 1903. *Surveyors and Architects of the Past in Sheffield: A lecture.* Unpublished text: Sheffield Local Studies Library

Leader, R E 1905. *History of the Cutlers' Company in Hallamshire* Pawson and Brailsford Sheffield

Leader, R E 1905. *History of the Company of Cutlers in Hallamshire.* Vol. 1. Sheffield

Leader, R E 1906. *History of the Company of Cutlers in Hallamshire.* Vol. II. Sheffield

Linstrum, D 1978. *West Yorkshire Architects and Architecture.* London: Lund Humphries

Linton, M (ed.) 1956. *Sheffield and Its Region: A Scientific and Historical Survey.* London: British Association for the Advancement of Science

Lloyd G I H 1913. *The Cutlery Trades.* London. Reprinted 1968, London: Cass Library of Industrial Classics, 87–92

Lloyd-Jones, R and M J Lewis 1983. Industrial Structure and firm growth: the Sheffield Iron and Steel Industry 1880–1901. *Business History* 25, 260–262

Magnusson, L 1994. *The Contest for Control: Metal Industries in Sheffield, Solingen, Remscheid and Eskilstuna during Industrialisation.* Oxford, Providence, U.S.A: Berg Publishers

Maiwald, K 1954. An Index of Building Costs in the United Kingdom 1845–1930. *Economic History Review,* seven, 187–203

Mantoux, P translated by M Vernon 1929. *The Industrial Revolution in the 18th century.* London: J Cape

Marshall, R J 1993. *A History of the City of Sheffield.* Sheffield: Sheffield Academic Press, 17–34

Mathias, P 1993 (reprint) 2nd edition. *The First Industrial Nation.* London: Routledge

Melton, V L 1973. Trade Unionism and the Sheffield Outrages. *Local History Sheet, no. 6,* Sheffield

Middleton, G A T (ed) 1900–1924. *Modern Buildings, their planning, construction and equipment.* Caxton

Miller, W T 1949. *The Watermills of Sheffield,* (4th edition). Sheffield: Pawson and Brailsford

Moore, S and G Tweedale 1997. The Cutlery Collection in the Cutlers' Hall. In Binfield, C and D Hey (eds) *Mesters to Masters: A History of the Company of Cutlers in Hallamshire.* Oxford: Oxford University Press, 205

Moore, S 1999. *Cutlery for the Table*

Musson, A E 1976. Industrial Motive Power in the UK 1800–70. *Economic History Review,* 2nd Series XXIX, 415–439

Mynors, C 1995. *Listed Buildings and Conservation Areas.* London: FT Law and Tax Pearson Professional Ltd

Nassaney, M S and M R Abel Lessons from New England's Nineteenth-century Cutlery Industry'. In Delle, J S A, Mrozowski and R Paynter *Lines That Divide: Historical Archaeologies of Race, Class, and Gender.* Knoxville: University of Tennessee Press, 239–276

Newbould, H B 1930. *Modern Building Practice.* London: Caxton

Newton, L, *The Financing of Manufacturing in the Sheffield Region.* PhD Thesis, University of Leicester. Unpubl

Nicholson File Co 1878. *A Treatise on Files and Rasps.* Providence U.S.A.

Norton, J 1984. *Guide to the National and Provincial Directories of England and Wales before 1856.* English Historical Documents 5

Nunn, P 1985. *The management of some S. Yorkshire Landed Estates in the 18th and 19th centuries linked with the central economic development of the area (1700–1850).* PhD Thesis, University of Sheffield. Unpubl

Oxley, J 1951. Notes on the History of the Sheffield Cutlery Industry, part 1. *Transactions of the Hunter Archaeological Society,* Vol. VIII, 1–4

Palmer, H J August 1884. Cutlery and Cutlers at Sheffield. *The English Illustrated Magazine* Quotation, transcribed onto the internet by Eric Youle: http://freepages.history.rootsweb.com/ .../cutlery_and_cutlers.htm

Palmer, M 1989. Houses and Workplaces: the framework knitters of the East Midlands. *Knitting International,* Vol. 96, 31–35

Palmer, M 1994. Rolt Memorial Lecture 1993:Industrial Archaeology: Continuity and Change. *Industrial Archaeology Review,* Vol. XVI no 2 Spring, 135–170

Palmer, M and P Neaverson 1992. *Industrial Landscapes of the East Midlands.* Chichester: Phillimore

Palmer, M and P Neaverson 1994. *Industry in the Landscape 1700–1900.* London: Routledge

Palmer, M and P Neaverson 1994. *Managing the Industrial Heritage.* Leicester Archaeological Monographs 2, University of Leicester

Palmer, M and P Neaverson (eds) 2001. *From Industrial Revolution to Consumer Revolution: international perspectives on the archaeology of industrialisation.* The International Committee for the Conservation of the Industrial Heritage, Millenium Congress. Cambridge: Maney Publishing, for the Association for Industrial Archaeology, 10

Palmer, M and P Neaverson 1998. *Industrial Archaeology: Principles and Practice.* London and New York: Routledge, 14

Parry, D 1984. *Victorian Sheffield in Advertisements.* Moss Valley Heritage Publications

Passmore, R S 1975. *The mid Victorian Urban Mosaic- Studies in Functional Differentiation and Community Development in three Urban Areas.* PhD thesis, University of Sheffield. Unpubl

Pawson, E 1977. *Transport and Economy.* London: Academic Press

Payne ,P L 1967. The Emergence of the Large Scale Company in Great Britain 1870–1914. *Economic History Review* 20, 519–542

Paynter, R 1988. Steps to an Archaeology of Capitalism: Material Change and Class Analysis. In Leone, M and P Potter, Jnr, (eds) *he Recovery of Meaning: Historical Archaeology in the Eastern Unite States.* Washington D.C.: Smithsonian Institution Press, 407–33

Pearce, D 1989. *Conservation Today.* London: Routledge

Pearson, R 1990. Thrift or dissipation? The business of life assurance in the early nineteenth century. *Economic History Review* 2nd series XLIII, 236–206

Peatman, J 1985. *Abbeydale Industrial Hamlet.* Sheffield City Museums Publication

Peatman, J 1984. *Shepherd's Wheel.* Sheffield City Museums Publication

Perry, V A 1993. *The Archaeology of the Domestic Workshops of the Boot and Shoe Industry in Leicester and its Satellite Villages.* 3rd year dissertation, University of Leicester (With M Palmer Dept. of History) Unpubl

Pevsner, N 1973. *An Outline of European Architecture.* London: Art Book Society Readers Union

Phelps-Brown, E H and S V Hopkins 1955. Seven Centuries of Building Wages. *Economica,* vol. 22 (August), 195–206

Phelps-Brown, E H and S V Hopkins 1956. Seven Centuries of the price of consumables compared to Builders Wage-rates. *Economica,* (November) vol 23, 296–314

Pollard, S 1957. Real Earnings in Sheffield 1851–1914. *Yorkshire Bulletin,* 55–62

Pollard, S 1959. *History of labour in Sheffield.* Liverpool: Liverpool University Press, 50

Powell, C G 1980. *An Economic History of the British Building Industry 1850–1979.* London: Architectural Press

Pragnell, H 1995. *Britain: A Guide to Architectural Styles from 1066 to the Present Day.* London: Ellipsis London

Pressnell, L S 1956. *Country Banking in the Industrial Revolution.* Oxford: Clarendon Press

Prival, M 1994. *Couteaux et Couteliers.* Thiers

Public Art Research Archive: Sheffield Hallam University. *Sheffield's Cutlery Collection.* http://www. shu.ac.uk/services/lc/slidecol/pubart/canteen3.html

Pugh-Smith, J and J Samuels 1993. PPG16: Two Years On. *Journal of Planning Law*, 203–210

Putsch, J and M Krause, 1995. The Cutlery Industry from Production to Industrial Museum: Solingen and Sheffield Compared. *Engineering in Germany: Proceedings of a conference held in Cologne on 28th October 1994. Transactions of the Newcomen Society*, Vol. 66 1994–95, Supplement no 1 Science Museum, London, 43–52

Rapoport, A 1980. Cultural Determinants of Form. In King, A D (ed) *Buildings and Society.* London: Routledge and Kegan

RCHME 1990. *Recording Historic Buildings: A Descriptive Specification*. London: RCHME

RCHME n.d. *Historic Building Report; Truro Works.*

Reeder, D 1988. The Industrial city in Britain: urban biography in the modern style. *Urban History,* 25, 3, 368–378

Reid, C.1976. Middle Class Values and Working Class Culture in nineteenth century Yorkshire. In Pollard, S and C Holmes (eds) *Essays in Economic and Social History of South Yorkshire.* South Yorkshire County Council

Renfrew, C and P Bahn 1991. *Archaeology- Theories, Methods and Practice.* London: Thames and Hudson

Reynolds, T S 1983 (reprinted 1988). *Stronger than a Hundred Men: A History of the Vertical Water Wheel.* Baltimore, US: Johns Hopkins University Press.

Richards, J M 1958. *The Functional Tradition in Early Industry Buildings.* London: Architectural Press

Rimmer, W G 1960 *Marshalls of Leeds: Flax Spinners.* Cambridge: Cambridge University Press

Ripper, W 1903 (3rd edition). *Steam Engine Theory and Practice.* New York: Longman Green and Co

Rix, M 1967. *Industrial Archaeology.* London: The Historical Association

Robinson, W 1890. *Gas and Petroleum Engines.* London: Finsbury Technical Manuals E and FN Spon

Rudmose Brown, R N 1936. Sheffield its Rise and Growth. *Geography* 21, 174–184

Rule, J 1992. *The Vital Century.* London: Longman

Saint, A 1983. *The Image of the Architect*. London: Yale University Press

Schmoller, T 1992. *Sheffield Papermakers:_Three centuries of paper making in the Sheffield area.* Wylam Allenholme Press.

Shackel, P A 1996. *Culture Change and the New Technology: An Archaeology of the Early American Industrial Era.* New York: Plenum

Shaiken, H 1985. *Work Transformed: Automation and Labor in the Computer Age.* New York: Holt, Rinehart and Winston

Shaw, G 1994. The evolution and availability of directories. *Local History Magazine,* April vol 44, 14–17

Shaw, G and A Alexander 1994. Directories as Sources in Local History. *Local History Magazine,* Sept. vol. 46, 12–17

Shaw, G and T Coles 1994. Methods of complication and the work of large-scale publishers. *Local History Magazine,* July vol. 45, 10–14

Sheffield Archives 1784. MD571–574, Freemen's protest

Sheffield Archives OR2 Elizabeth Parkin inventory

Sheffield Archives Tibbett Collection 762, Contract

Sheffield City Council 1991. *Sheffield: A City for the People: Unitary Development Plan (draft).* Sheffield: SCC

Sheffield Independent, 17 June 1875. 'How Sheffield Lost the American Trade'

Silvester, J W H and P H Bennett 1972. Crucible steelmaking at Abbeydale. *Local History Sheet, no. 2,* Sheffield

Silvester, J W H and P H Bennett 1975. Shepherd, a cutlery grinding wheel. *Local History Sheet, no. 9,* Sheffield

Simons, E and E Gregory 1940. *Steel making simply explained.* London: Pitman and Sons

Smith, D 1995. Victorian Valuations.*Transactions of the Hunter Archaeological Society* Vol. 18, 35–46

Smithurst, P 1983. *Sheffield Industrial Museum, Kelham Island and a guide to Sheffield's Industrial History.* Sheffield

Smithurst, P 1987. *The Cutlery Industry.* Shire Album Series 195. Princes Risborough, Aylesbury: Shire Publications Ltd

Stocker, D 1995. Industrial Archaeology and the Monuments Protection programme in England.*Managing the Industrial Heritage*

Strass, G L M et al 1864. *Workshops of England.* London: Groombridge and Sons

Surrey-Dane, E 1973. *Peter Stubbs and the Lancashire Hand Tool Industry.* Altrincham: Sherratt and Son Ltd

Symonds J 1999 Songs Remembered in Exile? Integrating unsung archives of Highland life. In Gazin-Schwartz, A and Cornelius J Holtorf (eds) *Archaeology and Folklore.* London and New York: Routledge, 106–128

Tann, J 1970. *The Development of the Factory.* London: Cornmarket Press

Tarlow, S and S West 1999.*The Familiar Past? Archaeologies of Later Historical Britain.* London and New York: Routledge

Taylor, J 1879. *The Illustrated Guide to Sheffield and the Surrounding District.* Sheffield: Pawson and Brailsford

Taylor, S A 1988. *Tradition and Change the Sheffield Cutlery Trades 1870–1914.* PhD thesis, University of Sheffield. Unpubl

Taylor, W 1927. *The Sheffield Horn Industry.* Sheffield: J W Northend Ltd, 11

The Great Exhibition, London 1851. *Official Descriptive and Illustrated Catalogue of the Great Exhibition, 1851,* Vol. II

Timmins, J G 1976. *Commercial Development of the Sheffield Crucible Steel Industry.* MA, University of Sheffield. Unpubl

Timmins, J G 1979. Handloom Weavers' cottages in central Lancashire: some problems of recognition. *Post Medieval Archaeology*, 13, 251–272

Townsend, H 1954. Economic Theory and the Cutlery Trades. *Economica,* 224–239

Townsend, H 1954. The structures and problems of the Sheffield Cutlery Trade. *District Bank Review* (Local History Pamphlets 198/9)

Pollard, S 1971. Trade Union Commission: *The Sheffield Outrages,* facsimile

Trinder, B 1982. *The Making of the Industrial Landscape.* Dent

Tunzelmann, G N von 1978. *Steam power and British Industrialisation.* Oxford: Oxford University Press

Tunzelmann, G N von 1993. Technological change in Industry during the early Industrial Revolution. In Patrick, K (ed.) *The Industrial Revolution and British Society.* Cambridge: Cambridge University Press

Turner, C A 1986. *A Sheffield Heritage: An Anthology of Photographs and Words of the Cutlery Craftsmen* Sheffield: Division of Continuing Education, University of Sheffield and Sheffield Trades Historical Society

Tweedale, G 1987. *Sheffield Steel and America: A Century of Commercial and Technological Interdependence, 1830–1830* Cambridge: Cambridge University Press.

Tweedale, G 1993. *Stan Shaw Master Cutler: The Story of a Sheffield Craftsman.* Sheffield: Hallamshire Press.

Tweedale, G 1994. Strategies for Decline: George Wostenholm and Son and the Sheffield Cutlery Industry. *Transactions of the Hunter Archaeological Society,* Vol 17, 43–56

Tweedale, G 1996. *The Sheffield Knife Book a History and Collectors' Guide.* Sheffield: The Hallamshire Press.

Unwin, J 1999. The Marks of Sheffield Cutlers, 1614–1878. *Journal of the Historical Metallurgy Society*, Vol .33, No 2

Unwin, J and K Hawley 1999. *Sheffield Industries - Cutlery, Edge Tools and Silver.* Stroud

Unwin, J 1995. Apprenticeships and Freedoms: the computer analysis of the Records of the Cutlers' Company in Sheffield. *The Local Historian*, Vol. 25, No 4

Unwin, J 1999 'The marks of the Sheffield cutlers, 1614–1878.' *Journal of the Historical Metallurgy Society.* 33 No 2. 93–102

Unwin, M J 1988. *The Pen and Pocket Knife Industry, an investigation into the historical tradition of working practices and trade organisation.* MA thesis, University of Sheffield (CECTAL). Unpubl

Warhurst, M E 1987. Changing Occupational and Social Structure of Sheffield, 1650–1780. *Hallamshire Historian*, Vol. 1, No 2

Watson, J S 1987. (reprint) *The Reign of George III 1760–1815.* Oxford: Clarendon Press

Willan,T S 1965. *The Early History of the Don Navigation.* Manchester: Manchester University Press

William, R 1989. *Limekilns and Limeburning.* Aylesbury: Shire

Wilson, J 1856. On the manufacture of articles from steel, particularly cutlery. *Journal of the Society of Arts*, Vol. IV, no 177, 357–366

Worshipful Company of Cutlers, London 1993. *Handlist of the Permanent Exhibition*

Woodward, L 1979. reprint of 2nd edition, *The Age of Reform.* Oxford History of England Book Club Associates by arrangement with Oxford University Press

Wray, N 2001. *One Great Workshop: The Buildings of the Sheffield Metal Trades.* English Heritage

Yorkshire Electricity 1986. *100 years of Electricity.* Yorkshire Electricity Board

Selected bibliography

Binfield, C and D Hey (eds) *Mesters to Masters: A History of the Company of Cutlers in Hallamshire*, Oxford: Oxford University Press

Bradbury, F 1912 *History of Old Sheffield Plate*, London. Reprinted in 1968, Sheffield

Crossley, D N Cass, N Flavell and C Turner (eds) 1989 *Water Power on the Sheffield Rivers*, Sheffield: University of Sheffield Division of Continuing Education and Sheffield Trades Historical Society

Dyson, B R 1936 *A Glossary of Words and Dialect Formerly Used in the Sheffield Trades*, Sheffield. Reprinted 1979, Sheffield Trades Historical Society

Flather, D 1934 *Old Sheffield Craftsmen: Their Tools and Workshops*, Sheffield: Society for the Preservation of the Old Sheffield Tools

Grayson, R with K Hawley, 1995 *Knifemaking in Sheffield and the Hawley Collection*, Sheffield: PAVIC Publications, Sheffield Hallam University

Hey, D 1991 *The Fiery Blades of Hallamshire: Sheffield and its Neighbourhood 1660–1740*, Leicester: Leicester University Press

Hey, D 1998 *A History of Sheffield*, Lancaster: Carnegie Publishing

Himsworth, J B 1953 *The Story of Cutlery: From Flint to Stainless Steel*, London: Earnest Benn (for the Hardware Trades Journal)

Housley, H 1998 *Back to the Grindstone: Personal Recollections of the Sheffield Cutlery Industry*, Sheffield: Hallamshire Press

Leader, R E 1905 *History of the Company of Cutlers in Hallamshire in the County of York. Volumes I-II*, Sheffield: Cutlers' Company. Printed by Pawson and Brailsford

Lloyd, G I H 1913 *The Cutlery Trades: An Historical Essay in the Economics of Small-Scale Production*, London. Reprinted by Frank Cass, London, 1968

Magnusson, L. 1994 *The Contest for Control: Metal Industries in Sheffield, Solingen, Remscheid and Eskilstuna during Industrialisation*, Oxford: Berg Publishers

Pollard, S 1959 A *History of Labour in Sheffield*, Liverpool: Liverpool University Press

Pybus, S et al, 1982 *Cutlery: A Bibliography*, Sheffield, Sheffield City Museum

Singleton, H R 1973 *A Chronology of Cutlery, Sheffield*. Sheffield: Sheffield City Museum

Smithurst, P 1987 *The Cutlery Industry*. Shire Album Series 195, Aylesbury: Shire Publications Ltd

Turner, C A.1978 *A Sheffield Heritage: An Anthology of Photographs and Words of the Cutlery Craftsmen*, Sheffield: Sheffield Trades Historical Society and University of Sheffield Division of Continuing Education

Tweedale, G 1995 *Steel City: Entrepreneurship, Strategy and Technology in Sheffield, 1743–1993*, Oxford: Oxford University Press

Tweedale, G 1996 *The Sheffield Knife Book: A History and Collectors Guide*, Sheffield: Hallamshire Press

Unwin, J 1999 The Marks of Sheffield Cutlers, 1614–1878. *The Journal of the Historical Metallurgy Society*. 33:2, 93–103

Unwin, J and K Hawley 1999 *Sheffield Industries: Cutlery, Silver and Edge Tools*, Stroud: Tempus Publishing Ltd

Wray, N B Hawkins and C Giles 2001 *One Great Workshop: The Buildings of the Sheffield Metals Trades*. English Heritage and Sheffield City Council

Primary sources

Local Studies Library, Sheffield

Sheffield Independent 1855
Sheffield Local Register 200-1857 Vol 1 1857
Sheffield Times 1846-7 Vol 1
Photographic Collection (Various - see text)
The Sheffield Society of Architects and Surveyors List of Members and Rules 1887 (107130 042S)

Trade Directories

Kelly's Directories 1888
Robson's Directory 1839
Sheffield General and Commercial Directory for 1821 Gell and Bennett
White's Trade Directories, 1833,1841, 1852, 1856, 1860, 1862, 1868,1871, 1879,1883, 1888, 1893, 1898
Yellow Pages 1995/96

Maps

1850s 1:500 series CCXCIV.4,5,7,8,11,12 each is divided into 25 squares.
1890s 1:500 series CCXCIV.4,5,7,8,11,12 each is divided into 25 squares.
First Edition OS Maps for Sheffield, Grenoside (CCLXXXVIII.7) and Ecclesfield (CCLXXXVIII.8)
Godfrey reprints of 2nd edition OS Maps 294.4, 294.5, 294.7, 294.8, 294.11, 294.12, 295.1, 295.5

Sheffield Archives

Appleby (Building Firm) list of clients 91/B1/1
Arundel Castle S.383 Agreements for Long Leases 1785-1816
Building Registers CA205 and Plans CA206
CA598(1) Annual Report of Planning Dept 1888
Church Burgess Leases CB 111 & CB1634
Deeds of Thomas Sambourne for Howard Street ACM SD 26
Fairbank Collection. Fieldbooks (FB), Building Books (BB), Correspondence (CP), Miscellaneous Books (MB), Notebooks (NB) and Account Books (AB). For specific references see text.
Flood Claims 1864 CA7
Gas Company Records GCR (1-24)
German Wilson Papers PhC 530/1&2
Goad's Fire Plans 674/B1/1-32
Harrison Bros and Howson Building,1900, AP 84 (1-2) AP85 (1-9)
Letter from Broadhead sister to Fairbank re spending money on tanners workshop
Mattias Spencer Records, LD 1926 Memoranda Book of John Spencer 1830-49
NVT12 Needham Veal and Tyzack, outworkers agreements 1914-18
Papers of James Dixon, Dixon Series A&B
Sheffield Deeds Catalogue Books 1-4
Sheffield Ratebooks
Soho Minute Books MD709
Soho Rent Books (A143)
Special List on Building Societies
TC762 Wages Agreement
Trinity Works Plans AP82(1-2)
W.D. 474 Sheffield Reform Freehold Benefit Building Society papers

Trade Directories

Business Directory of Sheffield 1862
Drake's Directory 1862 and 1863
Gell R Directory of Sheffield 1825
Melville and Co's Directory of Sheffield and Rotherham 1859

Pigot J Yorkshire Directory 1828
Rodgers Directory 1841
Sheffield Directory and Guide 1828
White's Directory 1838, 1841, 1849, 1852, 1862, 1864, 1868, 1871, 1876,   1884, 1894

Hawley Collection, University of Sheffield/Hawley Trust

Sheffield Illustrated Lists
1797 Directory of Sheffield (J Montgomery)
Photographs accredited in text.

Rotherham Archives

Robert Lowe and William Stead Papers in the Merryweather and Corbett Collection.

Midland Bank Archive, London

Records of the Sheffield Union Bank AD 2-4
Records of the Sheffield and Hallamshire Bank AM5-12

National Monuments Record, Swindon

George Watkins' Note book.

Parliamentary and official papers

Parliamentary

Enclosure

Act of Enclosure for Ecclesfield 1779

Employment
1852-53 Parliamentary Papers Vol LXXXVIIIpt2 Occupations of the people
1889 Select Committee on Sweated Labour (XIII)

Factory Acts & Children's Employment
Extension of the Factory Act 1867 {30&31 Vict. 1867 (Chapter 103)]
Extension of the Factory Acts 1856 [19&20 Vict. 1856 (Chapter 38)]
Factory Act 1844 [7 Vict. 1844 (chapter 15)]
Factory and Workshop Act 1878 [41 Vict. 1878(Chapter 16)]
Factory Commission 1833
Report to the Commissioners upon the Metal Manufactures of the Sheffield District by JE White
(Appendix to the 4th report)
Report to the Commissioners on Roads &c. In England and Wales 1840 (PPF11)
Reports to the Commissioners on the Employment of Children 1843 (Appendix to 2nd Report, Trades
and Manufactures)
Reports to the Commissioners on the Employment of Children 1864

Local
1844 Bye-Laws
1853 Smoke Bye-Laws in Pursuance of the Municipal Corporation Act
1889 Bye-Laws with regard to New Streets and Building and Drainage thereof
1890 Sheffield Corporation Act

Glossary of Sheffield manufacturing terms

This is a short list of words used by manufacturers, found in trade catalogues, price lists for the various processes and probate inventories. Many words are different from those used by the London trades.

aggon	inverted chisel set into a forger's anvil, for cutting off the mood
blister steel	product of a cementation furnace – steel bar with surface 'blisters'
buffing polishing	process using a cloth wheel dressed with a fine abrasive
bolster	decorative metal junction between the blade and the tang
cementation	process of converting wrought iron to steel by packing iron bars with charcoal and heating in an enclosed chest in a furnace for several days
cooltrough	trough containing water and/or oil for quenching blades during hardening
cross-rolling	machine process of thinning spoon blanks prior to pressing into a bowl-shape
crucible steel	homogeneous steel produced by melting broken up pieces of blister steel bar in a crucible in a furnace
cutler's thumb print	at the base of the knife blade showing the junction between the steel blade and iron for the bolster and tang
cutlery	initially, items which 'cut', i.e. knives
cutling	assembling and hafting knives
electroplating	electrolytic process of depositing a thin layer of silver on base metals
engraving	incised decoration using small chisel-like tools
flatstick	shaped piece of wood, with which the grinder presses the blade to the wheel
flatware	forks and spoons
forging	hammering heated steel into the shape of a blade
glazer/glazier	leather-headed wheel dressed with emery to give finish to blades
goff hammer	fast-running powered hammer used in forging
grinding	using an abrasive wheel to put a sharp edge on a blade
hackhammer	chisel-faced hammer to correct defects in the surface of a grindstone
holloware	dishes, bowls, trays, teapots, generally in silver or plated metals
horsin/saddle	seat in a grinding trow
hull	the building housing the trows, the grinding wheels, drive belts and seating
mark side	side of the blade on which the maker's identifying mark is struck
mood	rough forging of a knife blade
parser	drill rotated using a fiddle bow to bore a hole
pentrough	water container above the water wheel - the flow of water can be regulated
pile side	reverse side of the blade from the mark side, often shows the cutler's thumb print
pressing	a metal-forming process using dies in a fixed stroke ram
prints	pair of dies used to form a knife bolster
run steel	cast steel

saw piercing	decorative fretwork designs made by sawing into spoon tops, fish eaters
scales	two flat pieces of bone, wood, etc rivetted to form handles of knives
shear steel	blister steel bars, layered, heated and hammered to make a more homogeneous steel
shut	forged welding wrought iron to steel blades
shuttle pole	control rod allowing the grinder inside the grinding hull to open and close the shuttle on the pentrough
smithing	the striking of a blade with a chisel-faced hammer to correct any errors in flatness caused by the hardening process
sours	goods and items for which the craftsman has been paid in advances
stamping	a metal-forming process using dies in a free-fall weight
stiddy/stithy	an anvil
stock	wooden or stone base for an anvil
striker	a man wielding a heavy striking hammer to assist the forger in two-handed forging
sweets	goods delivered for which the craftsman has not yet been paid
tang	metal extension of the bolster which lies with the knife or fork handle
tilt	water-powered hammer regulated by cams on the drive axle
trow	grinding wheel, water trough and seat
tup	heavy metal head of a tilt hammer
tuyere	nozzle or pipe carrying draught from bellows to hearth
workboard	small wooden trays used to hold parts of knives for assembly